Becoming Human

Becoming Human
New Perspectives on the Inhuman Condition

EDITED BY PAUL SHEEHAN
FOREWORD BY STEVEN CONNOR

Westport, Connecticut
London

Library of Congress Cataloging-in-Publication Data

Becoming human : new perspectives on the inhuman condition / edited by Paul Sheehan ;
    foreword by Steven Connor.
        p. cm.
    Includes bibliographical references (p.) and index.
    ISBN 0–275–97899–0 (alk. paper)
        1. Philosophical anthropology. I. Sheehan, Paul, 1960– .
    BD450.B4112   2003
    128—dc21   2002193004

British Library Cataloguing in Publication Data is available.

Library of Congress Catalog Card Number: 2002193004
ISBN: 0–275–97899–0

First published in 2003

Praeger Publishers, 88 Post Road West, Westport, CT 06881
An imprint of Greenwood Publishing Group, Inc.
www.praeger.com

Printed in the United States of America

The paper used in this book complies with the
Permanent Paper Standard issued by the National
Information Standards Organization (Z39.48–1984).

10 9 8 7 6 5 4 3 2 1

In truth, there are only inhumanities, humans are made exclusively of inhumanities, but very different ones, of very different natures and speeds.

—Gilles Deleuze and Felix Guattari, *A Thousand Plateaus*

Contents

FOREWORD Coming to Be   ix
   Steven Connor

INTRODUCTION Contingencies of Humanness   1
   Paul Sheehan

Part I   The Backgrounds of Human Being   13

1   Humanism and Human Being: Beyond Essentialism   15
   Tom Rockmore

2   The Rehumanization of Art: Modernism, Technology,   29
   and the Crisis of Humanism
   Michael Hollington

3   Is Humor Human?   43
   Simon Critchley

Part II   Naturalizing Human Dominion   53

4   *Philosophie au Naturel*   55
   John Mullarkey

5   Nature and Culture: The Mythic Register   67
   Kate Soper

6   The Way of the World: Nature, History, Human Ontology   81
   Joseph Margolis

Part III   Screen Narratives of Human Becoming   91

7   Death Twenty-four Times a Second: The Inorganic Body   93
    and the Cinema
    Laura Mulvey

8   Toward a New Demonology   103
    Steven Connor

9   Rights of Sacrifice   113
    Richard Kearney

Part IV   Politics of Human Becoming   125

10 The Project of Humanity   127
    Zygmunt Bauman

11 Value, Justice, and the Wilderness Ideal   149
    John O'Neill

12 On Critical Humility   165
    Thomas Docherty

Further Reading   181

Selected Bibliography   183

Index   189

About the Editor and Contributors   197

FOREWORD

Coming to Be

Steven Connor

For Plato, the proper study of philosophy was the realm of Being, of that which always is, not the realm of nature, which is always merely becoming. By the time of Hegel, who described Becoming as the unity of Being and Nothing, philosophy was finding it much harder to turn aside from the sphere of becoming. Indeed, we seem nowadays to have set up our nomadic habitation in the midst of becoming. There are books to advise one about the process of becoming anything and everything: a man, a woman, a Black American, a Mexican American, a Jew, a father, a reader, a writer, Irish, Catholic, Anglican, feminine, and "orgasmic."

For no human being can simply be, and leave it at that. The nature of human beings, it is often said, is not to be but to subsist in a state of becoming, by which is meant coming about, coming-to-be, being in transit, being on the way to what one will have been. Humans are customarily said to be not "creatures" but beings. Humans are beings who are in the midst of their being, who have a relation, a relation of care or concern, Heidegger says, to that being. When one uses the expression "being" with respect to the nonhuman—spiritual beings, or beings from another world—we are ascribing to them that same state of vexed uncompletedness. Beings are creatures who experience themselves in terms of the verb "to be," who are incomplete yet on their way to full, inclusive being; we might even refer to them as "becomings."

Becoming signifies more than a simple transformation, a movement from one condition to another. It involves development, an unfolding of what has lain previously enfolded or ready to be unfolded. If human beings experience and characterize themselves as standing out, or ex-isting, being ex-posed, or turned to the future in this way, then the force of the simple word "come" in the word *becoming* also establishes the prejudice that what one is coming to be will be what one will have come, with the sense of "returned" rather than "gone to." How appropriate that when one regains one's senses, one should be said to "come to" ("or rather from," says Beckett, in glum exactitude) them. The sense of teeter in that oddly uncompleted preposition "to" in that phrase, like a bridge or arch thrown out into midair, is braced by the idea of coming, which always signifies a movement toward a place that one already occupies in actuality or imagination; it is a *here* that one must move to in coming and a *there* toward which one moves in going. Strikingly, phrases that mean taking leave of one's self or one's senses attract idioms of going rather than coming: going to the dogs, round the bend, and so on. So becoming is always necessarily a kind of coming to oneself, a return to where one already was all along, in either actuality or anticipation. Although the futurity of human being is clear in the French word for this becoming, *devenir,* which echoes the *ad-venire,* that which is to come in *l'avenir,* the suffix *de-* seems to imply that one's coming is a derivation, a departure or setting out from the shore, *de ripam,* rather than an arrival—*ad ripam*—at it.

The sense that in becoming, one is "coming to," or "coming back to," is perhaps partly due to the lingering in English of the force of the past tense that the *be-* prefix originally signified. In such words, the principal force of the *be-* prefix is to convey the ideas of extension and intensification. To be bedazzled, bedecked, or beshat is to be those things in high degree, all over, from top to bottom; to bemoan one's fate is to lament it utterly, to belabor opponents is to give them a comprehensive going over. There is almost, at times, the sense of something overdone in the *be-*. Becoming may therefore be thought of as a doubled coming, a second, or over-coming. (Interestingly, there are also usages in which the *be-* signifies a privation rather than an extension—as, most notably, in the verb "to behead.")

To become human thus implies the fulfilling of some promise or predestination. But what? The irony is that most accounts of what it means to be human also stress its arbitrary or nongiven nature. "Are we to assume," fretted Aristotle at the beginning of the *Nicomachean Ethics* (perhaps for a moment darkly suspecting that we are), "that, while the carpenter and the shoemaker have definite functions or businesses belonging to them, man as such has none, and is not designed by nature to fulfil a function?"[1] If the human being is the unnecessary animal, then it is subject to the necessity of unrolling possibilities that do not lie necessary or immanent in its given biological conditions. Human beings, we have become accustomed to feel at least since Kant, become themselves most authentically in entering into their freedom, which is, as Sartre glosses it, a nothingness, a condition of not being a thing but rather a continuing potential, a not-yet, an unformedness, a nothing-in-particular. But if one simply and necessarily *is* this freedom, how is one to choose or embrace it, make it a necessity, other than by vacuously willing whatever happens to happen? I once heard an old tramp roar out to a niggardly donor the words "I wish your life on you!" Can a more vicious curse be conceived? To wish someone long life is to wish them the continuing chance of exposure to new possibility. Simply, pitilessly, to wish someone their own life, the life that is no more than the one that will always anyway have been in store for them, is to condemn them to death-in-life, the death of being no more than their life, reducing them to the poor, arbitrary total of what they merely will have added up to. It is this irony above all that lies coiled within the notion of becoming—that one must end up seeming to have chosen what one never quite did or fully could but for all that could not have chosen not to. Being in becoming, becoming the kind of being that must become conscious and consciously become, means acceding to the necessity, the *it-will-have-been* of this undetermined condition.

Becoming human is also an ambivalent notion because it means more than coming to be human. It implies a swelling, an opening in one of something that one is not yet. If I report the sensation of becoming ill, or weak, or strong, I am referring to a process that is taking place in some sense without my volition, or supervision. When I say "I am becoming," what I am is not quite synchronous with what I am becoming. Though I may be doing things to promote the process of becoming ill or strong—actively pursuing, for example, the studies that will help me become a hairstylist or a nurse—to report the process as a "becoming" is to report a development that is taking place in as well as from me. Just as we tell our children that all their growing is done at night, so the work of becoming seems to be going on in the intervals between self-inspections and self-declarations. To become human is always to become more, or less, than human.

Many of the writers in *Becoming Human* are interested in the condition of passive action and active passivity that seems to be implied in becoming human. This perhaps partly awakens an obsolete intransitive use of the verb—"to come about or come to pass"—as defined by Palsgrave: "It becometh, it happeneth, it chaunceth." Among these contributors, Thomas Docherty identifies a kind of passionate passivity or responsiveness in the critic, which seems to point to the larger lesson that "we can be determined as ourselves by something—indeed *only* by something—that is other than ourselves."

FUTURE PERFECTS

Becoming is the bridge, not so much between Nothing and Being as between the present and the future perfect tense. To be what you are becoming is to attempt to will and be in advance what it is you will end up having been. Here one might note the "lean" or prejudice toward futurity in the verb "to be" in English. "To be" is formed from the irregular union of three originally distinct verbs: a verb with the stem *es-*, another with the stem *wes-*, and a third with the stem *be-*. In the form *be-on*, this third was still an independent verb in Old English, which had all the present but no past tenses, and meant "to become," or "come to be." The verb which originally had reference to future actions unfolding in the present now covers the whole of the verb complex *am-was-be*. The fact that *be-on* has now come to occupy the position of the infinitive of this complex of verbs seems to install unfolding into futurity, or coming to be, into being as such. That the verb features in the future tense ("will be") and in perfected and pluperfect tenses—"have been" "had been," "will have been" (yet why no future pluperfect, "will had been"?)—also makes for an inclension, or infolding, in the very grammar of being. Only a creature capable of the trick of plucking out that pleat or ruck in the fabric of time that we call the future perfect, first placing itself imaginatively at a point in the future, then looping beyond (another doubled-up *be* word) to a vantage point in the yet further future from which to look back on it, is open to the predicament and the possibility of becoming that we think of as distinctively human.

This distinctively doubled, here-and-there, *fort/dasein* condition of human being is brought about by the complex relations of being and knowing. Many of the problems of becoming human that are reflected on in this collection arise from attempts to make human knowing coincide with human being. Unlike animals, whose lives are entirely exhausted in their existences (so we say to ourselves), humans partly know what and that they are—and even find that they know that, too. Pascal was one of the first to announce the superiority of man to nature on these grounds: "Even if the universe were to obliterate him, man would be nobler than that which kills him, in that he knows he is dying. . . . All our dignity consists in thought."[2] Since Hegel, the relations between doing and knowing have been taken up in a project of knowing as the highest form of doing (this, of course, being just the kind of argument one would expect from professional thinkers). Between Hegel and Adorno, becoming human had meant the infinite expansion of self-consciousness; the attempt to make thinkable what was residually unthought in the human—the animal, the natural, instinctive, the unconscious. The current efforts to render entirely transparent the genetic construction of man, a process in which, as Michel Serres has recently put it, the flesh is being "carnated," or made word, is paralleled by the effort to make the physical bases of thought and consciousness itself available to consciousness.[3] Becoming human means consciousness attempting to coincide with itself, which, to the degree that human beings see themselves as lonely or redemptive exceptions in a world driven by blind process, often means differentiating oneself from what is not-human ("nature").

However, since St. Francis, Christian thought has also offered resources for thinking of the human as not only an anomalous gash in the sweet nescience of nature but also the means of raising nature back to Godhead. This notion survives into the postreligious metaphysics of Bergson, for whom "man is the 'term' or the 'end' of evolution,"[4] and of Heidegger, who famously declared, "We are too late for the gods and too early for Being. Being's poem, just begun, is man."[5] This confidence in evolutionary becoming has become a feature of much popular ecological writing.[6] It has recently been given a technological dimension in Michel Serres's *Hominescence*, a book the title of which is a rendering of the phrase "Becoming Human." Serres sees the possibility in human technology of the aggregation and integration of all the forms and degrees of life on the planet into what he calls the "Biosom." In this model, human beings encroach on the natural, not in order to objectify and eliminate it but to draw it into the condition of becoming that had previously been the ambivalent prerogative of the human. For so long the prefect rather than the shepherd of Being, humanity, in the "exodarwinism" of technological development, now perfects nature by disclosing a drive to transcendence that henceforth will have been immanent in it all along: "Are we coming at the indistinct idea," suggests Serres, "of the world's faculty for self-understanding, of which we are the mediators?"[7]

The immoderate claim that man is the agent or organ through which nature takes thought is, of course, open to the suspicion that it vastly and narcissistically overestimates the power or value of human thought. (But should we be suspicious that we find it so natural to suspect our thought in this way?) In the second half of the twentieth century, the effort to draw up the maximum of existence into consciousness has also on occasion mutated into a desire to moderate this appetite. Becoming human might also mean, as Kate Soper puts it, finding a way to acknowledge and indulge the "envy of immanence" as well as the desire for transcendence. If the human has involved reaching out beyond what it merely, self-evidently is, a reaching for what is presently unfitted or unbecoming to it, then it might also involve accommodation to what "negatively transcends" it, transcends it downward, as it were, accommodating it to animal or natural existence. A distinctive feature of the essays in this collection is their acknowledgement of the need for an ironic or comic embrace of the intermittent or interrupted nature of human self-consciousness. Simon Critchley, Richard Kearney, Laura Mulvey, and Steven Connor all, in various ways, outline the prospects for a humanity that has learned to temper its appetites and pretensions by tolerating the nonhuman in itself. There are perhaps continuities here with the ecological withdrawal from phallic dominance over nature, the new determinism in evolutionary studies, whether in psychology or sociology, and the new naturalism that, in his contribution to this volume, John Mullarkey detects in Continental philosophy. All of these signal a more chastened, less expansive view of the claims of the human.

Zygmunt Bauman, by contrast, is less confident of our capacities to become more human by becoming less so, in mitigating the will-to-consciousness. We cannot be sure, he warns, that new forms of political organization appropriate to the new structures of global interconnection and dependence—new ways, in other words, of knowing and regulating those global conditions—will simply arise or spontaneously come about. Rather we must strive to assist the process of growing a world-mind that can be a match for the new world-body of global communications and economic power. Rather than a given, or an inevitable precipitate of present conditions, the "[g]lobalization of humanity . . . is a task to be undertaken." In reading the necessity of becoming human in such starkly political terms, Bauman may seem to cut across the arguments of some of the other contributors to this volume. But he also discloses the inescapable prejudice within all efforts to limit the powers of the human for a humanity that has become bigger and more authoritative by having assimilated its own limits, and so has continued its work of overcoming, overreaching, and overdoing in the very effort to accept passivity and a measure of immanence. For no creature can choose immanence or freely choose a restriction of its freedom in the way that a human can. "Man cannot be an animal," writes Emil J. Fackenheim; "he can only be a philosopher or anthropologist who asserts that men are animals."[8] Rather than the sleep of reason, this would always be a kind of regulated, lucid dreaming.

KNOWING ONE'S MIND

If becoming signifies the emergence of awareness and continuous self-relation out of mere, momentary existences, this can suggest the idea of a progressive increment of knowing—including the knowledge of what we cannot ever know—over existing. The growth of self-awareness is often figured implicitly as the occupation of a territory, the steady encroachment of light into the previously dark spaces of blind existence—*Wo es war, soll ich werden*, in Freud's hopeful slogan. The extension of the territory of consciousness—by which is meant both that of which one is conscious and that of which one is *conscious* of being conscious—also results in a thickening of that administered space of awareness. Where there is no consciousness of being, there are no connections or relations. Without consciousness of being, the world (though there can be no such thing as a world under these circumstances) must be a mere blizzard of unsynthesizable particulars, which are not even ordered by succession, for this requires as a minimum an ordering time sense. Where there is becoming, though, as opposed to mere agitation, past, present, and future can be knitted together in ever more complex ways.

Given this territorial model for thinking the relations between human expansion in and through consciousness, there would seem to be three possible relations between the human and the nonhuman: (1) infinite and unchecked expansion of the human at the expense of the nonhuman; (2) a recession of human becoming-into-consciousness, either through deliberate policy, or involuntarily, through some such historical convulsion as Foucault famously imagines at the end of *The Order of Things*; or (3) the striking and maintenance of a stable balance or rapprochement between the human and the nonhuman, through something like Michel Serres's "natural contract" or some other settlement or voluntary restriction of powers on the part of the human.[9]

This scheme of outcomes is unsatisfactory not just in its possible overestimation of the power and value of the cognitive but also because it measures the advance of human self-knowledge on a single, progressive scale. But human becoming may not be best thought of as a one-way street or as a gathering spate. Perhaps it is not to be seen as a simple increment or recession, as on a tidal coastline, but a turbulent coming and going in many directions and dimensions simultaneously. Even the most highly and agonizedly self-aware of thinkers has regularly to go to sleep or perform actions (riding a bike, smoking, reading, swimming) in which a certain abatement of conscious attention is actually a requirement. Consciousness and human self-relatedness are not homogenous or always plugged in. An increase in self-consciousness and consequent tightening of the circuits between action and awareness in one area will usually bring about or be accompanied by a diminution in another; thus, the huge growth in forms of artificial memory and the accessibility of information at the level of the human network is accompanied by a significant loss in stand-alone memory in individual nodes of the network—that is, individual human beings. Do we have more or less memory in total as a result, more or less capacity for self-relation, more or less aptitude to become or remain human? Surely what occurs under these circumstances is a change in the configuration or rhythm of self-relatedness. It is difficult to see how one might take the measure or do the calculation of how human—which is to say, how fully self-reflective or self-related—we are in sum becoming, since there is no basis on which to add up all the different components of the sum or integrate all the different shifts and fixings of minds in time. Because it is entrained by these rhythms of self-relation, the shape of human becoming may then be less like a tide advancing on a shore than a flame, flickering and fluctuating, leaping and subsiding. Just as the quantities or degrees of self-relation may be inconstant, so too the forms of self-relation by which being appears to gather itself into Being may also be more diverse than we have found ways to acknowledge. Might one not see the history of human self-disgust, from Swift to Beckett and Coetzee, as testimony, for example, to a form of syncopated self-relation rather than a simple abnegation of the human?

Finally, there is the compromised model of the individual mind, which has dominated so much of the thinking about human becoming. The synchronicities, interrelations, and codependencies of the networked world that is currently taking shape may make it implausible to continue to imagine the self-relations of collectivities as scaled-up single minds. Confronted with the many forms of the question "How is one to become human?" or

"How is one to help becoming human?" the essays in this collection perhaps proffer collectively Humpty Dumpty's response to Alice's protest that one cannot help growing older: "*One* can't perhaps ... but *two* can."[10] If it is implausible to think of human becoming in terms of a simple bipolar march or retreat of mind, or irreversible reaching of thought into the unthought, the different perspectives enlarged by the essays in *Becoming Human* help bring about a sensitivity to the rhythms as well as the ratios of human becoming. If the face of the human is being effaced in the sand, it may yet be possible to say of the human that nothing becomes it so well as the manner of its taking leave of itself.

NOTES

1. Aristotle, *The Nicomachean Ethics*, trans. H. Rackham (Cambridge, Mass.: Harvard University Press; London: William Heinemann, 1934), 31, 1097b.

2. Blaise Pascal, *Pensées*, ed. Philippe Sellier (Paris: Mercure de France, 1976), 134 (my translation).

3. Michel Serres, *Hominescence: Essais* (Paris: Le Pommier, 2001), 79.

4. Henri Bergson, *Creative Evolution*, trans. Arthur Mitchell (London: Macmillan, 1911), 278.

5. Martin Heidegger, *Poetry, Language, Thought*, trans. Alfred Hofstadter (New York: Harper & Row, 1971), 4.

6. For one example among many, see Heather Couzyn, *The Cosmic Microbe: Towards a Becoming Life on Planet Earth* (New York: Headway Books, 1995).

7. Serres, *Hominescence*, 153.

8. Emil J. Fackenheim, *Quest for Past and Future* (Bloomington: Indiana University Press, 1968), 88.

9. Michel Serres, *The Natural Contract*, trans. Elizabeth MacArthur and William Paulson (Ann Arbor: University of Michigan Press, 1995).

10. *Alice through the Looking Glass*, in *The Annotated Alice*, ed. Martin Gardner (Harmondsworth: Penguin, 1976), 266.

INTRODUCTION

Contingencies of Humanness

Paul Sheehan

"Man's inhumanity to man"—the slogan has resonated through much of the nasty, brutish and short century that has just expired. The moral certitude of the phrase—more self-secure than its coiner, the poet Robert Burns, could ever have envisaged—is matched by other, epistemological assurances: that "man" as an entity is knowable and that the kinds of conduct appropriate to such an entity are definable. The legal accompaniment of the slogan "human rights legislation" has attempted to provide licit support for these assurances, but instead it only raises further doubts. For the various abuses and breaches necessitating that such a thing as human rights be enshrined in law in the first place suggests that some of us do not know what it means to be human or do not feel it strongly enough to use it as a guiding principle for social interaction. Man—the human—cannot be both "perfectible," as William Godwin claimed in his *Enquiry Concerning Political Justice*,[1] and knowable. "Human rights" are therefore better seen as provisional reports on an ever-changing entity, an entity that is forever in the process of becoming. But becoming what, exactly? And is the process of this becoming a destiny, a condition, or a predicament? These are the sorts of questions that this book is designed to tackle, approaching them from a number of different directions: sociological, philosophical, ecological, literary, cultural.

A CENTURY OF ANTIHUMANISM

The various upheavals of the twentieth century, from scientific and philosophical hubris to political extremism and total war, prompted Emmanuel Levinas to attend to a "crisis of humanism." If God, *cogito*, and cosmos once provided support for the human, they can no longer be taken for granted: "[T]heories on the death of God, the contingency of humanness in philosophical reflection and the bankruptcy of humanism—doctrines already voiced by the end of the last [nineteenth] century—have taken on apocalyptic proportions."[2] The latter two upheavals, the contingency of humanness and the bankruptcy of humanism, are points of departure for the essays in this collection.

Levinas was right to locate the turn away from humanism in the nineteenth century. Such a disposition governs the fiction of Dostoevsky and Thomas Hardy and is writ large in the German philosophical tradition, principally in the work of Schopenhauer and Nietzsche. Each of these figures questions what it means to be human and, for the most part, comes up with negative results. Being human, they all insist, is a punishing and debilitating experience. But what lies adjacent to this experience?

A similar abandonment of traditional humanist beliefs occurred early in the twentieth century, among enthusiasts of technological modernity. As Michael Hollington's chapter shows, the seedbed for this "naïve modernism" was preindustrial European culture. Comparable attitudes also unsettle English letters of this period, in the novels of D. H. Lawrence and Joseph Conrad and the critical polemics of Wyndham Lewis and T. E. Hulme. The latter figure provides a link of sorts with postwar antihumanism, in his accentuation of the arrogance and narcissism behind human self-understanding. Hulme conducted a single-minded campaign to bring this aspect to the forefront of contemporary thought. More than any of his peers, he theorized explicitly about the potential snares of humanism, with an ardor rivaling that of his French successors.

Hulme attacked humanism by denouncing Romanticism, which he saw as the apogee of the humanist tradition: "Here is the root of all romanticism: that man, the individual, is an infinite reservoir of possibilities."[3] Romanticism, according to Hulme, derived from Rousseau's insistence that man is a wondrous being, a possessor of unlimited powers: "The whole subject has been confused by the failure to recognize the gap between the regions of vital and human things, and that of the absolute values of ethics and religion. We introduce into human things the Perfection that properly belongs only to the divine, and thus confuse both human and divine things by not clearly separating them. . . . We place Perfection where it should not be—on this human plane."[4] Humanism is thus an ironic overcoming, an unwarranted ascription of transcendence to a being congenitally unfit for such power.

For Hulme, humanist arrogance impels man to seize for himself the role of surrogate divinity—just as he does in the purview of the generation of theorist-philosophers across the Channel, half a century hence. Hulme's Romanticist bête noire is replaced in the 1960s by the Gallic targets of the *cogito*, its freedom-besotted Kantian descendant, and, closer to home, Sartrean *engagement* and self-making. The God of the Old Testament was not being contested here, as it was in Hulme's diatribe, but rather His successor—the metaphysical deity implied in the self-grounded Cartesian or transcendental subject, which professes to command godlike powers of being.

Postwar theory assumed this attitude because it discovered a severance in Western thought, a fissure that widened as the century progressed. By these lights, the proposition that culture could be inherently civilizing, not to say humanizing, was rendered unthinkable in the wake of the stark facts of the *Shoah*. German culture and thought, widely regarded as the apogee of Western civilization, was seen to contain unfathomable depths of barbarism. This recoil from humanist confidence, a condition of possibility for postwar French thought, was given overt expression by Theodor Adorno. Kate Soper's chapter shows how his famous collaboration with Max Horkheimer, the seminal *Dialectic of Enlightenment*, drew on mythical narratives to elucidate the moral compromises of modernity. In the later *Negative Dialectic*, Adorno argued that what had taken place at Auschwitz provided irrefutable evidence for the failure of culture. His disgust was unqualified:

> That this could happen in the midst of the traditions of philosophy, of art, and of the enlightening sciences says more than that these traditions and their spirit lacked the power to take hold of men and work a change in them. There is untruth in those fields themselves, in the autarky that is emphatically claimed for them. All post-Auschwitz culture, including its urgent critique, is garbage. In restoring itself after the things that happened without resistance in its own countryside, culture has turned entirely into the ideology it has been potentially—had been ever since it presumed, in opposition to material existence, to inspire that existence with the light denied it by the separation of the mind from manual labor.[5]

Adorno was unsparing in his vehemence: "Whoever pleads for the maintenance of this radically culpable and shabby culture becomes its accomplice, while the man who says no to culture is directly furthering the barbarism which our culture showed itself to be."[6] Bearing in mind Jean-François Lyotard's description of the Holocaust as an earthquake so powerful as to destroy all the instruments of measurement,[7] Adorno's cultural apostasy is, for all its bitterness, an immensely sane and fitting response.

Across the Rhine, a similar attitude is discernible in the postwar Gallic intellectual. Here, disquiet at political turpitude (and the public acquiescence silently supporting it) emerges from the simple fact that for most of the war years, France was an occupied nation. Four decades later, Michel Foucault came to describe the experience as akin to "spending one's entire childhood in the night, waiting for the dawn." It instilled in him the belief that the present world, in all its precariousness, would soon have to end—

to be replaced, somewhat ominously, by another in due course: "That prospect of another world marked the people of my generation, and we have carried with us, perhaps to excess, a dream of Apocalypse."[8]

OEDIPUS IN PARIS

Foucault's direful dream was not just a reaction to the Vichy experience but also a retort to its most prominent intellectual nemesis, Jean-Paul Sartre. It might be said, then, that the agenda of post-Sartrean French philosophy and theory was determined to a great extent by the man himself. If, as Sartre declared in 1946 in a renowned essay, "Existentialism Is a Humanism," then existentialism's successors would be, as part of their self-definition, an "antihumanism." Martin Heidegger's *Letter on Humanism* (1947) was the first counterstrike, a thoroughgoing denunciation of Sartre's tract. As Tom Rockmore's chapter argues, this essay was targeted at a French readership, setting the standard for a new generation of French theoretical reflection. Foucault's own offensive, a salvo aimed at Sartre's *Critique of Dialectical Reason,* was intended for *The Order of Things,* in 1966. But at the last minute he thought better of such a crude assault and withdrew it from the manuscript.[9] Jacques Derrida was more resolute. His 1968 essay on "The Ends of Man" begins with a critical fusillade, a devastating juxtaposition of Sartre with Third Republic ideology and American imperialism.[10]

The Oedipal challenge hinted at here is apparent in Foucault's quest to renew the status of the intellectual. Hindsight has shown this undertaking to be as much a move to distance his project from Sartre's as a challenge to the latter's position as the reigning philosopher-king. Sartre had staked his position on an idea of the writer as both engaged and responsible. This had the effect of elevating the writer to the same status as the politician; indeed, by having the freedom to mount critical diatribes, the writer could claim moral superiority over the politician. The portentous responsibility he assumed was underwritten by the almost subliminal rapport he had with his audience. Sartre's writer, the "general intellectual," was thus a kind of postwar Resistance fighter, addressing the whole community the way Vichy dissidents—including, of course, Sartre himself—had done during the Occupation. He was an intrepid, heroic figure, given to reminding the oppressed and confused masses how free they really were.[11]

Foucault repudiated this view in every respect. He conceived of the writer as someone averse to conventional activism and responsibility. Instead of being a representative figurehead, Foucault's writer was an impersonal space, at ease with his anonymity. Part of the reason for writing *The Order of Things,* he noted, was "to conquer the anonymous, to justify for ourselves the enormous presumption of one day finally becoming anonymous."[12] Elsewhere, he declared that the "author function," once it has disappeared, will enable discourses to "develop in the anonymity of a murmur," behind which "we would hardly hear anything but the stirring of an indifference."[13] Far from possessing an omnipotent political identity, this writer was perpetually straining against impotence. Foucault's version of the modern-day intellectual, the "specific intellectual," emerges fully formed into the arena of dissensus. An elusive figure, he operates in the locales of everyday life, where theory and practice coincide: housing projects, hospitals, asylums, laboratories, universities.[14] He reports from within, avoiding the rhetoric of breast-beating or sanctimoniousness; the specific intellectual recognizes that there is no privileged place to stand, no vantage point where knowledge is not contaminated with power.

Foucault's cultural authority to make such pronouncements ensued from the massive public exposure brought by *The Order of Things*. Over nearly four hundred remorseless pages, Foucault chipped away at the foundations of humanist assurance. Arguing that "man" was a recent invention, of less than two centuries' standing, he demonstrated the accidental nature of his condition and the uncertainty of his future survival. The dense, elliptical prose delivered itself toward the end of a final avowal, the most famous and quoted passage of all antihumanist polemics. Foucault's "dream of apocalypse"—the sublimated uncertainties of the war years—is realized in a stark, unforgettable image:

> If those arrangements were to disappear as they appeared, if some event of which we can at the moment do no more than sense the possibility—without knowing either what its form will be or what it promises—were to cause them to crumble, as the ground of Classical thought did, at the end of the eighteenth century, then one can certainly wager that man would be erased, like a face drawn in sand at the edge of the sea.[15]

Foucault renders the figure of the human ephemeral and evanescent, fatally exposed to the incoming tide of history and contingency. The image is as emblematic of postwar French antihumanism (and as succinct and quotable) as Sartre's apologia had been for existentialist humanism twenty years earlier. The book became a best-seller in France, turning its author into an academic superstar and a sought-after media intellectual. Anonymity was no longer an option, much less an enforced condition.

Not the least of Foucault's talents was his superb sense of timing, since the *Order* coincided with theoretical antihumanism achieving national notoriety. The year 1968 is often cited as the watershed, the moment when the seeds sown earlier in the century reached full bloom (see Ferry and Renaut). But although the *événements* provided an explicit enactment of the antinormative assertions of Althusser, Barthes, and Deleuze, purely in terms of theoretical discourse 1966 might be seen as the year of antihumanism. As well as marking the publication of Foucault's *Order* and (in Germany) of *Negative Dialectic*, Adorno's desolating lament for a morally diminished mankind, it heralded the arrival of Lacan's collected *Ecrits,* which announced that "the true centre of the human being is no longer in the same place assigned to it by the whole humanist tradition."[16]

All these works venerated pluralism and difference, in their manifold forms of undecidability, dispersion, and radical heterogeneity. But the various modes of theoretical antihumanism share some common strategies; they are counterintuitive, sometimes programmatically so, and they are (therefore) relentlessly problematizing. Counterintuitiveness and problematization work together to demonstrate that what has been taken for reality by the Western mind is really something quite other. In Foucault's words, if one "listens to history, he finds that there is 'something altogether different' behind things."[17] Theory shows how we habitually trade real for virtual, oblivious to the fact that such exchanges take place and leave us stranded on terra incognita when our folly is exposed.

As if catching up with such reflections, a spate of recent science-fiction films has conjoined this mistrust of commonsense actuality with the new understandings of cyber-technology. *Dark City, Cube, The Matrix, eXistenZ, Pi,* and *The Thirteenth Floor* disclose doubts that certainty is ever attainable, so lethal and indomitable are the technologies of illusion. Richard Kearney, in his chapter, makes clear the link between late-millennial film narratives of angst and foreboding, and questions of otherness and "monstrosity." Laura Mulvey clarifies the link between theory and film technology by elucidating a "technological uncanny," a zone of uncertainty that "embalms" time and suspends life and death, producing an unnerving confusion of animate with inanimate.

CHARTING TERRA INCOGNITA

After Sartre, after Foucault, what? Whether the watershed is dated as 1966 or 1968, it is clear that the theoretical framework constituting contemporary antihumanism has been in place for over thirty years. The primary concern of this book is the series of related questions that bolsters this framework. If we could get outside our human envelope, what would we see? How would the human appear, from the perspective of the inhuman? Would it even be recognizable? Might the human then manifest itself as a representation, a mere signification, instead of something inherent, intrinsic, and indivisible?

In addressing these questions, the essays that follow could broadly be described as "post-theoretical." They take as a given the rise of theoretical and philosophical antihumanism but resist the programmatic assertions that often accompany such thinking. This means acknowledging, first and foremost, that what theory has bequeathed us is a mixed blessing. On the one hand, we have inherited the tools for taking apart much that has hitherto been thought of as "natural," commonsensical, and intuitive about the human and its others. But on the other hand, there is a frustrating lack of ethical and political commitment in much of this writing. In terms of the account given above, this was one of the key attitudes the specific intellectual set out to dismiss. Prescribing positive alternatives was the bailiwick of the general intellectual—the "rhapsodist of the eternal," in Foucault's words, against whom he wagered his entire political cache. Prescriptive statements work in tandem with normative mechanisms of control, blindly perpetuating the power/knowledge dyad looped into the switchboard of Western thought.

The so-called ethical turn taken by deconstruction in the late 1980s, after the Paul de Man affair, was an attempt to rectify this deficiency. But there was much to attend to, more than the heroic labors of Derrida and a few fellow thinkers could adequately address. In criticizing "man," theorists exposed themselves and their endeavors to charges of political and/or ethical vacancy, and we are the reluctant inheritors of this divestiture. Zygmunt Bauman implicitly questions this in his chapter, by addressing the intractable difficulty of establishing moral parameters within the mobile boundaries of sociopolitical communities. The politics of wilderness appropriation is at the heart of John O'Neill's argument, which also adumbrates the interests governing land that has technically escaped human intervention. On the other side of ethics, Joseph Margolis shows what is at stake in philosophical debates about "naturalism," by framing the human cultural milieu in terms of what he calls the "Intentional." John Mullarkey finds alternative ways of exploring humanity's place in nature and of circumventing the either-or logic of immanence/transcendence.

The antihumanist impetus, such as it is, derives from a scepticism that human ways of being are either admirable or inevitable. "Humanism" is seen to be grounded in assumption, a de facto doctrine derived from the "human." More specifically, humanist doctrines are seen as a series of beliefs and practices derived from one assumption in particular—that we know what the human is, and hence that we know what it means to be human. Antihumanism, by contrast, does not deny the ongoing existence of beings capable of defining themselves and their world, and who experience the relationship between the two as something unique and intrinsic. Rather, it puts into question the designation of "human" for this type of being. This designation (natural and inevitable to the humanist) does not for the antihumanist simply codify something actual but rather fulfills a particular need, an ideological urge to make certain qualities or attributes appear admirable: the moral law, agency, reason, choice, responsibility, all of them tied into universal patterns of behavior. "Humanism," then, is placed under suspicion for being a doctrinal codification of what the "human" has claimed for itself.

Can this be dismissed by saying, "We are all human, so to presume to inhabit the being of the inhuman is a manifest absurdity, an outright impossibility"? Of course, this is true. But although this does characterize

certain enquiries into the inhuman, it does not define the project as a whole.
The discourses of contemporary antihumanism do not attempt to invent
new forms of life as much as question or problematize the envelope that
has come to be known as the "human." New forms of life do not need to
be invented, because they are already extant, concealed by the ideology of
"humanism."

It is not the human, then, that is under interrogation but the "human"—
the process that produces the name, and everything that has been done in
that name. Theory seeks to examine this being as it is, without the metaphysical occlusions and spiritual disfigurations of truth and profundity. The
"human" and its accompaniment, the ideology of "humanism," are the
metaphysical shields protecting us from an inclement environment. If we
were to peer inside the epithelium of the "human," what would we find
there, hidden behind the metaphysics of subjectivity?

The realm of the human is the realm of conscious discourse; beyond it
lies the mysterious and unknowable, a kind of portable other, immanent
to each individual. Freud recognized the inhuman quality of the unconscious
in his description of symptoms as "all-powerful guests from an alien world,
immortal beings intruding into the turmoil of the mind." He elaborated this
in a formulation, the law that "always and everywhere the sense of the
symptoms is unknown to the patient and that analysis regularly shows that
these symptoms are derivatives of unconscious processes but can, subject
to a variety of favorable circumstances, be made conscious."[18] Determined
to prove that the unconscious really existed and could not be dismissed as
something imaginary or makeshift, Freud was anxious to bring unconscious
processes to the surface of the psyche. This, he believed, would prove the
existence of "psychical predeterminants," issuing from the very real locus
of the unconscious. In following this procedure of unconscious made conscious, Freud endeavored to recuperate the unconscious for a therapeutic
humanism, whose aim was to rehumanize the sufferer of obsessional neuroses. Knowing about the existence of the unconscious meant that it could
be "tamed" and its effects neutralized.

In theoretical antihumanism, the activity of the Freudian unconscious is
taken out of the realm of the human and placed in a more impersonal do-
main, where extrahuman discourse is produced: social structures, history,
technology, and so forth. Language is the most cogent paradigm of this shift,
a labyrinthine archive never entirely present to consciousness yet structur-
ing and offering the materials for all thought and utterance. Based on this
model, theoretical antihumanism posits its own "unconscious," an agglom-
eration of antihumanist (i.e., human-decentering) forces: the inhuman en-
croaching on, and partly constituting, the human. This elusive, indistinct
unconscious—which can never be named or made present—is implicit in
any attempt at theorizing antihumanism. In recognizing conscious discourse
as nothing more than clusters of symptoms, as coded signals from an

extrahuman unconscious, we have touched down on the perilous ground of terra incognita, stripped of our human passports.

Sartre's tenacious insistence on the subject as a conscious and free agent capable of self-determination exemplifies his distance from theoretical antihumanism in another important respect. The master tool in Sartre's armory was *mauvaise foi,* the bad faith of denying responsibility for one's life choices (everything from career paths to political allegiances). The term appeared originally in chapter two of *Being and Nothingness,* where it was delineated as a surrogate unconscious. Living with *mauvaise foi* is a debilitating, self-diminishing affair, so "to escape from these difficulties people gladly have recourse to the unconscious." Psychoanalysis, he declares, "substitutes for the notion of bad faith, the idea of a lie without a liar; it allows me to understand how it is possible for me to be lied to without lying to myself."[19] This early refusal of Sartre's to acknowledge the validity of anything outside of conscious, willful decision making and acting furthers the Oedipal relationship separating Sartrean French thought from its successor.

A conscious-unconscious differential is produced through the intervention of power. Steven Connor's chapter shows the historical determinations of power in its "demonic" guise, its maintenance of the division between human and inhuman, self and other. The progenitors of this notion were the "masters of suspicion," Marx, Nietzsche, and Freud. Power, in their terms, is the inevitable by-product of class interest, *ressentiment,* and psychosexual division. What has been sublimated is, however, resistant to both Freudian self-enlightenment (recuperation through analysis) and Marxian disalienation (emancipation through revolutionary praxis). It is the Nietzschean emphasis that has taken root in theory, where power precedes and surpasses agential causation—the conscious, willed activity that enables the "talking cure" to be practiced or nonalienated labor to be performed.

This power-irradiating unconscious behaves like the Freudian unconscious, in that it determines human behavior and can be "read" through symptoms on the surface of the human and its life-world. But it is a virtual unconscious, every bit as alien as Freud's metaphor above suggests, though outside human grasp, out of reach of the agencies of therapy and praxis. It is a true terra incognita, no less with the following consequences: "Anything visible is thus based on the invisible, any presence on absence, any appearance on withdrawal—condemning from then on as naive the idea of absolute transparency and mastery. Any conscious discourse possesses, like the cube, its hidden side, its beyond."[20]

This virtual unconscious makes evident, in short, why the human mind is unable fully to master what the human mind has made. To the contrary, this seditious unconscious has the potential to dismantle the shafts of agency, causality and rationality holding together the "human," indicating the unwitting human propensity to give rise to the inhuman. Thus, at the

heart of human understanding is a hidden shadow, an inhuman other prop-
ping up human self-identity. Simon Critchley's chapter on the paradoxical
nature of humor unravels this doubling up of human and inhuman. He
foregrounds the uneasy coexistence of limitation and overcoming, where
the need for human containment is allied with the desire to exceed it, the
urge to overstep the boundary between human and animal. Humor, too,
informs Thomas Docherty's conception of the human, and it provides a
crucial background to his formulation of a resilient yet tractable critical
agency.

"WHAT OCCASIONALLY IS HUMAN IN MAN"

It has become a truism of the theoretical era (c.1960 to the present) that
what has been and still is nominally regarded as human is never self-present
or "pure," because it is already cohabited by its others. But the converse
also applies. Attempts to think the inhuman can never be unmitigated, because of the resistance offered by our humanist inheritance: "Inescapably,
Western man is metaphysical man. For us, then, the possibility of freedom
must be understood ironically within the framework of metaphysics."[21] Our
metaphysical background thus functions as another kind of unconscious.
Since we cannot rid ourselves of it any more than we can the "antihumanist" unconscious, by knowing both more intimately we can attempt
to re-create ourselves within the forces of their determinations.

Antihumanism possesses cultural force because it is "correct," in the
sense of its being a prior condition, anterior to humanism. The snares of
the unconscious entrap us before the discourses of humanism have begun
to form, exposing us to the exigencies of forces greater than ourselves—
some of which have come from our own hands. We cannot but be help-
lessly changed by our own creations, that is our "facticity." Bearing this
in mind, the human is not the center of the universe, nor is man the measure of all things. Thus, as a diagnosis of the human predicament, antihumanism is both right and necessary. As a response to it, however, and
for the kinds of understanding it has engendered, it is something less than
adequate. Orthodox or "vulgar" humanism ignores the antihumanist unconscious and transfigures human beings into sacred, unique possessors of
meaning and value. At the other extreme, where theory is programmatically revered, the virtual unconscious is exalted for transforming what is
considered to be "human" into a discursive by-product or excrescence.

Theory has given us the tools to mount an ongoing critique of "metaphysical man" (the cardinal tenet of which is that the metaphysical disposition is, indeed, the "natural" human one). The current state of affairs owes
a debt to earlier counterhumanist forays; to repudiate them, as vulgar humanists do, is to deny their acute insights into our present circumstances.
Without theory, current debates about the humanist project would be lim-

ited by the specular distortions of earlier arguments. Contingencies of humanness suggest an alternative to the ahumanisms, antihumanisms, and
posthumanisms of the past century. If rather than being human we are, more
modestly, *becoming* human, then we do better to speak not of "man's inhumanity to man" but, in Emmanuel Levinas's phrase, of "what occasionally is human in man."[22] The chapters that follow seek to apprehend this
wavering, fugitive quality, to chart its disappearance and reemergence in
the ideas and cultural forms of the last century.

NOTES

1. See William Godwin, *Enquiry Concerning Political Justice and Its Influence
on Modern Morals and Happiness* (Harmondsworth: Penguin, 1976), 156–63.

2. Emmanuel Levinas, *Proper Names,* trans. Michael B. Smith (London: Athlone
Press, 1996), 4.

3. T. E. Hulme, *Speculations: Essays on Humanism and the Philosophy of Art*
(London: Routledge and Kegan Paul, 1987), 116.

4. Ibid., 32–33.

5. Theodor Adorno, *Negative Dialectics,* trans. E. B. Ashton (London: Routledge
and Kegan Paul, 1973), 366–67.

6. Ibid., 376.

7. Jean-François Lyotard, *The Differend: Phrases in Dispute,* trans. Georges
Van Den Abbeele (Manchester: Manchester University Press, 1988), 56.

8. Otto Friedrich, "France's Philosopher of Power," interview with Michel
Foucault, in *Time,* 16 November 1981, 148.

9. James Miller, *The Passion of Michel Foucault* (London: Flamingo, 1994),
44.

10. Jacques Derrida, "The Ends of Man," in *Margins of Philosophy*, trans. Alan
Bass (New York: Harvester Press, 1982), 115–17.

11. See Sunil Khilnani, *Arguing Revolution: The Intellectual Left in Postwar
France* (New Haven, Conn., and London: Yale University Press, 1993), 53–56.

12. Michel Foucault, *Foucault Live: Interviews 1961–1984,* trans. Lysa Hochroth
and John Johnston, ed. Sylvère Lotringer (New York, Semiotext[e], 1989), 30.

13. Michel Foucault, "What Is an Author?" trans. Joseph V. Harari, in *Modern
Criticism and Theory,* ed. David Lodge (London and New York: Longman, 1988),
210.

14. Michel Foucault, *Power/Knowledge,* trans. Colin Gordon (Brighton, Sussex:
Harvester Press, 1980), 126.

15. Michel Foucault, *The Order of Things* (London: Routledge, 1970), 387.

16. Jacques Lacan, *Ecrits: Selections,* trans. Alan Sheridan (London: Routledge,
1989), 401.

17. Michel Foucault, "Nietzsche, Genealogy, History," in *The Foucault Reader,*
trans. Donald F. Bouchard and Sherry Simon, ed. Paul Rabinow (Harmondsworth:
Penguin, 1991), 78.

18. Sigmund Freud, "General Theory on the Neuroses," in *The Standard Edition of the Complete Psychological Works of Sigmund Freud,* vol. 16, 1916–17,
trans. James Strachey (London: Hogarth Press, 1963), 278–79.

19. Jean-Paul Sartre, *Being and Nothingness: An Essay on Phenomenological Ontology,* trans. Hazel E. Barnes (London: Routledge, 1969), 50–51.

20. Luc Ferry and Alain Renaut, *French Philosophy of the Sixties: An Essay on Antihumanism,* trans. Mary H. S. Cattani (Amherst: University of Massachusetts Press, 1990), 9.

21. Stephen Yarborough, *Deliberate Criticism: Toward a Postmodern Humanism* (Athens and London: University of Georgia, 1992), 26.

22. Emmanuel Levinas, *The Levinas Reader,* ed. Seán Hand (Oxford: Blackwell, 1989), 290.

PART I

The Backgrounds of Human Being

1

Humanism and Human Being: Beyond Essentialism

Tom Rockmore

Humanism, like love and analogous terms, is widely mentioned but little understood. Everyone is in favor of it, since no one is in favor of its polar opposite, inhumanism; but few observers have more than a hazy idea of what humanism represents. There is no natural, or nonnormative, way to use the term, which takes on different meanings in different contexts. Humanism seems to have an intrinsic reference to practice. Yet a concern with humanism over many years seems not to have been useful in bringing about a better, more humane world. Among the many myths about humanism is the view that it is necessarily associated with what is best about people. It is too easy to forget that it is associated with not only the best but also the worst instincts of human beings, as in the "irrationalist" current, in reaction to positivism, which attracted the Nazi ideologue Alfred Rosenberg, the Munich philosopher Ludwig Klages, and others, and which later led to National Socialism.[1]

The least one can say is that the long humanist tradition has mainly been ineffective in preventing or even in impeding the rise and spread of many forms of inhumanism that singly and collectively constitute the warp and woof of our time. At the beginning of the new millennium, it behooves us to take a fresh look at the concept of humanism in order to determine if and under what conditions it still speaks to us, or if it does not, how it could be reformulated or adjusted to acquire new meaning, perhaps even a certain usefulness, for our lives. I will be arguing that humanism as it has usually been understood implies an essentialist conception of human being that, in our postessentialist environment, is no longer a meaningful approach, so that we require a new, different, nonessentialist view of humanism if the idea is to remain relevant.

WHAT IS "HUMANISM"?

It is not possible here to provide a complete or even an incomplete account of humanism.[2] But it will be useful at least to clarify the term. Any fluent speaker of English knows how to use the word, but, perhaps surprisingly, few people have more than a hazy idea of what it means. Like beauty, humanism comes in various shapes, sizes, and varieties. The concept, which is unclear and difficult to define, is routinely used in different, often incompatible ways. We can distinguish between "humanism" and related words, and between the history of humanism and the various meanings of the term.

"Humanism" refers implicitly or even explicitly to the idea of the human, or to the authentically human, or again to the specifically human, although as we begin the new century there is no agreement—in fact there is considerable disagreement—about what this means. To begin with, the term needs to be differentiated from such near cognates as humanitarianism, or the love of humanity in general. In the Western tradition, humanism goes back at least to Roman times, and perhaps appears a good deal earlier. Socrates' reported concern that the unexamined life is not worth living is perhaps an early example of philosophical humanism directed toward the meaning of human existence, which anticipates existentialism by several thousand years.

The term "humanism" appears in widely separated contexts, including religion, Marxism, and so on. Ethical humanism is associated with a broadly agnostic or atheist approach in which values are presumably justified on wholly rational, or secular, as opposed to nonsecular, religious grounds. Marxist humanism stresses the interest of Marx's remarks about the conception of human being in his early writings, especially the so-called *Manuscripts of 1844,* for his position. It implies a philosophical approach to Marx and Marxism, an implicit rejection of the Marxist view of materialism, by extension an implicit critique of Stalinism, and so on.[3]

There is a long but still not sufficiently clarified association between philosophy and humanism. In Western philosophical circles, tendencies associated with humanism include the philosophical conception of communism, as distinguished from real communism, which in principle would abolish man's self-alienation; pragmatism, because of its anthropocentric view; personalism (also called "spiritualism"), which centers on a conception of the human person; existentialism, which affirms that there is no other universe than the human universe; and so on.

In Western philosophy, humanism is further associated with such ideas as naturalism, freedom, and responsibility. If naturalism is construed as referring to the natural world, then a view that understands man as a natural being belonging to nature can be considered humanist. If it is understood as relating to freedom, then it covers a wide variety of theories, including Kantian ethics, Marx and Marxism, and so on. If it concerns responsibility, then virtually any Christian view, in which responsibility is accorded to individuals, is humanist, as is the entire ethical tradition since Aristotle, who associated responsibility with the capacity to do otherwise.

A concern with humanism is already present in the Roman tradition. Cicero and Varro distinguish between humanitarianism and humanism (*humanitas*), understood in the sense of the Greek *paideia,* meaning education. In standard usage, "humanism" refers both to the revival of ancient learning in the High Middle Ages and the Renaissance, featured in Petrarch, Ficino, Erasmus, More, Rabelais, and many others,[4] and the idea of human being. If "humanism" means the recovery of ancient wisdom, it presupposes a difference between the educated, the humanists, or the supporters of humanism, and the uneducated; on this elitist model there is a difference in kind between the humanists and everyone else.

In the latter sense, humanism is associated with the discovery of the idea of human being in the Renaissance and the emergence of various kinds of individuality in the second part of the fourteenth century. The idea of human being is an idea that later spread throughout Europe, and that development is often taken to mark the end of the Middle Ages. Yet as the older view of classical studies did not disappear when the conception of human being emerged, this whole period is marked by a continual oscillation between the concern in Christian circles to revive the humanist tradition—which is not a philosophy but rather a concern with curriculum, pedagogy, as well as classical literature and language—on the one hand, and the secular or nonsecular emergence of a philosophy of human being, on the other.

Both senses of humanism are present in Høffding's typical effort to define the term: "Humanism denotes, then, not only a literary tendency, a school of philologists, but also a tendency of life, characterized by an interest for the human, both as a subject of observation and as the foundation of action." Høffding's definition evokes both the return to classical studies as well as the novel conception of the human individual as personally responsible that emerges in Christian thinking around the time of Augustine. Yet it omits the further idea—that a certain conception of philosophy is indispensable for the good life in society—which goes all the way back to Socrates as interpreted by Plato.

HUMANISM AND HUMAN BEING

Merely to point out that "humanism" refers either to the recovery or to a conception of "human being" does not resolve but only postpones the problem of what is meant, in other than an imprecise, general way. The concept of culture refers to a view of human being as its subject, which is understood quite differently by, say, a believing Christian, a Kantian, a political nationalist, a biologist, and a neurosurgeon.

The two main anthropological views of human being as a rational being and as made in God's image are now questionable. Suffice it to say that
the religious approach to human being has been decisively undermined since
the end of the Middle Ages, through the continued, increasing seculariza-
tion of modern industrialized society, in a way that apparently cannot be
recovered. There is no reason to think that, say, the rise of militant forms
of Islam in certain underdeveloped regions of the world is likely to reverse
this trend that at the time of this writing affects all, or virtually all, forms
of organized religion.

The generalized turn away from religion in modern industrialized society
removes or at least diminishes its appeal as an explanatory category for the
comprehension of the human world. As Dewey notes, in the West this un-
deniable fact has, since the end of the Middle Ages, prevented organized
religion from exercising its traditional integrative role as a source of orientation in the modern world.[5] This same fact also casts doubt on any contemporary effort, outside confessional circles, to understand man as made
in God's image. In our largely secular environment there is an obvious dichotomy between the believer and the nonbeliever: the former appeals to
the religious dimension to account for ordinary and even extraordinary
features of daily life that for the nonbeliever are explicable in a wholly
different way. An example among many is the difference between the
comprehension of human and animal life for a creationist and for an evo-
lutionist, who represent strictly incommensurable views, with no point in
common. It seems highly unlikely in this new century that the general approach to human being in terms of God will ever again win general favor
in the modern world.

For very different reasons it is just as difficult to accept the venerable
philosophical idea of man as a rational animal. At first glance, this approach
is appealing. Unlike the idea of humanism as the recovery of ancient wisdom, which points to the radical difference between the educated and the
uneducated, the view of man as a rational animal presupposes a radical
equality, whether in the sight of God or as concerns a quality, reason, that
is in principle widely, or universally distributed—as witness Descartes'
famous claim, at the beginning of the *Discours de la méthode,* that good
sense is equally possessed by us all.

Yet the idea that people are intrinsically rational is difficult to defend.
Chomsky, who favors what he calls Cartesian linguistics,[6] claims that human beings can learn natural languages only because the capacity to do so
is hardwired in what he originally called "deep grammar."[7] As interpreted
by Pinker, this means that people differ from other animals in that each of
us possesses a so-called universal grammar.[8] The distinction between man
and other animals on the basis of reasoned speech or even plain language
is increasingly tenuous, since the difference between human and animal
forms of communication is unclear. It is well known that certain higher

vertebrates have naturally occurring forms of communication and that, under the right conditions, human or quasi-human forms of language can be learned by animals.

The idea of reason, which is difficult to define, is understood differently by different observers. Although it is often attributed to human beings, reason is not clearly exhibited in what we do. It is further difficult to isolate a single form of rationality shared by all human beings. Kant's view of reason as the faculty of inference[9] suggests that those less intellectually gifted individuals who are incapable or only partly capable of judging mediately would not be fully human.[10]

The main philosophical argument in favor of a view of human being as a rational animal, which derives from Platonism, rests on a claim for a particular type of human reason, a claim that cannot be demonstrated. In the *Republic*, Plato describes an influential conception of truth and knowledge he may not himself hold. According to this theory, some among us—call them "men of gold"—on grounds of nature and nurture have direct intuition of, hence can be said to know, mind-independent reality. Although no one now accepts the naive Greek view of ontology, the idea that to know is to know mind-independent reality is still strongly influential in, for instance, various forms of metaphysical realism and scientific realism.[11] In the latter, science is regarded as rational because it correctly informs us about the nature of the independent external world. For Platonism, human beings are rational in that at least some of them know the way the world is. Since it has never been shown that or how we know mind-independent reality, the claim that man is a rational animal in this sense has never been demonstrated. Further, the whole idea of defining human beings in terms of a specific capacity they exhibit is clearly circular. For it presupposes that people have this capacity in order then to define them in terms of it.

PHILOSOPHY AS HUMANIST

Humanism is associated with particular philosophical periods or even whole traditions. It is often regarded as central to the Enlightenment. Pope's famous couplet is frequently taken as a motto of Enlightenment interest in the study of man. "Presume not then the ways of God to scan / The proper study of mankind is man." Enlightenment humanism understands the thought of this period as resolutely rationalist, secular—in fact, the realization of reason in its highest form as a means of human progress without limit, already suggested in the Cartesian view of philosophy. Elsewhere I have argued that from the time of Montaigne and Descartes, who were concerned with the entire French intellectual tradition, there is a central preoccupation with understanding the subject and the world from the perspective of human being—a concern that is, therefore, broadly humanist.[12]

Is philosophy in general, or at least Western philosophy, or again a strand of Western philosophy, humanist? The anthropocentric approach to humanism, which goes all the way back to Protagoras's view of man as the measure, runs forward throughout the modern debate. It is, to begin with, a main theme in moral theory from Aristotle, who perhaps for the first time makes responsibility depend on the freedom to do otherwise, to the present. The idea of freedom presupposed in any meaningful conception of ethics is widely influential in religious conceptions of human responsibility and in conceptions of human being as intrinsically free. In a famous passage, Pico della Mirandola stresses the idea of human freedom:

> I have given you, Adam, neither a predetermined place nor a particular aspect nor any special prerogatives in order that you make take and possess these through your own decision and choice. The limitations on the nature of other creatures are contained within my prescribed laws. You shall determine your own nature without constraint from any barrier, by means of the freedom to whose power I have entrusted you. I have placed you at the center of the world so that from that point you might see better what is in the world. I have made you neither heavenly nor earthly, neither mortal nor immortal so that, like a free and sovereign artificer, you might mold and fashion yourself into that form you yourself shall have chosen.[13]

This view of the moral individual as free is central to Kant's theory of practical reason. It is further the basis of the M'Naughten rule (1843), according to which an individual is legally responsible if and only if he possesses the capacity to distinguish right and wrong at the moment of the act.

The anthropocentric approach is further central to modern epistemology. Theory of knowledge, which is a main philosophical concern, always depends on a conception of the knower. We have already noted the ancient Greek view of knowledge as suggesting a direct grasp of mind-independent reality by a select group of properly trained, gifted individuals. After the rejection of the naive Greek ontology, modern thinkers argue for knowledge not in independence but rather on the basis of the subject. Modern philosophers since Montaigne and Descartes typically stress the relation of objective cognition to the subject. The modern view of the importance of the subject was considerably strengthened in the turn to history in the wake of the French Revolution. The anthropocentric approach to knowledge is typical of modern science and philosophy. It is associated with the introduction of the Copernican worldview, according to which the earth, hence human being, was displaced from the center of the universe, which could only be understood from the human perspective. Various forms of this idea are formulated independently in Vico's anti-Cartesian claim that man, who cannot know nature, can know only history; in the British empiricist concern with human knowledge; in Kant's famous claim, central to the critical philosophy, that we can know only what we in some sense "construct," "produce," or "bring forth"; in Hegelian historicism; in Marx; in the contextualism of the later Wittgenstein; in the empiricist naturalism typical of American pragmatism; and so on.

HEIDEGGER'S ATTACK ON DESCARTES AND HUMANISM

Heidegger, who equates traditional, anthropological forms of humanism with metaphysics, rejects more traditional essentialist views of man in favor of his own, rival, nonanthropological view of man's true nonmetaphysical essence.[14] Heidegger's commitment to an essentialist conception of human being is well known, even notorious. He has been criticized for remaining committed to an essentialist conception of man,[15] which has been further identified as the source of his turn toward Nazism, which was supposedly also humanist.[16]

Heidegger's attack on anthropological approaches to human being, directed against the Cartesian subject, modern philosophy and anthropocentric humanism,[17] is a constant theme in his position early and late. His attack includes four elements: a critique of Cartesian subjectivity, which is later expanded into a critique of subject-centered philosophy; his own rival, anti-anthropological view of the subject; and his own view of humanism.

His critique of the Cartesian *cogito* develops his claim that in the formula *cogito ergo sum*, Descartes forgets the *sum*.[18] He expands this idea in the claim that Descartes begins the consummation and completion of Western metaphysics in the idea of man as a subject, which is presupposed in every future anthropology.[19] In his early philosophy, he posits a conception of the subject as *Dasein*, always already there in the world that, after the obscure turning in his thought, he later abandons in suggesting that anything resembling a Cartesian approach to subjectivity—hence, on his reading, an anthropological approach to metaphysics deriving from Christianity—must be abandoned.[20] In his discussion of humanism, officially motivated by his desire to distinguish his own position from Sartrean existentialism, Heidegger proposes a new, allegedly deeper, ontological humanism according to which human being was to be understood in terms of 'being' in general.[21]

I believe, although I cannot argue the point here, that Heidegger's critique of Descartes derives from a fundamental misreading of the position. It is incorrect to claim that he reduces the subject to a thing but correct to claim that he does not clearly understand the cognitive subject, or *cogito*, as either a spectator or an actor but in both cases as a human being already in the world. The anthropological approach, which does not begin in Descartes, can also not simply be abandoned as Heidegger implies. For as Descartes points out, the road to objectivity necessarily runs through subjectivity.

I further believe that Heidegger's own view of humanism has been mainly misunderstood, since its historical background has been covered up. His *Letter on Humanism* is doubly determined by two factors: his determined effort to curry favor with French readers when after the war he was called to account for his active support of National Socialism, and his continued commitment to Nazism. In the 1930s, as part of the rise of National Socialism, another form of humanism, the "third humanism of Nazi man," arose, in connection with an explicitly political rereading of Plato that was proposed by Jaeger and others.[22] This idea, which distantly derives from the pan-German Graecophilia influentially kindled by Winckelmann,[23] led to a view of humanism as the alleged historical realization of a new kind of human being, supposedly associated with ancient Greek philosophy, to which contemporary German philosophy was allegedly the heir. In Werner Jaeger's authoritative rereading of Plato, the German Nazis were understood as the true heirs to the Greeks. Heidegger rejects this reading of Plato as failing to do justice to the specificity of the Nazis.[24] But he significantly does not reject, in fact affirms, the idea that National Socialism represents an opportunity to realize the German essence, what he calls the Germanness of the Germans.[25]

What Heidegger calls "humanism" echoes the religious view of man as dependent on God in his conception of *Dasein* as dependent on being. For Heidegger, man is what he calls the "shepherd of being,"[26] and "what counts is *humanitas* in the service of the truth of Being, but without humanism in the metaphysical sense."[27] "Humanism" in this theory does not mean anything like a view of man as independent, hence as free, as exemplified by Pico, but rather a view of man as dependent. Heidegger interprets his rejection of the anthropocentric approach to man as requiring him to reject modern philosophy, indeed philosophy as such in all its forms, for thought (*Denken*) is hoist with its own petard. For his ontological view of humanism does not improve on, but rather falls to, his own view that the sciences and other traditional forms of anthropology presuppose a conception of human being, which Heidegger also presupposes in his view of being.

HUMAN BEING AND ESSENTIALISM

The essentialist approach to human being is widespread but perilous, since it is difficult to make out the very idea of an essence. This is a postessentialist period, in which doubt is rampant that we ever discover any essences, or even that there are any essences to be discovered.[28]

The traditional anthropological and the Heideggerian nontraditional, anti-anthropological views of the subject are both essentialist. Each claims to grasp the essence of human being in a way deeper than, say, the various sciences, which cannot discover, uncover, or determine what they inevita-

bly already presuppose as a condition of their investigations.[29] Essentialism is rampant in efforts to understand human being, including human
capacities, such as language—for instance, in Chomsky's view that there is
a fixed set of hardwired capabilities. Heidegger's effort to think the essence
of man more primordially[30] does not evade problems that arise within essentialism.

Essentialism is often understood as the view that objects have essences
and that there is a distinction between what is essential and what is nonessential. Aristotle was already concerned with the distinction between what
an object is, its essence, and *how* it is, which is nonessential. This distinction is often rendered as the difference between essential (*kath'auto*) and
inessential (*kata symbebekos*) predication. Recent discussions of essentialism in the context of the problem of semantic reference, focusing on *de re*
modality, or necessary truth in all possible worlds, is very different from
the Aristotelian and post-Aristotelian focus on what something is and how
it is.

In a recent discussion of essentialism, the distinguished phenomenologist
J. N. Mohanty distinguishes three main varieties of essentialism, according
to whether the essence is posited as unknowable within experience (Plato),
as a theoretical entity within a scientific theory (Saul Kripke), or finally as
experiencable and experienced (Edmund Husserl).[31] Plato is usually understood to hold that the epistemological knowledge of particulars depends
on an ontological relation of participation (*methexis*). He is routinely taken
as suggesting that ideas are the condition of knowledge of what he calls
"appearances," although on grounds of nature and nurture some among
us can in principle directly grasp reality as the necessary condition of knowledge. Kripke, who is concerned with definite reference, in his language
"rigid designation," addresses essentialism as the intuitive belief in modality
de re. Husserl maintains that we can and do pick out particulars by virtue
of a prior grasp of universals. The common thread in various types of essentialism seems to be the idea that it is only on the basis of a prior universal that we can identify a particular as one—that is, in current jargon,
as a token of a type.

When essentialism is understood in this way, it is vulnerable on two
grounds: the decision to accept a particular view of essence (say, the essence
of human being), and the problematic nature of the very idea of an essence.
As soon as an essence is identified by an observer, others can disagree. Disagreement can take different forms, such as the failure to agree on the essence in question or even the denial that there is an essence to be observed.
Heidegger is a case in point, since, on the basis of his anti-anthropological
approach to man, he disagrees with the main forms of the anthropological
approach.

This disagreement can be explained in different ways. One is to suggest
that essences, like facts, simply cannot be determined apart from prior

conceptual frameworks, schemes, frames of reference, perspective, or points of view. I am assuming here that a distinction between contents and frameworks can be drawn.[32] An essence is like a fact. In the same way as what counts as a fact depends on a conceptually prior framework, so what counts as an essence, hence the nature of that essence, depends on the conceptual framework, which is never neutral.

Since a disagreement about essences presupposes the prior existence of essences about which to disagree, essentialism resembles metaphysical realism, according to which the mind-independent world consists of a totality of mind-independent objects.[33] Just as one could hold that our theories of the external world offer different interpretations of the same mind-independent world, one could also hold that theories of the essence of human being are no more than different readings of the same mind-independent human essence. But there is no more reason to think there is a mind-independent human essence than to think that there is a mind-independent world. The essentialist approach to human being, hence the essentialist approach to humanism, fails because there is no way to show that mind-independent essences exist.

CONCLUSION: HUMANISM AND A NONESSENTIALIST IDEA OF HUMAN BEING

It is widely but incorrectly presupposed that essentialism is unproblematic. Even such a radical thinker as Heidegger assumes but does not demonstrate that an essentialist approach to human being requires no particular justification. Understood in different ways, essentialism is widely utilized in possible world semantics, in Husserlian phenomenology. It is further applied to a wide variety of domains, such as politics.[34] I have been arguing that since essentialism is problematic and even indefensible, forms of humanism based on a conception of the essence of human being are also difficult to defend. If humanism is to recover its plausibility it must either be understood apart from human being or, if it is understood through human being, "human being" must be grasped in a different, nonessentialist manner.

If "humanism" is to be understood in a way resembling the meanings this term has taken on in modern times, we cannot understand it other than through some conception of human being. If "human being" cannot be understood in an essentialist manner, we need either to understand it nonessentially or to abandon humanism. There are various nonessential models of human being. One is Sartre's Romantic but unrealistic idea that human beings, who have no essence, simply freely decide what they will be through their choices and actions in a way unimpeded by their surroundings.[35] Sartre is correct to hold that there is no fixed human essence but incorrect to contend that for this reason there are no constraints. For all of us are always already in a context by which we are shaped and within which we live out our lives.

My suggestion is to understand human beings on a roughly Marxian model as beings with multiple capacities or potentials, which they express, manifest, or develop in the concrete situations into which they are born and that continue to shape the ways they later develop in the course of meeting their needs and of realizing (to the extent that any of us can) their hopes, aspirations, and dreams. On this nonessentialist view of human being, a person lives, flourishes, and dies within a human context "constructed" in the interaction with others and nature, within which one can strive for freedom but no one is ever wholly free.

A model of human being that understands human freedom in context has two clear advantages. On the one hand, it avoids disagreements about the fixed nature of human being that arise in any essentialist conception of human beings. Disputes about man's nature cannot arise if man literally has no nature. On the other hand, it offers an interesting take on humanism as the concern to preserve and to increase the extent of real human freedom, not outside but rather within the real context, providing within the constraints of real possibility for the realization of human capacities, hence for human beings as really individual.

NOTES

1. See "The Occult Origins of National Socialism," in George L. Mosse, *The Fascist Revolution: Toward a General Theory of Fascism* (New York: Howard Fertig, 1999), 117–37.

2. See, for a representative discussion, Nicola Abbangnano, "humanism," in *The Encyclopedia of Philosophy*, ed. Paul Edwards (New York: Macmillan, 1967), vol. 4, 69–71. The article provides further references.

3. See, e.g., Adam Schaff, *A Philosophy of Man* (New York: Dell, 1963).

4. For a discussion of the rise of Renaissance humanism in the High Middle Ages, see Michael R. Allen, "humanism," in *The Columbia Encyclopedia of Western Philosophy*, ed. Richard H. Popkin (New York: Columbia University Press, 1999), 282–93.

5. See John Dewey, *The Quest for Certainty: A Study of the Relation of Knowledge and Action* (New York: Putnam, 1960).

6. See Noam Chomsky, *Cartesian Linguistics* (New York: Harper & Row, 1966).

7. Chomsky has often written about his view. For a recent, accessible discussion, see Noam Chomsky, *Language and Problems of Knowledge: The Managua Lectures* (Cambridge, Mass.: MIT Press, 1994).

8. See Steven Pinker, *The Language Instinct: How the Mind Creates Language* (New York: Harper Perennial, 1995).

9. See Immanuel Kant, *Critique of Pure Reason*, trans. Paul Guyer and Allen W. Wood (Cambridge and New York: Cambridge University Press, 1998), B 386.

10. Ibid., B 172.

11. See, e.g., Michael Devitt, *Realism and Truth* (Princeton, N.J.: Princeton University Press, 1997).

12. See Tom Rockmore, *Heidegger and French Philosophy: Humanism, Antihumanism and Being* (London: Routledge, 1995).

13. Pico della Mirandola, "Oration on the Dignity of Man," in *On the Dignity of Man: On Being and the One, Heptaplus*, trans. C. G. Wallace, P.J.W. Miller, and D. Carmichael (Indianapolis: LLA, 1955), 4–5.

14. See Heidegger, "Letter on Humanism," in *Basic Writings*, ed. David F. Krell (San Francisco, Calif.: HarperSanFrancisco, 1993), 229.

15. He has been criticized for maintaining an essentialist approach to human being. See, e.g., "Les Fins de l'homme," in Jacques Derrida, "The Ends of Man" in *Margins of Philosophy*, trans. Alan Bass (Chicago: University of Chicago Press, 1982), 109–36.

16. See Philippe Lacoue-Labarthe, *La Fiction du politique* (Paris: Christian Bourgeois, 1988).

17. There is an extensive discussion of Heidegger's view of humanism. See Tom Rockmore, Gail Soffer, "Heidegger, Humanism, and the Destruction of History," in *Review of Metaphysics* 49 (March 1996): 547–76.

18. See Martin Heidegger, *Being and Time*, trans. John Macquarrie and Edward Robinson (Evanston, Ill.: Harper & Row, 1962), 71, 122–34.

19. See "The Age of the World Picture," in Martin Heidegger, *The Question Concerning Technology and Other Essays*, trans. William Lovitt (New York: HarperCollins, 1982), 140.

20. See Heidegger, *The Question Concerning Technology*, 153.

21. See "Letter on Humanism," in Heidegger, *Basic Writings*, 189–242.

22. For Heidegger's initial reaction to this rereading of Plato, which he opposed, see Martin Heidegger, *Hölderlins Hymnen >>Germanien und der Rhein<<* (Frankfurt a.M.: Vittorio Klostermann, 1980), 48–49.

23. See J. J. Winckelmann, *Gedanken über die Nachahmung der grieschischen Werke in der Malerei und Bildhauerkunst* (Stuttgart: Philipp Reclam, 1969).

24. See Martin Heidegger, *Hölderlins Hymnen >>Der Ister<<* (Frankfurt a.M.: Vittorio Klostermann, 1984), 98, 106.

25. See Martin Heidegger, *Heraklit* (Frankfurt a.M.: Vittorio Klostermann, 1987), 107–108, 123.

26. See Heidegger, *Basic Writings*, 221, 222.

27. Ibid., 231.

28. See, e.g., Richard Rorty, *Philosophy and the Mirror of Nature* (Princeton, N.J.: Princeton University Press, 1979), 357.

29. See Heidegger, *Being and Time*, 71–75.

30. See Heidegger, *Basic Writings*, 224.

31. See J. N. Mohanty, *Phenomenology: Between Essentialism and Transcendental Philosophy* (Evanston, Ill.: Northwestern University Press, 1997).

32. For a counterargument, see "The Very Idea of a Conceptual Scheme," in Donald Davidson, *Truth and Interpretation* (New York: Oxford University Press, 1991), 183–98.

33. See Hilary Putnam, *Reason, Truth and History* (New York: Cambridge University Press, 1990), 49.

34. For discussion of Heidegger's effort to develop an essentialist theory of politics, see Miguel de Beistegui, *Heidegger and the Political: Dystopias* (London: Routledge, 1998).

35. See Jean-Paul Sartre, *Existentialism and Humanism*, trans. Philip Mairet (London: Methuen, 1980).

2

The Rehumanization of Art: Modernism, Technology, and the Crisis of Humanism

Michael Hollington

Like much else associated with our current Age of Theory, debts to the modernist art of the first half of the twentieth century are still being tallied. Modernism, however, distinguishes itself from artistic and intellectual movements before and since by its persistent leaning toward auto-theorization. In the urge to produce statements of artistic intent in the form of decrees, manifestos, programs for renewal and other self-justifying tracts, an overt theoretical edge was added to the challenges to orthodoxy issued by the artworks themselves. This forward-looking movement contrasts with more recent theoretical reflection, whose transformative praxis is mobilized through readings of the past that attempt, as it were, to alter the past, via "secret" histories or counterhistories, following Benjamin's directive to brush history—not to mention philosophy, sociology, political enquiry, gender construction, and so on—against the grain. Modernist poetics might also seem to part company with postwar theoretical discourse in its gesturing toward the rigors of system—but such gestures were, more often than not, rhetorical figures rather than coherent programs for change. Even so, they exerted a powerful influence on subsequent understandings of the era.

This chapter offers a reexamination of the fortunes of humanism in the period of modernism, considering the relationship between the human and the mechanical as a central strand of the crisis of humanism in the early twentieth century. It then seeks to uncover a broader spectrum of attitudes toward this relationship in writers and artists of the period, rather than assuming that humanism is simply extinguished or supplanted. I propose, then, to undertake an immanent reading of modernist theory, reading modernism as it read itself—or through the kinds of rhetoric that reveal, nonetheless, much of modernism's attitude to the human and its others.

Three main tendencies can be identified, in terms of modernist responses to the machine. The first, most obviously descended from Romanticism, reflects a mood of profound defeatist cultural pessimism about the impact of the machine upon modernity, taking as its prime instance the horrors of the First World War. The second is its diametrical opposite, the enthusiastic embrace of modernity and new technology by such writers and artists as the Italian and Russian Futurists. But there is also in modernism a third, more "sophisticated" tendency, represented by ironic writers, artists, and thinkers such as Joyce, Thomas Mann, and the practitioners and theorists of the Bauhaus. Here, defeatism and triumphalism give way to a greater detachment and cooler, often humorous contemplation of attempts to negotiate the new world of machines. I suggest that this could also be seen as an attempt, if not to rescue humanism in its pristine form, then to keep it alive in a period of crisis.

A generation ago, Robert Weimann stated that the "need for theory and method is usually felt most acutely when, in a time of rapid changes, the object of theoretical inquiry no longer functions in its traditional context."[1] Weimann sought an historical explanation for the preoccupation with theory in the preceding quarter-century or so. As a Marxist critic working in the German Democratic Republic, he believed that it was chiefly the function of literature in a capitalist society that was problematic, the analysis of that problem rather less so. Soon after he made this observation, continental theory infiltrated Anglo-American critical practice, indicating a radical uncertainty about method itself, a lack of confidence in established critical concepts and a restless search for new ones.

In the case of modernism, the cardinal problem in terms of critical understanding is the continuing proximity of the object of inquiry and the difficulty of achieving independent perspective. Whether we are in a postlapsarian stage and are now experiencing the "brass and iron ages" of the modernist cycle, or whether writers as diverse as Günter Grass, Thomas Bernhard, Gabriel García Márquez, and Harold Brodkey have indicated what might be thought of a renaissance of modernism, I would contend that "postmodernism" is hardly a convincing name to designate any fundamentally compelling artistic or intellectual movement of broad international scope. Many contemporary critical systems—particularly those that emphasize autonomy and/or absence of referentiality as a feature of literary works—also seem to stem essentially from the modernist period. From New Criticism and Northrop Frye's "anatomy of criticism," to certain versions of structuralism and poststructuralism, the crucial insights of modernism could be seen as becoming refined and developed—occasionally achieving the intellectual beauty of poems the Symbolists themselves were unable to complete—rather than as being fundamentally altered. As a result, some contemporary criticism can still sound like *mitsingen,* the vicarious reformulation of modernist aesthetic polemics. As Harry Levin once wrote, "We may well count ourselves fortunate . . . that we can so effortlessly enjoy those gains secured by the pangs of our forerunners."[2]

This proximity may help to explain what I shall characterize as the pervasively binary approach of much writing on the modernist period. I am thinking here of a parallel to Jack Goody's critique of Lévi-Strauss and *La Pensée Sauvage*. Goody thinks that the structure of European languages, in which the "we/they division penetrates so deeply our everyday speech," determines an ethnocentric habit of thinking in terms of a "set of categories, such as primitive and advanced, simple and complex, developing and developed, traditional and modern, pre-capitalist etc."[3] that circumscribe our perception of difference: "the dichotomising of 'we' and 'they' in this manner narrows the field both of the topic and its explanation."[4] Paul Fussell, in *The Great War and Modern Memory*, provides an historical explanation of thinking in terms of "them and us" when he suggests that the prolonged nervous consciousness of the enemy in the frontline trenches of the First World War promoted "the modern *versus* habit"—"the mode of gross dichotomy [that] came to dominate perception and expression elsewhere."

Fussell goes on to quote supporting testimony from Carl Jung, who analyzed one of his own dreams in the 1920s as a symptom of the general condition of man in which "the war . . . was not yet over, but was continuing to be fought within the psyche."[5] One might say that the wars of modernism continue likewise to be fought in the psyches of many contemporary critics, so common is the habit of defining it in terms of some single, static concept or set of relations—nonreferentiality, the image, spatial form, etc.—and polarizing these against some equally static antithesis—mimesis, linear plot, temporal form. Though the adoption of such positions was clearly a necessary part of the *self*-definitions of modernist artists, we run the risk of cliché, oversimplification, and overgeneralization if we merely continue to repeat them as definitions from the standpoint of now.

As already indicated, I shall address a federal bundle of laterally related "modernisms," rather than one central monolithic concept. This is all the more necessary in view of the fact that, although some modernist practitioners adopted a single-concept self-definition, many others were conscious of living in a "multiverse" that could not be reduced to single-perspective unity—the essence of the doctrine and practice of cubism, for instance, though to make all modernists cubists, as some critics once tried to do, is to risk reintroducing paradoxical monism. There are of course some valuable contributions to a plural taxonomy of modernism, but one can hardly think of such approaches as having established themselves as normative. The fact again is, perhaps, that the writers and artists of modernism were so fond of making up labels for *themselves* and announcing their *own* distinctness that they make life difficult for the would-be taxonomist of the movement as a whole. Besides this, the whole area of modernism is so vast and so mined with paradox that it offers radical challenge to *any* conventional logic classification.

I take as my central theme the question of how the artists of modernism come to terms with the crisis of relations between science and human values, and treat that crisis within their work. This is familiar territory, but I am attempting to make a limited contribution to the discussion of this subject by exploring a larger spectrum of attitudes than is perhaps generally invoked. It seems to me that within this spectrum certain reasonably clear-cut distinctions are discernible: first, between those artists who simply loathe and reject modern technology and its social and cultural consequence, and those who celebrate both of these with enthusiasm; and second, between both these kinds of artists and a smaller, more sophisticated, and more critically discriminating group of artists who attempt some new ways of adjusting, if not of synthesizing, the relations between science and human values. Of course there are many artists who will not fit simply into one category or who will seem to change course once or even several times during their careers. But within this framework some kind of reassessment of the role of humanism within the period becomes possible, one in which it perhaps does not die out altogether (though it obviously takes a battering) but goes underground to express itself chiefly in a more complex ironic mode than ever before. I give irony a significant, if not predominant, role in modernist art, and it seems to me to retain the essential critical spirit of humanism.

I begin by juxtaposing passages by four poets about the challenge of modern science to the poet's art and sensibility. The first is from Wordsworth's (updated) *Preface to the Lyrical Ballads* (1850): "If the time should ever come when what is now called science, thus familiarized to men, shall be ready to put on, as it were, a form of flesh and blood, the Poet will lend his divine spirit to aid the transfiguration, and will welcome the Being thus produced, as a dear and genuine inmate of the household of man."[6] The second is from Matthew Arnold's 1882 essay "Literature and Science":

> But how, finally, are poetry and eloquence to exercise the power of relating modern results of natural science to man's instinct for conduct, his instinct for beauty? And here again I answer that I do not know how they will exercise it, but that they can and will exercise it I am sure. . . . [S]uch is the strength and worth, in essentials, of their authors' criticism of life,—they have a fortifying, and elevating, and quickening, and suggestive power, capable of wonderfully helping us to relate the results of modern science to our need for conduct, our need for beauty.[7]

The third is from a piece by Hart Crane entitled "Modern Poetry," and its date is 1930: "The function of poetry in a Machine Age is identical to its function in any other age; and its capacities for presenting the most complete synthesis of human values remains essentially immune from the so-called inroads of science. . . . For unless poetry can absorb the machine, i.e., *acclimatize* it naturally and casually as trees, cattle, galleons, castles and all other associations of the past, then poetry has failed of its full contemporary function."[8] The fourth is from David Jones's preface to his *In Parenthesis*, first published in 1937 and referring to the First World War:

> It is not easy in considering a trench-mortar barrage to give praise for the action proper to chemicals—full though it may be of beauty. We feel a rubicon has been passed between striking with a hand weapon as men used to do and loosing poison from the skies as we do ourselves. We doubt the decency of our own inventions, and are certainly in terror of their possibilities. . . . We stroke cats, pluck flowers, tie ribands, assist at the manual acts of religion, make some kind of love, write poems, paint pictures, are generally at one with that creaturely world inherited from our remote beginnings. Our perception of many things is heightened and clarified. Yet must we do gas-drill, be attuned to many new-fangled technicalities, respond to increasingly exacting mechanical devices; some fascinating and compelling, others sinister in the extreme, all requiring a new and strange direction of the mind, a new sensitivity certainly, but at a considerable cost. We who are of the same world of sense with hairy ass and furry wolf and who presume to other and more radiant affinities, are finding it difficult, as yet, to recognize these creatures of chemicals as true extensions of ourselves, that we may feel for them a native affection which alone can make them magical for us.[9]

Perhaps the most striking thing that emerges from this juxtaposition is the remarkable degree of continuity in the consciousness of this problem that the passages exhibit. Within this continuity, however, clear differences emerge, already sufficiently marked in the progression from Wordsworth to Matthew Arnold. For Wordsworth there is a Christian metalanguage capable of relating the spheres of science and human value; the problem is made analogous to the process of Christ's incarnation, and the poet is a divinely inspired priest assisting at the transubstantiation.

Matthew Arnold's confidence is surely less convincing; unlike Wordsworth, he cannot say how poetry will exercise its power, and his optimistic liberal rhetoric, relying on adverbial echoes of the language of religious miracle, sounds a bit hollow and imprecise. But of course the chief distinction is between the two nineteenth-century writers, who attempt prophecy about a crisis still seen as some way off, and the two modernists, who are in the middle of it. Neither of them succumbs to pessimism, but they are both conscious of an urgent task of synthesis, the failure of which may render poetry irrelevant. Jones in particular employs dichotomized registers of language—the concrete versus the abstract, the humanly ordinary versus the technological—that underline the extent of the divorce. There enters into his writing a trace of an irony of understatement, as the reasonableness of his tone confronts the evident magnitude of the task.

Jones and Crane write after the decisive modernist loss of faith in the nineteenth-century liberal vision of the endless advance of scientific progress. "Progress, therefore, is not an accident but a necessity. . . . [S]urely must the things we call evil and immorality disappear; so surely must men become perfect," wrote the positivist Herbert Spencer in 1851.[10] This kind of language has sounded useless for little but parody to the ears of modernist artists. Describing New York in his autobiography of 1905, Henry Adams employs the clichés of positivism in a way that makes them echo newspaper headlines and incorporates them in sentences with cadences that are mockingly bathetic: "Prosperity never before imagined, power never yet yielded by man, speed never reached by anything but a meteor, made the world irritable, nervous, querulous, unreasonable and afraid."[11] From there it is only a short step to the terse and bitter ironies aimed at the language of progress in the war sections of Pound's *Hugh Selwyn Mauberley* ("disillusions as never told in the old days").[12]

The war itself put paid to naïve realism, revealing, as Henry James recognized as soon as it was declared, that "what the treacherous years were all the while really making for and meaning" was not a new level of civilization but a new level of barbarism. The glib ethical abstractions of the optimistic tradition were immediately rendered inoperative, as Yeats (along with countless others) registered in his poem *Nineteen Hundred and Nineteen*, with its reference to "The Weasel's twist, the weasel's tooth."[13]

Behind the discredited faith in science and progress many modernist writers diagnosed a fatal obsession not only with empty abstractions but with the syllogism and the linear structure of Western logic. "All our mental consciousness is a movement onwards," wrote D. H. Lawrence in *Apocalypse*, "a movement in stages, like our sentences, and every full stop is a mile-stone that marks our 'progress' and our arrival somewhere. On and on we go, for the mental consciousness. Whereas of course there is no goal. Consciousness is an end in itself. We torture ourselves getting somewhere, and when we get there it is nowhere, for there is nowhere to get to."[14]

This kind of preoccupation with linear logic was itself widely parodied, as in Brecht's "Legend of the Dead Soldier," where the hero's death is a syllogistic absurdity, "the logical thing" for him to do.[15]

Among the extreme postwar generation of Dadaists and Surrealists were figures like Jacques Rigaut, prepared to act out in real life absurd demonstrations of the meaning of cause-and-effect logic by predicting in 1919 that he would commit suicide ten years later, and carrying this out on November 5, 1929. Rigaut was also the author of an interesting piece of humorous science fiction called "Un Brillant Sujet," which attempts to sabotage the linear logic of Western history by sending its hero back to the Garden of Eden so that he may start again and remove the stages of the argument by cutting off Cleopatra's nose, having Homer write the works of Tristan

Tzara rather than the *Iliad* and *Odyssey*, poisoning Jesus Christ as a young man, and, of course, discovering steam and electricity in South America so that indigenous Indians rather than Europeans might enjoy its "benefits."[16]

With Rigaut we encounter as extreme a representative as I care to uncover of that *double* reaction—against both the rationalism of the eighteenth century and the materialism of the nineteenth century—that Yeats defined as the cardinal principle of the Symbolist movement. The example may help to suggest why I want to argue the pluralist case that Symbolism supplies only one of the strands, or poles, of definition of modernism rather than the dominant aesthetic that, subject to no more than qualification and revision, is thought by some to inform modernist art as a whole. This latter view stems from the prestige and influence exercised in some Anglo-American quarters by, until recently, Edmund Wilson's *Axel's Castle* (first published in 1931).[17] Unlike many of his followers, Wilson was critical of the Symbolist aesthetic and moreover allowed Naturalism a lesser but still significant place in the inspiration of works like *Ulysses,* but his book does not—perhaps could not, in view of its date—take account of the radical discontinuities within the modernist tradition, with movements like Imagism in England and *Neue Sachlichkeit* in Germany effecting major shifts away from the Symbolist tradition.

The character of Symbolist thinking is strikingly binary or dualistic. The primary antithesis is a Platonist opposition between the world of matter and the world of spirit. Walter Pater recognized this as the perpetual flux of change, from his preoccupation with Heraclitus (whom he translated and whose philosophical outlook Pater traced through Plato and into Hegel and Darwin). In *Plato and Platonism* he writes: "The principle of disintegration, the incoherency of fire or flood ... are inherent in the primary elements alike of matter and of the soul."[18] This basic antimony points toward most of the Symbolist antitheses. Art has no mediating function, as it has in all the passages above, from Wordsworth to David Jones. On the contrary, it is decisively aligned only with one side of the binary—with the world of the spirit. Art thus turns its back on modern science. Even more, art turns its back on humanity itself, as W. B. Yeats observed of the Rhymers' Club in 1892: "To them literature had ceased to be the handmaid of humanity, and become instead a terrible queen, in whose service the stars rose and set, and for whose pleasure life stumbles along in the darkness."[19]

This arresting passage also serves to characterize the extreme binary form of Symbolist politics, postulating as it does an unmediated divide between the unspeakable base, materialistic herd of man and woman in the mass, and the exceptional autocratic individual, often a projection of the artist himself, who should rule them. George Moore expresses this kind of attitude when he writes in jocular complaint of the troubles that are caused to him by Davitt's protesting Irish land tenants, "That some wretched farmers and miners should refuse to starve, that I may not be deprived of my *demi-tasse* at *Tortini's*, that I may not be forced to leave this beautiful retreat, my cat and my python—monstrous."[20] But despite some other exceptions, such as Huysmans and Oscar Wilde, many of the aesthetes of the latter part of the century thought that humor itself was something rather impure. The lack of irony in the Symbolist position—there is no surer sign of its inadequacy as a touchstone for the whole of modernism—may have contributed to the tragedy of Ezra Pound, who adopted antidemocratic politics at an early stage, applying them first to the Great War and then going on to aestheticize the Second World War as well, with calamitous personal consequences.

But the main significance of Symbolism as an index to a cultural crisis seems to me to reside in its attempt to make art into a substitute for religion. Seen in this way it takes its place alongside such characteristic phenomena of the late nineteenth century as theosophy and Rosicrucianism, Madame Blavatsky and Joseph Peladan, the self-styled "sandwich board man of the beyond." T. S. Eliot, himself thoroughly schooled in the Symbolists through reading Arthur Symons, uses its habitual language in *Gerontion* to provide a brilliant satire of the search for bogus transcendence. The reference to "Hakagawa, bowing among the Titians,"[21] is a perfect ironic adaptation of the Symbolist doctrine of freeing poetry from the task of conveying meaning in order to provide the symptoms of a deep cultural crisis. For all the subtlety and sophistication of its aesthetic discoveries, and without denying the immense importance it has in the history of modernism, in particular for the study of the language of modern poetry, it seems to me that there is a good deal of naïvete in the Symbolist approach to the modern world and its ills.

The same is more obviously true of another version of modernism that seems perhaps to turn the Symbolist movement on its head. Instead of retreating from the world of the machine, from the modern city, or from the sense of power unleashed by modern science and outside of human control, the Futurists of Italy and Russia unreservedly embrace it. In the Futurist Manifesto of 1909, Marinetti declares the characteristic Futurist enthusiasms:

We will sing of great crowds excited by work, by pleasure, and by riot; we will sing of the muticolored, polyphonic tides of revolution in the modern capitals; we will sing of the vibrant nightly fervor of arsenals and shipyards blazing with violent electric moons; greedy railway stations that devour smoke-plumed serpents; factories hung on clouds by the crooked lines of their smoke; bridges that stride the rivers like giant gymnasts, flashing in the sun with the glitter of knives; adventurous streamers that sniff the horizon; deep-chested locomotives whose wheels paw the tracks like the hooves of enormous steel horses bridled by tubing; and the sleek flight of planes whose propellers chatter in the wind like banners and seem to cheer like an enthusiastic crowd.[22]

The energy of such conceptions of the modern world is perhaps refreshing after the pallid withdrawal from it that most of the Symbolists practiced. But the contrast between Futurism and Symbolism, it seems to me, is not an absolute one; at another, perhaps deeper level, there is a considerable degree of similarity between the two aesthetics. In the same manifesto Marinetti claims the realization of the Symbolist search for a transcendent absolute—it has arrived, not in art but in the modern city: "We stand on the last promontory of the centuries! . . . Why should we look back, when what we want is to break down the mysterious doors of the Impossible? Time and Space died yesterday. We already live in the absolute, because we have created eternal, omnipresent speed."[23] The same cardinal Symbolist word "mysterious," the same flight from the limiting contingencies of time and space, the same fundamentally aesthetic attitude toward the modern world, is apparent. We may remember that in Huysmans's *A Rebours* the hero Des Esseintes, searching for some new erotic sensation, falls in love with a pair of railway engines—a sign, I think, that the more sophisticated amongst the aesthetes and decadents had already mapped out the Futurist position.

Again the Futurists, like the Symbolists, make no attempt to rise to the challenge of achieving the kind of synthesis between science and human values projected in Wordsworth's preface. Whereas the Symbolist flight is away from the machine and the city into the artist's subjectivity, the Futurist flees toward technology, to celebrate its inhumanity. "Instead of looking for the new human phenomenon, they will only look for the phenomena of the science of physics to be found in human being. They are crassly stupid," wrote D. H. Lawrence in criticism of their failure to make any human use of their perceptions of the new urban environment.[24] "Do people imagine they have found the psychic basis common to all humanity?" asked Tristan Tzara, in the Dada Manifesto of 1918. "After the carnage," he declared, echoing the Futurist sensibility, "we are left with the hope of a purified humanity. . . . [E]veryone makes his art in his own way, if he knows anything about the joy that rises like an arrow up to the astral strata, or that which descends into the mines strewn with the flowers of corpses and fertile spasms."[25]

Even more than Tzara and his fellow Dadaists, the Futurists possessed a certain naïvete, stemming perhaps from the fact they originated from countries where the industrial process was still at relatively early stages of development, and making them (like the Symbolists) suitable satiric material. Their simplistic reading of Nietzsche and enthusiastic championing of themselves as the new supermen of civilization, for instance, can be set against the sharper wit of Henry Adams writing about New York: "The new man seemed close at hand, because the old one had plainly reached the end of his strength, and his failure had become catastrophic."[26] Similarly, albeit less ironically than Adams, Tzara too extolled the glories to come: "On the one hand there is a world tottering in its flight, linked to the resounding tinkle of the infernal gamut; on the other hand, there are: the new men."[27]

In describing Symbolism and Futurism, at least in their abstract theoretical positions, as naïve versions of modernism, I imply no dismissal of their capacity to stimulate and sustain highly significant and original creative work. What Pound wrote of Jouve may certainly be applied to the Futurists, for instance: "Whatever may be said against automobiles and aeroplanes and the modernist way of speaking of them. . . . [S]till it is indisputable that the vitality of the time exists in such work."[28] Naïvete was an essential aspect of modernism, the prerequisite, perhaps, of the decreative side of the movement and a vital part of the creative struggle for new forms. Nevertheless, it seems to me important to try to accommodate within modernism artists of a very different temper whose response to the modernist crisis of relation between science and human values is more complex. I think first of the three great novelists of the period, Proust, Joyce, and Mann, and of their respective masterpieces, *A La Recherche du temps perdu, Ulysses,* and *Der Zauberberg,* but it would not be difficult to extend the list with names like Svevo and Musil, Chekhov and Brecht. Erich Kahler provides us with useful orientation to these masterpieces in his description of *Ulysses.* He writes that Joyce attempts "to give a comprehensive picture of his whole contemporary world. . . . In order to represent this anarchic, incoherent whole, all styles, from the naturalistic to the surrealistic, are employed, all the accumulated knowledge of our time, the elements of ten languages."[29]

The essential tendency of the above works—and perhaps the tendency of the modern novel as a whole—is toward a form that is encyclopaedic. Though they break with the immediate past of the novel, they link up with the tradition of Rabelais and Sterne, which provides a manifest alternative to positivistic realism.[30] Encyclopaedic form, with its Enlightenment background, seems inevitably to reflect a version of humanism; the tendency to voluminous referentiality expresses the urge to humanize scientific and technological development (not that they achieve anything like the synthesis envisaged by Wordsworth and Matthew Arnold). Irony supplies the unifying tone, connecting and ordering a multiple set of perspectives on the modern world while denying any of them authoritative validity. Dispensing with any normative metalanguage, its inclusive power nevertheless finds a place and relevance for ethical values.

To give these works their proper place in modernism implies, I think, the abandonment of the view that the novel in this period aspires to the condition of the Symbolist lyric and thence of course to music. It seems perverse, for one thing, to try to claim that *Ulysses* is a lyric novel when Joyce at the outset of his career relegated the lyric to the bottom of a hierarchy of genres. I repeat that the role of the Symbolist aesthetic in the modernist period must not be overgeneralized and that by the twenties, the great climax of the age, a reaction had set in as a result of the First World War against the more romantically inspired movements of the period (this seems to me to include Symbolism as well as Expressionism) in favor of a harder, more objective and classical style. Its temper is memorably announced in a diary note of Brecht's, dated June 1920: "I hunt around for new forms and experiment with my feelings just like the very latest writers. But then I keep coming back to the fact that the essence of art is simplicity, grandeur and sensitivity, and that of its form coolness."[31] Brecht too, far from aspiring to the intense concentration of lyric form, allowed the looseness of epic to enter into both his lyric and dramatic art.

Part of the distortion here, I think, in Anglo-Saxon criticism at least, is the historical neglect of the German contribution to culture as a whole and to modernism in particular. Those who venture across the Channel or the Atlantic at all rarely get beyond Paris. The result is that the powerful contribution of Weimar Germany—the world of Thomas Mann, the Bauhaus, Brecht and Benjamin, to name but a few—to modernism, both in the twenties and later, during the exile rarely gets sufficient attention in accounts of the period. A more expansive sense of cultural geography might seek to examine the relation of Imagism to *Neue Sachlichkeit,* explore the correspondences between Pound's idea of Chinese poetry and Brecht's, or set T. S. Eliot's sense of tradition alongside Thomas Mann's. It is also instructive to note that the first, belated, authentically English wave of modernism (as opposed to Anglo-American or Anglo-Irish)—the generation of Auden, Isherwood, and Spender—took its orientation not from Paris but from Berlin.

Of course, the central drama of Weimar Germany, as Peter Gay expounds in his seminal *Weimar Culture,* was the struggle to establish, in the city of Goethe, a modern society based on humanist principles, against the background of fanatic, extremist opponents of modernity. Its anxieties were characteristic of the age: "The most insistent questions revolved around the need for man's renewal, questions made most urgent and practically insoluble by the disappearance of God, the threat of the machine, the incurable stupidity of the upper classes, and the helpless philistinism of the bourgeoisie."[32] But here, for once, argues Gay, were some clear representatives of the classical version of modernism—in the form of the Bauhaus artists, for instance, whose object (in the words of Gropius) was "to eliminate every drawback of the machine without sacrificing any one of its real advantages." Their guiding principle was "that artistic design is neither an intellectual nor a material affair, but simply an integral part of the stuff of life."[33] Here, perhaps, is a glimpse of the kind of synthesis that Wordsworth imagined.

But to mention Weimar and the Bauhaus, which survived it only by six months, is to highlight the extreme fragility of the humanist position in the modernist period. It would be foolish, and quite misleading, to present it as more than one of the strands of modernism, shrunk at times to the point of invisibility. It was so thoroughly implicated in the catastrophe of the war that it had to withstand devastating criticisms, involving a rejection not only of logic and the historical process but also of the whole tradition of written culture without which the humanist critical tradition could not have arisen. But just as Thomas Mann perceived of Freud that it was not necessary to be an antirationalist to explore the irrationality of the human psyche, so there were some figures in the period who realized that it was not only antihumanists who could analyze the failings and inadequacies of humanist culture. The artists of this humanist modernism took as their heroes neither supermen nor artist-priests but tragicomic clowns—the Good Soldier Schweik, Leopold Bloom, Charlie Chaplin. But they were not the less capable of providing "a conscience for a scientific age."[34]

NOTES

1. Robert Weimann, *Structure and Society in Literary History: Studies in the History and Theory of Historical Criticism* (Charlottesville: University Press of Virginia, 1976), 18.

2. Harry Levin, *Refractions: Essays in Comparative Literature* (London, Oxford, and New York: Oxford University Press, 1966), 277.

3. Jack Goody, *The Domestication of the Savage Mind* (Cambridge and New York: Cambridge University Press, 1977), 2, 146.

4. Ibid., 147.

5. Paul Fussell, *The Great War and Modern Memory* (London: Oxford University Press, 1975), 79, 113.

6. William Wordsworth, *The Prose Works of William Wordsworth,* ed. W.J.B. Owen and Jane Worthington Smyser (Oxford: Clarendon Press, 1974), 141.

7. Matthew Arnold, *Discourses in America* (London and New York: Macmillan, 1889), 121–23.

8. Hart Crane, *The Collected Poems of Hart Crane* (New York: Liveright, 1946), 177.

9. David Jones, *In Parenthesis* (London: Faber and Faber, 1963), xiv.

10. Herbert Spencer, *Social Statics; Or, the Conditions Essential to Human Happiness* (New York: D. Appleton, 1886), 80.

11. Henry Adams, *The Education of Henry Adams: An Autobiography* (Cambridge, Mass.: Riverside Press, 1961), 499.

12. Ezra Pound, *Selected Poems* (London: Faber and Faber, 1975), 101.

13. W. B. Yeats, *The Poems* (London: Everyman, 1992), 255.

14. D. H. Lawrence, *Apocalypse* (Harmondsworth: Penguin, 1974), 50.

15. Bertolt Brecht, *Poems and Songs from the Plays*, ed. John Willett (London: Methuen, 1990), 3.

16. See Jacques Rigaut, "Un Brillant Sujet," in *Ecrits* (Paris: Gallimard, 1970), 34–36.

17. See Edmund Wilson, *Axel's Castle* (Harmondsworth: Penguin, 1993).

18. Walter Pater, *Plato and Platonism: A Series of Lectures* (New York: Greenwood Press, 1969), 15.

19. From an 1892 newspaper article quoted in Richard Ellmann, *Yeats: The Man and the Masks* (Harmondsworth: Penguin, 1987), 144.

20. George Moore, *Confessions of a Young Man* (London: William Heinemann, 1952), 92.

21. T. S. Eliot, *Selected Poems* (London: Faber and Faber, 1954), 32.

22. R. W. Flint, ed., *Marinetti: Selected Writings*, trans. R. W. Flint and Arthur Coppotelli (London: Secker and Warburg, 1972), 42.

23. Ibid., 41.

24. D. H. Lawrence, G. J. Zytaruk, and J. T. Boulton, eds., *The Letters of D.H. Lawrence*, vol. 2 (Cambridge: Cambridge University Press, 1981), 183.

25. Tristan Tzara, *Seven Dada Manifestoes* and *Lampisteries*, trans. Barbara Wright (London: John Calder, 1977), 5.

26. Adams, *Education*, 499.

27. Tzara, *Seven Dada Manifestoes* and *Lampisteries*, 7.

28. Ezra Pound, review of Pierre Jean Jouve's *Présences*, in *Poetry* 1, no. 5 (February 1913), 165–66.

29. Erich Kahler, *Man the Measure: A New Approach to History* (Cleveland and New York: Meridian, 1967), 513–14.

30. See Erich Kahler, *The Inward Turn of Narrative*, trans. Richard and Clara Winston (Princeton, N.J.: Princeton University Press, 1973), 177–79.

31. Herta Ramthum, ed., *Bertolt Brecht Diaries 1920–1922*, trans. John Willett (London: Eyre Methuen, 1979), 4–5.

32. Peter Gay, *Weimar Culture: The Outsider as Insider* (Westport, Conn.: Greenwood Press, 1981), 7.

33. Ibid., 101.

34. Levin, *Refractions*, 295.

3

Is Humor Human?

Simon Critchley

Animals come when their names are called. Just like human beings.
—Wittgenstein

Humor is human. Why? Well, because The Philosopher, Aristotle, says so. In "On the Parts of the Animals," he writes, "No animal laughs save Man."[1] This quotation echoes down the centuries from Galen and Porphyry, through Rabelais to Hazlitt and Bergson. Now, if laughter is proper to the human being, then the human being who does not laugh invites the charge of inhumanity, or at least makes us somewhat suspicious. Apparently Pythagoras and Anaxagoras never laughed, neither did the Virgin Mary, and Socrates laughed rarely. If laughter is essentially human, then the question of whether Jesus laughed assumes rather obvious theological pertinence to the doctrine of incarnation. One of Beckett's more monstrous antiheroes, Moran, debates the point with one Father Ambrose:

> Like Job haha, he said. I too said haha. What a joy it is to laugh, from time to time, he said. Is it not? I said. It is peculiar to man, he said. So I have noticed, I said. A brief silence ensued. . . . Animals never laugh, he said. It takes us to find that funny, I said. What? he said. It takes us to find that funny, I said loudly. He mused. Christ never laughed either, he said, so far as we know. He looked at me. Can you wonder? I said.[2]

As M. A. Screech shows in impressive detail, the theological importance of showing Christ's humanity, and therefore his sense of humor, led many mediaeval scholars to trawl the Evangelists for evidence of levity.[3] Some support for the case can be found in the first of Christ's recorded miracles, the marriage at Cana (John 2:1–11). Discovering that the wine has run out, the distraught host somehow alerts Mary, who orders her son to do something about the problem, presumably knowing that he can. This is in itself interesting, as there is no evidence heretofore that Mary was aware that her Son could perform such impressive party tricks. She says to him, "They have no more wine"; to which Jesus replies somewhat coldly, from his full messianic height, "Woman, my time has not yet come." However, like the good Jewish mother who knows what's best for her-Son-the-Messiah, Mary turns to the servants and says, "Do whatever he tells you." At which point, the water is miraculously turned into wine, and the party can continue.

This is an odd moment, bearing a family resemblance to a scene from Monty Python's *Life of Brian,* where Brian's mother insists, "He's not the Messiah, he's just a very naughty boy." Although the joke is on Jesus to some extent insofar as he is made to look slightly foolish by his mother, the marriage at Cana might nonetheless be seen as evidence of humorous humanity on Christ's part. It might indeed appear curious that Jesus' ministry begins with an encouragement to imbibe. However, to the perfervid imagination of mediaeval Christendom, this first miracle was seen analogically as a New Testament response and recompense for the Old Testament tale of the drunkenness of Noah (Genesis 9:20–29). Noah was, of course, the first human being to cultivate the vine and sample its fruits, "and he drank of the wine, and was drunken." Noah's son, Ham, looked on his inebriated father "uncovered within his tent" and told his two brothers, who walked in backward and covered his nakedness with a garment. A presumably rather hung-over Noah was none too pleased with Ham and lay an awful curse of servitude on him and all of his Canaanite progeny. Hence the Old and New Testament stories are connected both by theme (wine) and location (Cana). Now, was Ham's sin that of laughter? The Bible does not say.

ECCENTRIC HUMANS

Any philosophical and theological assurance that laughter is unique to the human being becomes somewhat unsure when one turns to the anthropological literature. One need only observe the behavior of chimpanzees and dogs to see that animals certainly *play,* and they do get frisky, but the question is: Do they laugh? They certainly don't seem to laugh at my jokes. But in her 1971 paper, "Do Dogs Laugh?" Mary Douglas sets out to trouble the assumption that we can divide human from animal along the faultline of laughter.[4] She cites Konrad Lorenz's *Man Meets Dog* and Thomas Mann's "A Man and His Dog" to show how the panting, slightly opened jaws of man's best friend look "like a human smile" and can give "a stronger impression of laughing." However, the evidence is anecdotal and, to my mind, not particularly convincing. The interpretation of the dog's laughter seems rather anthropomorphic and evidence of a crude learned response on the dog's part, particularly when Lorenz admits that the same facial expression of the dog that denotes "laughter" also indicates the beginning of erotic excitement—getting frisky in another way.

We are not going to be able to decide the issue here, and animals are full of surprises. So while we cannot say with any certainty whether dogs laugh or not, we can, I think, grant that humor is an anthropological constant and is universal, common to all cultures. There has been no society thus far discovered that did not have humor, whether it is expressed as convulsive, bodily gaiety or with a laconic smile. Thus, humor is a key element in the distinction of the human from the animal; it is a consequence of culture and indeed of civilization, as Cicero's Latin word for humor, *urbanitas,* would suggest. If, as ethnologists report, laughter originated in the animal function of the aggressive baring of teeth, then the transformation of the social meaning of this physiological act is one testament to the distance of human culture from animal life.

As Helmuth Plessner puts it, laughter confirms the eccentric *(exzentrisch)* position of the human being in the world of nature. Plessner's thesis is that the life of animals is *zentrisch,* it is centered. This means that the animal simply lives and experiences *(lebt und erlebt).* By contrast, the human being not only lives and experiences, he or she experiences those experiences *(er erlebt sein Erleben).* That is, the human being has a reflective attitude toward its experiences and toward itself. This is why humans are eccentric, because they live beyond the limits set for them by nature, by taking up a distance from their immediate experience. In living outside themselves, the reflective activity of human beings achieves a break with nature. Indeed, Plessner goes further and claims that the human *is* this break, this hiatus, this gap between the physical and the psychical. The working out of the consequences of the eccentric position of the human is the main task of a philosophical anthropology, which is why laughter has such an absolutely central role in Plessner's work.[5]

Plessner's thesis is pretty convincing, but is it true to say that animals always exist in sheer immediacy? Do they—even the cleverest of them— always fail to take up an eccentric position with regard to their life, even when they seem to *know* that they are going to die? In a word, are all animals incapable of reflection? I simply do not know, and if a lion could talk we could not understand him. I simply do not know how Plessner can *know* what he seems so sure of, namely, that animals are incapable of reflection. Let's just say that I have my doubts about Plessner's certitude.

A SMALL BESTIARY

If humor is human, then it also, curiously, marks the limit of the human. Or, better, humor explores what it means to be human by moving back and forth across the frontier that separates humanity from animality, thereby making it unstable and troubling the hiatus of which Plessner speaks. Humor is precisely the exploration of the break between nature and culture, which reveals the human to be not so much a category by itself as a negotiation between categories. We might even define the human as a *dynamic* process produced by a series of identifications and misidentifications with animality.[6] Thus, what makes us laugh is the reduction of the human to the animal or the elevation of the animal to the human. The fact that we label certain comic genres in animalistic terms, like "cock and bull" or "shaggy dog" stories, is perhaps revealing.

Examples of bestiality in literature are legion, from *Aesop's Fables* to Chaucer's Chaunticleer in *The Nun's Priest's Tale* and *Le Roman de Renard*. Animals litter the history of literature, in particular parrots, dogs, cats, and bears. A more bizarre example of the identification with animality, because of the unhappy mental state of the author and the fact that it was penned in Mr. Potter's madhouse in Bethnal Green, is Christopher Smart's *Jubilate Agno,* written sometime between 1758 and 1763. Smart begins a section thus,

For I will consider my Cat Jeoffry.
For he is the servant of the Living God duly and daily serving him.
For at the first glance of the glory of God in the East he worships in his way.
For is this done by wreathing his body seven times round with elegant quickness.

And so on, and so forth, for page after rambling page. My favorite lines are the following:

For by stroking him I have found out electricity.
For I perceived God's light about him both wax and fire.
For the Electrical fire is the spiritual substance, which God sends from heaven to
   sustain the bodies of both man and beast.
For God has blest him in the variety of his movements.
For tho' he cannot fly, he is an excellent clamberer.
For his motions upon the face of the earth are more than any other quadrupede.
For he can tread to all the measures upon the music.
For he can swim for life.
For he can creep.[7]

Smart was sadly less than smart when he wrote these lines, but their electrical warmth expresses something approaching humanity toward Jeoffry the cat.

The exploration of the hiatus between the human and the animal is obviously at the heart of Book IV of *Gulliver's Travels,* where the power of Gulliver's identification with the rational animals, or Houyhnhnms, is proportionate to his misanthropic disgust at his all-too-human Yahoo-ness.

Swift explores a similar paradox in "The Beast's Confession to the Priest" by way of a critique of Aesop's "libelling of the four-foot race":

For, here he owns, that now and then
Beasts may degenerate into men.[8]

This comic inversion of the human and the animal continues in the twentieth century in Orwell's *Animal Farm* and Kafka's *Metamorphosis*. The latter text Breton quite properly places in his *Anthologie de l'humour noir*, but he might also have included many of Kafka's ever-strange short stories, such as "Investigations of a Dog" and "Josephine the Singer, or the Mouse-Folk." This tradition continues on to a book like Will Self's *Great Apes*, not to mention a whole tradition of satirical cartooning of which a contemporary expression would be Gary Larson's *The Far Side*.

HORACE AND JUVENAL, URBANITY AND DISGUST

The two effects produced by such humor here might be considered in terms of the distinction between the benign mockery or *urbanitas* of Horatian satire and the brooding, black misanthropy of Juvenalian satire. In the eighteenth century, of course, this is the distinction between the satires of Pope and Swift and the accompanying genres of mock-heroic and travesty: the epic elevation of the insignificant and the deflationary belittling of the sublime. On the one hand we find the comic urbanity of the animal, where the humor is generated by the sudden and incongruous humanity of the animal. A wonderful example of this is given by Peter Berger:

A bear is charging this hunter in the woods. The hunter fires, and misses. The bear breaks his rifle in two, sodomizes the hunter, then walks away. The hunter is furious. The next day he is back in the woods, with a new rifle. Again the bear charges, again the hunter misses, again he is sodomized. The hunter is now beside himself. He is going to get that bear, if it's the last thing he does. He gets himself an AK-47 assault rifle, goes back into the woods. Again the bear charges and, believe it or not, again the hunter misses. The bear breaks the assault rifle, gently puts his paws around the hunter and says, "OK, come clean now. This isn't really about hunting, is it?"[9]

On the other hand, the Juvenalian reduction of the human to the animal does not so much produce mirth as comic disgust with the species. This is something that Petronius employs to great effect in "Trimalchio's Feast" from the *Satyricon*, where the slave Trimalchio—himself some sort of twisted reflection of Petronius's employer, the Emperor Nero—appears like a great, shining pig. His epitaph, composed himself in what Beckett would call pigsty Latin, describes his life in terms of a rags-to-riches narrative,

capped with "AND HE NEVER ONCE LISTENED TO A PHILOSO-
PHER."[10]

Whether we think of Yahoos defecating from trees, Gregor Samsa wrig-
gling on his back, or Orwell's further twisting of the animal-human coupling by presenting the tyrant Napoleon finally upright on two legs, the
history of satire is replete with Juvenalian echoes. In his oddly eighteenth-
century novel *Great Apes,* Will Self writes:

> Sarah sat at the bar of the Sealink Club being propositioned by men. Some
> men propositioned her with their eyes, some with their mouths, some with
> their heads, some with their hair. Some men propositioned her with nuance,
> exquisite subtlety; others propositioned her with chutzpah, their suit as obvi-
> ous as a schlong slammed down on the zinc counter. Some men's proposition-
> ing was so slight as to be peripheral, a seductive play of the minor parts, an
> invitation to touch cuticles, rub corns, hang nails. Other men's proposition-
> ing was a Bayreuth production, complete with mechanical effects, great flats
> descending, garishly depicting their Taste, their Intellect, their Status. The men
> were like apes—she thought—attempting to impress her by waving and kick-
> ing things about in a display of mock potency.[11]

When the animal becomes human, the effect is pleasingly benign, and
we laugh out loud, "OK come clean now. This isn't really about hunting,
is it?" But when the human becomes animal, the effect is disgusting, and
if we laugh at all then it is what Beckett calls "the mirthless laugh," which
laughs at that which is unhappy.

Staying with the example of Will Self, it seems to me that he combines
both Horatian and Juvenalian effects in a wonderfully macabre short story
called "Flytopia." One sultry summer, in the somnolent Suffolk village of
Inwardleigh, our hero Jonathan is trying to complete the index to a tome
on ecclesiastical architecture. Irritated by the insects that plague his cottage
and break his concentration, he resolves to destroy them with the use of
sundry toxic products. Then he awakens one morning, after insect-haunted
nightmares, to find a pullulating mass of silverfish on his draining board
shape themselves into the words, "WELCOME TO FLYTOPIA." He then
enters into a bizarre contract with the insects: they cease bothering him and
keep the house clean; he lets them live and even feeds them. The Horatian
humor consists in the sometimes protracted dialogues on the draining board
with the silverfish, with Jonathan pedantically correcting their spelling. But
the effect becomes more Juvenalian when we are treated to the image of
Jonathan's person being cleaned by his newfound insect friends: "He found
their assistance in his toilet not simply helpful, but peculiarly sensual."
Finally, after having agreed to give over a spare bedroom to his insects, for
breeding and feeding purposes, he happily sacrifices his girlfriend, unhappily
called Joy, in response to their request for "MORE MEAT": "Jonathan listened to her feet going up the stairs. He listened to the door of the spare

bedroom open, he heard the oppressive giant fluttering hum, as she was engulfed, then he rose and went out to pay the cab."[12]

OUTLANDISH ANIMALS

Humor is human. But what makes us laugh is the inversion of the animal-human coupling, whether it is Horatian urbanity or Juvenalian disgust. If being human means being humorous, then being humorous often seems to mean becoming an animal. But paradoxically, what becoming an animal confirms is the fact that humans are *incapable* of becoming animals. For, the sad truth is that in humor humans show themselves to be useless animals—hopeless, incompetent outlandish animals, defecating from trees and grunting like great apes. There is something charming about an animal become human, but when the human becomes animal, the effect is disgusting. All of which confirms the human being's eccentric position in the world of nature. Consider the following remark from Wittgenstein:

> Two people are laughing together, say at a joke. One of them has used certain somewhat unusual words and now they both break out into a sort of bleating. This might appear *very* extraordinary to a visitor coming from quite a different environment. Whereas we find it quite *reasonable*.
> (I recently witnessed this scene on a bus and was able to think myself into the position of the someone to whom this would be unfamiliar. From that point of view, it struck me as quite irrational, like the responses from an outlandish *animal*).[13]

There is something rather surreal about visualizing Wittgenstein on a double-decker bus thinking that thought while watching two people imitating sheep, but that is not the point. Satire works in precisely the way he describes. Namely, we are asked to look at ourselves as if we were visitors from an alien environment, to examine terrestrial existence from a Martian point of view. When we do this, we begin to look like outlandish animals, and reasonableness crumbles into irrationality. This can be linked to an idea dear to the French philosopher Gilles Deleuze, one that he calls "deterritorialization" and that he interestingly chooses to translate into English as "outlandish."[14] The critical task of the writer is to write from the place of the animal, to look at human affairs with a dog's or beetle's eye, as in Kafka's stories.

Satire transforms us into outlandish animals, and the natural history of humanity is the vast research archive of the writer. By crisscrossing the frontier between the human and the animal, writers like Swift or Kafka produce a kind of shock effect that shakes us up and effects a critical change of perspective. Satire stands resolutely against the self-images of the age. Adorno famously writes that the only thing that is true in psychoanalysis is the exaggeration. But this would seem to be even more true of satire. In

Book IV of *Gulliver's Travels,* Swift was not persuaded of the existence of talking horses. Rather, his critical point is that there is nothing to prevent this possibility once we begin to conceive of ourselves as rational animals. The truth of satire is obviously not to be assessed in terms of literal verifiability but rather to warn us against a danger implicit in our self-conception. To have an effect, the warning signals have to be deafening.

KANT'S PARROT

In this chapter, we have been pursuing an interesting paradox. On the one hand, humor is what picks us out as human; it is what is proper to the human being, situated as we are between beasts and angels. Humor confirms the human being's eccentric position in nature, as improper within it, as reflectively alienated from the physical realm of the body and external nature. Yet, on the other hand, what takes place in humor, particularly in satire, is the constant overstepping of the limit between the human and the animal, demonstrating their uneasy proximity. But, bringing together both sides of this paradox, we might say that the studied incongruities of humor show the eccentric position of the human in nature by recalling the benign humanity of the animal and the disturbing animality of the human. The human being is amphibious, like a boat drawn up on the shore, half in the water, half out of it. We are a paradox.

Mention of water brings to mind a final maritime example of humor, humans, and animals—in Thomas Bernhard's wonderful 1978 play *Immanuel Kant*. Kant is sailing to America, the country that was always for him *eine Perversität,* to receive an honorary doctorate from Columbia University and to have an operation for his glaucoma. Of course, absolutely none of this is true. Kant travels in the company of Frau Kant, his servant Ernst Ludwig, and his parrot Friedrich. Being Kant's parrot, Friedrich has awesome philosophical ability. Indeed, Kant says that the great Leibniz declined to give a lecture in Königsberg because he knew that Friedrich the parrot would be present. The whole piece has a wonderfully Dadaist, almost dreamlike, quality that is crowned by the mini-dialogues between Kant and his parrot, exchanges in which the animal bathetically mirrors the great philosopher's words. Let me give a flavor of the German alongside my translation:

Kant:	*Kant*:
Ich bin von Anfang an	From the beginning
nur mit Friedrich gereist	I only traveled with Friedrich
heimlich	clandestinely
naturgemäß	naturally
durch ganz Deutschlandthrough	all of Germany
Kant ist aus Königsberg	It is said that

nicht hinausgekommen	Kant never
wird gesagt	left Königsberg
aber wo Kant ist	but where Kant is
ist Königsberg	is Königsberg
Königsberg ist	Königsberg is
Wo Kant ist	where Kant is
zu Freidrich:	*to Friedrich:*
Wo ist Königsberg?	Where is Königsberg?
Friedrich:	*Friedrich:*
Wo Kant ist	Where Kant is
Kant:	*Kant:*
Und wo ist Kant?	And where is Kant?
Freidrich:	*Friedrich:*
Kant ist wo Königsberg ist.[15]	Kant is where Königsberg is.

Much could be said about parrots. They are surely the most unnerving of animals, because of their uncanny ability to imitate that which is meant to pick us out as a species: language. A comic echo of the human, holding up a ridiculing mirror to our faces, the parrot is the most critical beast of all the field. The first-century Neapolitan poet Statius described the parrot as "Prince among bird, delightful slave," who speaks like a person and makes sense by repeating our own words back to us.[16]

NOTES

1. See Aristotle, *De Partibus Animalum*, Book III, 673a: 8.
2. *Molloy*, from *The Beckett Trilogy* (London: Picador, 1979), 93.
3. See M. A. Screech, *Laughter at the Foot of the Cross* (Harmondsworth: Penguin, 1999). Thanks to Peter Howarth for his correspondence on this question.
4. Mary Douglas, *Implicit Meanings: Essays in Anthropology* (London and Boston: Routledge and Kegan Paul, 1975), 83–99.
5. See "Autobiographische Einführung" and "Der Mensch als Lebewesen" from *Mit anderen Augen. Aspekte einer philosophische Anthropologie* (Stuttgart: Reclam, 1982).
6. I owe this formulation to Sue Wiseman.
7. Christopher Smart, *Selected Poems*, ed. K. Williamson and M. Walsh (Harmondsworth: Penguin, 1990), 105–8.
8. Jonathan Swift, *The Complete Poems*, ed. P. Rogers (New Haven, Conn., and London: Yale University Press, 1983), 514.
9. Cited in Peter L. Berger, *Redeeming Laughter: The Comic Dimension of Human Experience* (New York: Walter de Gruyter, 1997), 55.
10. Petronius, *Satyricon*, ed. and trans. R. Bracht Branham (London: Everyman, 1996), 66.
11. Will Self, *Great Apes* (London: Bloomsbury, 1997), 15.
12. In Will Self, *Tough, Tough Toys for Tough, Tough Boys* (London: Bloomsbury, 1998), 23–42.

13. Ludwig Wittgenstein, *Culture and Value* (Oxford: Blackwell, 1980), 78.

14. See the first of the television programs that Deleuze recorded for the Franco-German channel Arte in the last years of his life: "A comme Animal," in *L'Abécédaire de Gilles Deleuze* (Paris: Vidéo Editions Montparnasse, 1997).

15. Thomas Bernhard, *Stücke 2* (Frankfurt a.M.: Suhrkamp, 1988), 273–74.

16. Cited in Raymond Geuss's hugely entertaining *Parrots, Poets, Philosophers and Good Advice* (London: Hearing Eye, 1999), 8.

PART II

Naturalizing Human Dominion

4

Philosophie au Naturel

John Mullarkey

What is the relationship between philosophy and nature? Must it be mediated by science and by physics in particular? What are the connections—historical and logical—between "natural philosophy," "the philosophy of nature," and "philosophical naturalism," and are there different concepts of "nature" at play in each of these domains? These are all huge questions, of course, but I will only question here whether one's initial approach to them—to the relationship of philosophy to physics, of philosophy to nature, and of philosophy to science—might be inescapably prejudiced by a more overarching opposition, of which one might call the dualism of philosophy and nature a mere subset. This broader position concerns the duality of *humanity* and *nature,* and, in particular, humanity's place, or lack of it, in nature. Specifically, though, I want to argue that this duality, qua duality, becomes less and less tenable when one broadens one's notion of the natural in philosophy, that there are nonreductive forms of naturalism available for thought, and that, at least until recent times, Continental philosophy has been overly narrow in its interpretation and consequent rejection of naturalism. All in all, I would like to point to a new line of (Continental) thinking that is happy to reunite humanity with its place in nature, but not at the price of reducing, but rather, aims at restoring an inherent value to both.

The relationship between humanity and nature is unquestionably problematic, and not simply because the history of its interpretation has been in large part an acrimonious one, with Western philosophers, for the most part (at least until the nineteenth century), taking every step possible to distance the human from the natural by deriding nature and exalting humanity. The phrase "human, hyphen, nature," is also perplexing, because of the ambiguity of its constituent terms.

What is the meaning of "nature" in respect to its opposition to humanity? The natural has been looked upon alternatively, or all at once, as the *nonhuman* animal or the animal in general, as our human physiology or biology in general, or as the unmanufactured environment around us (which can itself mean one's immediately environing landscape, the entire earth, or even the whole universe). Nature may equally be understood simply to mean "matter," the material stuff that makes up the physical world (a position we call "materialism"), and many materialist philosophers would also count themselves thereby as naturalists. In addition to this, "nature" may also include the various laws physicists and chemists use to describe this matter (a refined version of the materialist's position termed "physicalism" and also closely associated with the school of contemporary "naturalism" today).

Without in any way exhausting the list, one might add that nature can also be located within ourselves as the "irrational" or "nonrational" mind, or as in the Freudian notion of the "unconscious," with its opaque drives pushing us blindly toward goals set by instinct rather than intellect. Nature can also encompass the habitual ("what is always done") and the normative (what it is plainly "right to do"). Additionally, it can also be what is *contrasted* with the normative—a set of descriptive facts rather than values. This is what Hume understood by his "naturalism." Evidently, "nature" is an infuriatingly ambiguous term—Raymond Williams goes so far as to suggest that it is the most complex word in our language.[1]

As for definitions of the human, these have been no less wide-ranging, for alongside depictions that simply *oppose* those attributed to nature (the human as the nonanimal, the immaterial, etc.), humans have been *positively* described as sentient beings, conscious beings, rational beings, linguistic beings, political beings, temporal beings, and so on. This provides us with yet another list of attributes for the natural: the nonsentient, the nonlinguistic, the nonpolitical, the nontemporal, and so on. The task of elucidating simply the terms of the human-nature dualism may be endless.

But what is of real interest in any case is what lies behind the plethora of words, namely the *philosophical* strategies by which the human has been wrenched away from nature. The examples are too numerous to examine in detail, but it is needless to say that it was the philosopher *Aristotle* who described man as exclusively political; *Descartes* who said that we were exclusively sentient; *Kant* that we are exclusively rational—and so on. However, whereas most of the history of Western philosophy from Plato to Rawls has been clearly anti-naturalist, separating off humanity clearly from nature,[2] since the middle of the twentieth century the pressure from natural science to reunite human being with its "roots" in the natural world has become irresistible. As one commentator has remarked, "Nearly everybody nowadays wants to be a "naturalist."[3] But there is one highly significant point about this contemporary yearning to naturalize humanity: the nature in question is always one that has already been worked over by human hands. What welcomes us back is not the nature our prescientific forebears—animists, hylozoists, or pantheists—would have understood; it is more likely the *material* nature of physics, the evolutionary character of life (Darwinism), or the instinctive, unconscious character of mind (Freudianism) that reaches out to embrace the workings of the human soul. In short, when modern science replaces humanity within the natural realm, it is in a *scientific* nature that has already been *reduced* to a human interpretation of it.

Behind this contemporary naturalism/anti-naturalism split, of course, is often a concern regarding the *status* of humanity's place in nature. In this regard, both positions share a common prejudice. The naturalist and anti-naturalist each realize that humanity and nature share something—their material constitution—but both believe that it is of little moral value; they differ because the naturalist applauds that fact and tries to further its consequences with a total reduction of humanity, while the anti-naturalist fears and resists it by trying to offset the claims of nature with certain faculties, powers, and so on, that are exclusive to mankind (being "rich-in-world," exclusively having language, rationality, even a face, etc.). It is highly arguable that, in most cases, neither makes any serious reappraisal as to the original estimation of nature's value.

Yet there is a rarely pursued line of thinking that does not share this axiom of the poverty of nature; one finds it in those rare naturalistic philosophers who do not see nature as a purely inert realm or deny nature any immanent power. In Continental thought this type of nonreductive naturalism is practiced by figures like Bergson, Merleau-Ponty, Bachelard, and Canguilhem, as well as contemporaries such as Deleuze, Laruelle, and Stengers. The names here are of thinkers who were never aghast at philosophizing on the topics of science, matter, biology, or nature but who were, all the same, never scientistic or uncritical in their naturalism.

So before accepting or rejecting the idea that humans are only natural objects and nothing more, we might first investigate what it means to say that we really are "only" biological, chemical, or material. What is the import and foundation of the ethics of any naturalism, be it reductive or nonreductive? What is the basis for the use of the term "only"? Ultimately, we are asking whether there is only one way to be naturalistic in philosophy, one way of naturalizing humanity, and so whether there is but one approach to be accepted or rejected.

NATURE AND REDUCTION

Whereas traditional philosophy has mostly attempted to separate humanity away from its natural origins and *native* birthplace, contemporary philosophy has striven primarily to reverse this process, but only by depositing humanity within its reworked understanding of nature. Thus, for example, David Papineau's *Philosophical Naturalism* aims to defend the view that humans are material objects living in a material world. "Naturalism," and its related verb "to naturalize," are now connected with materialism, with the scientific view that all of reality ultimately boils down or reduces to matter/energy-in-motion. As a label, Naturalism *used* to imply the belief that everything could be explained through both the human and the nonhuman sciences without any recourse to *supernatural* entities; at present it signifies that even the human realm is reducible to the natural realm—or rather, that it is reducible to the scientific and materialistic view of the natural realm. To naturalize now means to reduce to matter, to take what was once exalted as independent from nature—human spirit, human rationality, or human language—and reduce its workings to those of material particles and forces in action.

Yet, while I have used this term "to reduce" a number of times, do we know exactly what "reductionism" means? In the introduction to one collection of essays on the topic, reductionist accounts are described as aiming "to show that where we thought we had two sets of concepts, entities, laws, explanations, or properties, we in fact have only one, which is most perspicuously characterized in terms of the reducing vocabulary."[4] For these writers, reduction is primarily a question of conceptual education. Another examination of the matter finds the motivation for "reductive analyses" to be in the contrast between concepts in one vocabulary appearing problematic and those in another avoiding the problem. An analysis represents the incursion of concepts from the latter into those of the former.[5]

But the benign epistemological motives these two explanations underline have been interpreted less positively by Robert Nozick. Seeing our times aptly represented by the title "the Age of Reductionism," he views its prevalence as part of an increasing tendency to deflate everything human to everything inhuman. While it is obvious that there have always been reductionist theories—materialism in ancient Greece, for example—more recently, Nozick observes, "such theories have moved to the center of the intellectual stage. These views, undermining, unmasking, and denigrating people's attachments, principles, motivations, and modes of action, have now come to shape people's own view of themselves."[6] Nozick argues that much of contemporary reductionism depends on the microscopic, inhuman, and general realms of impersonal psychic forces, dumb economic laws, or invisible neurological processes. So, in that it is usually toward a realm that is commonly held to be one of less value, it can be seen that hand in hand with the reductionist's benign epistemological motive, there comes a moral aim as well: to *devalue*. As Nozick remarks, "Reductionist views reduce the more valuable to the less valuable, the more meaningful to the less meaningful; the reduction is a reduction in value, in worth."[7] Simply leaving aside the negative connotations of the word "reduce," the normal strategy in reductionist texts is to talk of all "*x* being *no more* than *y*," "*merely y*," "*only y*," and so on. As Isabelle Stengers puts it, "[P]ropositions that contain the word 'only' are all, by nature, reductionist. Those who voice this word are attributing to themselves the power of judging."[8] There is also talk of "higher" levels being derived from "lower" levels.[9] The intent is not simply to debunk the opposing explanation but to devalue the realm in which that explanation resides.

But the whole of this argument, on the side of the reductionist as well as the anti-reductionist (like Nozick), simply assumes that, first, the natural realm *can be* equated with blind neurological, biochemical, or material forces, and that, second, neurological, biochemical, and material forces themselves are inherently lacking in any value, so that an equation between these and the human is necessarily one depreciating the human. Yet there are numerous other philosophical forms of naturalism that do not depreciate the natural realm while also embracing the fact that humans are natural objects, through and through.

It is not difficult to see that what really appalls so many Western thinkers like Nozick about the naturalization of humanity is the pragmatic consequences for the treatment that follow from it; because we know that any equation between nature and "dumb" material forces has usually been regarded as a license to mistreat nature at will, any subsequent equation between humanity and this dumb nature spells out an equally ominous fate for us. This European attitude toward nature as well as toward matter itself helps to mark a contrast with other societies, such as Japan's, where the continuing presence of animist thought in the culture allows for a less degraded view of matter, and with that, a less terrifying prospect for a materialized humanity. It has even been proposed that a "Japanese National Science" could "reconcile us with nature instead of opposing it."[10] Here we see the possibility of an identification of the human with the inert that would be less likely to bring with it the usual connotations of a reduction in value.

Nonetheless, such equanimity has not been the norm, and twentieth-century philosophy has been marked by a resistance, when it does occur, to *any* form of naturalism. This has taken many forms: philosophies of time proposing that humanity is quintessentially temporal, whereas scientific subject matter is not; philosophies of life (Husserl, Dilthey) maintaining the irreducibility of the human "life-world" to inert matter); philosophies of Being and Consciousness (Heidegger, Sartre), like philosophies of life and time, holding that the human realm has irreducible features, only adding a certain ontological import to this distinction. What is of note here is that most of these anti-naturalisms have emerged from the Continental quarter of current philosophy. Indeed, this is the reason that naturalism has been called, on the one side, the enduring persuasion of Analytic philosophy and, on the other, the very definition of nonphilosophy in many Continental circles.[11]

THE ORIGINS OF CONTINENTAL ANTI-NATURALISM

The origins of this Continental anti-naturalism are myriad. Cartesian Rationalism and post-Kantian idealism are strongly implicated, of course, but the source of its twentieth-century incarnation is not too hard to find. In as much as Heidegger's philosophy has dominated French thought for the last eighty years, so Heidegger's philosophy of science has also been dominant. Admittedly, Heidegger's anti-naturalism is a rather complex phenomenon. He actually links the infamous "end of philosophy" thesis to the triumph of science: since the eclipse of pre-Socratic thought (when philosophy lost its proper vocation and became "metaphysics"), it had been on a slippery slope, taking enframing, prediction, and control as its guiding lights. In this respect, philosophy is not destroyed by science but actually completed by it; it finds its end, or *telos,* in science because that is where its (fallen) essence lies.[12] Philosophy's new vocation can have nothing to do with naturalism, for such ontic realms are adequately uncovered by natural science. Science busies itself essentially with "theorising the regulation of the possible planning and arrangement of human labor."[13] But it is not *Seinsdenken;* it does not think the primordial.[14]

Of course, *Being and Time* is ambiguous in its anti-scientific views, which are discernible there mostly by implication of what Heidegger means by "essential" or "primordial" (do these terms imply a relation to "ultimate reality," "sole reality," or just a "prior reality"?). Undoubtedly, though, explicit statements of his anti-scientism are to be found in his later writings.[15] Admittedly, Heidegger does even there give extensive time to reflecting on the essence of science, on the meaning of the earth and of nature. But these writings make clear that, first, the best form of reflection of these topics is either through philosophy or poetry and, second, that that reflection additionally uncovers the status of science to be a merely regional form of enquiry in these fields. Science is ontic rather than ontological, the culmination of the history of metaphysics in its forgetfulness of the question of Being. Naturalism and traditional philosophy (metaphysics) fall together for Heidegger.

When one realizes, therefore, the centrality of Heidegger not only to German phenomenology but even more so and quite peculiarly within most forms of French thought, one begins to appreciate how Continental philosophy might have been steered away from any serious engagement with nature. Heideggerian thought constitutes, it has been said, "the horizon of contemporary French philosophy, the perspective within which French philosophers now tend to think and write."[16] We have no space here to distill the influence of Heidegger on philosophy in France through all its dimensions, but as Tom Rockmore has admirably demonstrated, aspects of this thinker's work that might appeal to an anti-naturalistic element of French thought are multifold. The religious echoes of his thought, the apparent anthropological and even anthropocentric thrust of *Being and Time*, the Hegelian brand of phenomenology already prevalent in Paris—these are all factors in explaining why his work should have received such a hospitable reception in France.

But as Rockmore has also shown, in France Heidegger is often studied hand in hand with Husserl,[17] and indeed, one can argue that, whereas the incredible breadth of Continental anti-naturalism is due to Heidegger's influence, its roots, like the roots of Heidegger's thought, are to be found in Husserl. Though Husserl's arguments against naturalism are extensively reproduced in later works like *The Crisis of European Sciences and Transcendental Phenomenology*, they gain a clear and concise expression in the 1911 paper "Philosophy as a Rigorous Science." Even the title of this paper presents the immediate paradox of Husserlian anti-naturalism, in that it combines it with a Cartesian scientism. Of course, Husserl has much in common with Descartes—significantly, the view that philosophy can only become *the* science of sciences by withdrawal from the empirical world into the pure, necessary realm of essential intuitions. Methodologically, this is a type of idealism.[18] The nature that Husserl rejects as a source of philosophical thought is nature considered as a unity of spatio-temporal being subject to the exact laws of the physical sciences.[19] This is the "nature" given passively in the naïve natural attitude shared by scientist and layperson alike, not the "nature" that is a concept that must be *actively*—that is, *phenomenologically*—constituted.[20]

I will not tackle here Husserl's magisterial progress between the twin evils of, on the one hand, this reductive, "naïve" naturalism that hopes to base philosophy on, or replace philosophy with, empirical science, and on the other, an anti-naturalist, anti-scientific "humanistic" position that tends to see everything in terms of historicism and *Weltanschauung* philosophy. But what remains remarkable in this essay is Husserl's delineation of two diverging cultures within European thought that have unfolded in our own era as the full-blown opposed traditions of Continental and Analytic thought.

A NEW NATURALISM?

As already mentioned, the Anglo-Saxon tradition has always been attracted to naturalism. Since the twentieth century that naturalism has often taken the form of *physicalism*. In this spirit one again finds Papineau's *Philosophical Naturalism*, for example, which connects the meaning of naturalism to "physicalism," the position that all natural phenomena are physical, as that term will eventually be explained by physics.[21] In other words, the nature in question is whatever forms the fundamental subject matter of a *reductive* physical science. As Roy Bhaskar points out in *The Possibility of Naturalism*, this is one of two species of naturalism currently prevalent: "*reductionism*, which asserts that there is an actual identity of subject matter [between the natural and social sciences] . . . and *scientism*, which denies that there are any significant differences in the methods of studying social and natural objects."[22]

Neither the reductive nor the scientistic approach are at all the forms of naturalism I am thinking of in relation to the minority of Continental philosophers who are open to naturalistic thought. They may or may not be materialist, but they are never reductionist or scientistic. As we will see, in fact, they naturalize the human by denaturing nature of its *unnatural qualities,* namely, its supposed intrinsic poverty and powerlessness.

Papineau himself provides a telling remark in this respect. While he asserts that nearly everybody wants to be a naturalist, he adds that "the aspirants to the term nevertheless disagree widely on substantial questions of philosophical doctrine."[23] One of the first philosophers to work within a Continental tradition of naturalism was Bergson. His constant plea to his colleagues was that they never neglect their philosophical duty to interpret the *underdetermined* findings of empirical science with new metaphysical ideas; in the absence of this, he argued, science would embellish them with an uncritical metaphysics. The role of the philosopher is to engage with this material and provide it with the new metaphysics that it deserves.[24]

It is obvious that nature itself is one such underdetermined concept. Consequently, the virtues of naturalism—the recourse to empirical evidence and the denial of supernatural explanations—are themselves open to multiple readings. Questions such as whether a naturalistic explanation has to be materialist or whether it can make reference to consciousness are still pertinent. Naturalism can also be both ontological (asserting what is) and epistemological (asserting the best method for studying what is). To think, then, that "nature" might be a wholly constructed concept belonging to an uncritical scientific establishment *that consequently needs no further philosophical engagement* represents a disastrous move for Continental philosophy as well as an artificial isolation of the cultural and human from the natural and material. This is not to stake a claim for scientism (traditionally the Achilles' heel of Analytic thought) in place of anti-scientism.[25] It is rather to maintain—as Bergson did—the absolute necessity of *some* positive conception of nature in philosophy, be it the scientific one or not.

Whereas there has been increasing talk of a crisis in Analytic philosophy in recent years with an observable shift in values among some practitioners,[26] a similar tendency is fast becoming evident in Continental circles, where a current of "postcontinental" thought is being initiated. The absence of any positive reference to nature is at long last becoming too heavy a burden for some Continental thinkers, and a yearning to engage seriously with science is progressively more evident. Perhaps this will come as no surprise; as early as the publication of Merleau-Ponty's *La Nature* in 1994, interest in the philosophy of nature and naturalism was discernible. There are now a growing number of writers—some working within the phenomenological tradition (the late Francisco Varela and Natalie Depraz being notable examples), some in the Nietzschean one (Keith Ansell Pearson, for instance)—who are no longer satisfied with dismissing either scientific investigations of nature and/or nature itself as simply ontic or conventional. Fields of research for their work include epistemology, cognitive science, and biology.

Such overtures to scientists from philosophers (whether Continental *or* Analytic)[27] have not always been welcomed, of course, especially when they are regarded as insubordinate. A work by Alan Sokal and Jean Bricmont, *Intellectual Impostures,* represents the most famous recent rejection of these advances—in their opinion, postmodern French philosophy has lacked any genuine intellectual credibility when it dares to engage with science.[28] In many respects, however, Sokal and Bricmont's *overall* thesis is weak, with only tenuous textual support, and only goes to show that if philosophers really did read scientific work as poorly as some scientists read philosophy, some of the criticisms made of philosophers might begin to ring true. In a far more serious book, *The Rise of Scientific Philosophy*, Hans Reichenbach points out that it was probably Kant who was the last philosopher who did, or could, produce a philosophical system that was "expressive of the science of . . . [his] time."[29] Since then, science has simply become too vast, too diversified, and too self-sufficient to require such systems of thought. The ideas of Fichte, Schelling, Hegel, Schopenhauer, Spencer, and turn-of-the-century *lebensphilosophie* are not on a par with those of Leibniz or Kant and never could be.

But this is precisely the interdiction that Continental naturalists continue to reject: they refuse to relinquish the demand for a critical naturalism by taking one metaphysical view of nature dogmatically. Moreover, Continental naturalism does not have to espouse a generalist attitude (as *lebensphilosophie* could be said to do), for it can perfectly well focus its analyses in specific fields, like the mind-body problem (Merleau-Ponty), evolution (Bergson), or physics (Deleuze). Not that it should be assumed that all continental encroachments into science and nature are equally successful—it should be on a case-by-case basis that these analyses are weighed. Hence, the cases that Sokal and Bricmont examine (Irigaray on fluid mechanics, Deleuze on calculus, and so on) as well as those they neglect (Heidegger's anti-biologism, the phenomenology of the flesh in Sartre and Levinas, for example) may be found in some instances to be genuine examples of charlatanry but in others to have been unfairly maligned. But it is surely unjust when a philosopher is accused of abusing science when he or she is practicing metaphysics. Gilles Deleuze is one such case, where all that has been found is a philosopher practicing metaphysics—that is, like Leibniz, he is taking certain empirical findings (microscopy in Leibniz's case) and extrapolating from them to go beyond *one* physical realm to all of reality (in the *Monadology*). He is not writing bad physics but *beyond* physics, though without ignoring it. One should call it a "metaphysicalism"; it is a true philosophy of nature that takes inspiration from natural philosophy.

By refusing to "devaluate nature" or take away any "immanent power" from it, Deleuze understands the body and nature in general as sites of simultaneously physical and conceptual forces. This is a nonreductive naturalism. It does not restrict certain powers to the human realm as exclusive properties. Indeed, if it seems to humanize nature, it is only because it is *restoring* what is inalienable to it; hence there is no deflation of humanity in naturalizing it so much as an inflation of nature. To this extent, Deleuze sees himself in a line of naturalists running from Spinoza to Nietzsche. What he wrote in his early work on Nietzsche is particularly telling in this regard: "Nietzsche had his own conception of physics but no ambition as a physicist. He granted himself the poetic and philosophical right to dream of machines that perhaps one day science will realize by its own means."[30]

I am of the opinion that the best chances for a *consistent* and truly philosophical naturalization of humanity lie in it reconnecting with a critical and nonreductive Continental naturalism. The significant transformation Continental thought is currently undergoing, through new readings of thinkers like Bergson, Bachelard, Merleau-Ponty, and Deleuze too, is indicative, I believe, of a new promise for Continental philosophy[31]—a naturalism of the plural and the multiple, one that transgresses the boundaries between the material and the human. The German thought that has dominated Continental thought for the last century—initially Husserlian phenomenology but very quickly its Heideggerian form—may consequently be regarded as a retrograde development in regard to this question. Though it clearly demonstrated its worth in fields less connected with nature and science (the arts and human sciences), the need to temper this unilinear thinking is evident. This is not a call for rampant reductive naturalism, which would just be another form of totalization, a single line of thinking that this time banishes *anthropos* to the outer regions. Rather, nonreductive Continental naturalism has always been pluralistic, forwarding a philosophical practice emphasizing the many faces of philosophy, human *and* natural simultaneously, without either reducing the one to the other. There is no place for a metaphilosophical elitism or a hierarchy of the essential and the nonessential, of the center and the regions. Be it a scientism, pan-culturalism, logicism or ontologism, there are no "first" philosophies. Having a place in nature does not spell a reduction of humanity as much as an explanation, one that provides us with a meaningful place.

NOTES

1. Raymond Williams, *Keywords: A Vocabulary of Culture and Society* (London: Flamingo/Fontana, 1983), 219.

2. See, for a catalogue of the various proposed definitions of what makes humanity different from any other animal or being, Peter Singer and Tom Regan, eds., *Animal Rights and Human Obligations* (Englewood Cliffs, N.J.: Prentice-Hall, 1989).

3. David Papineau, *Philosophical Naturalism* (Oxford: Blackwell, 1993), 1.

4. David Charles and Kathleen Lennon, "Introduction," in *Reduction, Explanation, and Realism,* ed. David Charles and Kathleen Lennon (Oxford: Clarendon Press, 1992), 2.

5. See Simon Blackburn, *Spreading the Word* (Oxford: Clarendon Press, 1984), 152–53.

6. Robert Nozick, *Philosophical Explanations* (Oxford: Clarendon Press, 1981), 629–30, my italics.

7. Ibid., 628. See also 627.

8. Isabelle Stengers, *Power and Invention*, trans. Paul Bains (Minneapolis and London: University of Minnesota Press, 1997), 137.

9. See Charles and Lennon, 5.

10. Stengers, 133. I should add that Stengers herself does not countenance this rather New Age idea.

11. Pascal Engel, "Interpretation without Hermeneutics: A Plea against Ecumenism," in *Topoi* 10 (1991), 138.

12. See Martin Heidegger, "The End of Philosophy and the Task of Thinking," in *Basic Writings*, ed. David F. Krell (San Francisco, Calif.: HarperSanFrancisco, 1993), 433–35.

13. Ibid., 434. It is said that Heidegger viewed modern science no differently from seventeenth-century Newtonian science. See Marjorie Grene, *Philosophy in and Out of Europe* (Berkeley: University of California Press, 1976), 42.

14. This Heideggerian position has been crucial in the development of Continental thought and the postphenomenological thinking that still dominates it today, such that, for it, the "naturalistic fallacy" is not simply a principle in meta-ethics, but all philosophy: to think in natural terms, that is, to understand life by reference to biology, the universe by reference to physics, and so on, is to fail to think essentially. So when Heidegger looks at death, for example, it is without regard for biology or psychology; it is, on the contrary, an existential analysis; see Martin Heidegger, *Being and Time*, trans. John Macquarrie and Edward Robinson (Evanston: Harper & Row, 1962), 292.

15. See Martin Heidegger, "The Age of the World Picture" and "The Question Concerning Technology," in *The Question Concerning Technology and Other Essays*, trans. William Lovitt (New York: HarperCollins, 1982).

16. Tom Rockmore, *Heidegger and French Philosophy* (London: Routledge, 1995), 2.

17. Hegel's narrow definition of "self-consciousness" as the "native realm of truth" (at the expense of sense-certainty, perception or Kantian rational understand-

ing) has arguably only encouraged the Continental withdrawal from any serious engagement with nature. This is notwithstanding his *naturphilosophie*, which Brunschvicg derided as an anachronism even prior to its formulation; see Rockmore, 28.

18. Edmund Husserl, "Philosophy as a Rigorous Science," in *Phenomenology and the Crisis of Philosophy*, trans. Quentin Lauer (New York: Harper, 1965), 73 n. 5.

19. Ibid., 79.

20. Ibid., 104 n. 40.

21. Papineau, 1, 2.

22. Roy Bhasker, *The Possibility of Naturalism* (London: Routledge, 1979), 2.

23. Papineau, 1.

24. Henri Bergson, *Mind-Energy*, trans. H. Wildon Carr (New York: Henry Holt, 1922), 50.

25. See Tom Sorell, *Scientism: Philosophy and the Infatuation with Science* (London: Routledge, 1991).

26. See John Rajchman and Cornel West, eds., *Post-Analytic Philosophy* (New York: Columbia University Press, 1985).

27. See Lewis Wolpert, *The Unnatural Nature of Science* (London: Faber and Faber, 1993).

28. See Alan Sokal and Jean Bricmont, *Intellectual Impostures* (London: Profile Books, 1998).

29. Hans Reichenbach, *The Rise of Scientific Philosophy* (Berkeley: University of California Press, 1951), 122.

30. Gilles Deleuze, *Nietzsche and Philosophy*, trans. Hugh Tomlinson (London: Athlone Press, 1983), 30.

31. Some of this work, it should be added, is focused on naturalizing Husserlian phenomenology in particular; see Jean Petitot et al., eds., *Naturalising Phenomenology: Issues in Contemporary Phenomenology and Cognitive Science* (Stanford, Calif.: Stanford University Press, 1999).

5

Nature and Culture: The Mythic Register

Kate Soper

My hope is that ecocriticism is too newly arrived on the academic scene to have established many conventions, and that I therefore do not have to worry unduly about the unorthodox nature of my contribution. I think, in fact, that it may just about qualify under the conveniently general definition offered by Richard Kerridge and Neil Sammells in their introduction to *Writing the Environment* (where "ecocriticism" is said "to evaluate texts and ideas in terms of their coherence and usefulness as responses to environmental crisis").[1] But there is no doubt, too, that my engagement will be rather different from the writing in that collection, and I want to begin by saying a word or two about how and why it does.

Much of the ecocritical writing I have encountered divides between two types of approaches, both concerned in differing ways with the understanding or representation of nonhuman nature. In the one—more ecocentric and nature-endorsing approach—literary and other texts are viewed as sources of revelation about the intrinsic value of nature or the importance of restoring human unity with it. This is associated with various calls to give "voice" to nature[2]; or to promote works that "privilege" nature over humanity or register its "otherness."[3] It is also aligned with what might be termed "redemptive Heideggerian readings" of texts for what they have to tell us about our human "alienation" or loss of "authentic" relations with nature and the conditions of their possible restitution. (Apart from Heidegger himself, important influences seem to be Lawrence Buell's work, Robert Pogue Harrison's *Forests*—described by Jonathan Bates as "the seminal eco-literary-critical book of our times"[4]—and the writings associated with the deep ecology perspective.)

The other approach is instantiated in the deconstructive-sceptical type of exercise that emphasizes the role of culture in the creation of what we term "nature" and seeks to expose dubiously Romantic, or anthropomorphizing, or ideologically distorting, cultural constructions and representations of nature. (As instances of this kind of critical exposure of our discourses on "nature" one might cite Alex Wilson's *The Culture of Nature*, the critical engagement with children's literature by Karin Lesnik Oberstein, or Karla Armbruster's piece on TV nature documentaries, in *Writing the Environment*. The contributions to that collection of Sammells, Kerridge and Greg Garrard also, I think, belong in this mode, though in rather more qualified ways.)

These two approaches are clearly in many respects antithetical; writers endorsing the "truth" or "value" of nature, or recalling us to a lost unity with it, are engaged in a something rather different from those exposing the cultural construction of that "truth" or the partial, and historically relative, quality of human feelings for the natural environment. Nonetheless, both approaches may be said to share a concern with clarifying our conceptions of the nonhuman world, or correcting misapprehensions about human relations to it. In the more nature-endorsing, Heideggerian mode, the appeal to the establishment of "authentic dwelling" or more "truthful" relations to nature is made fairly explicit. But the deconstruction of misleading cultural representations of "nature" is also implicitly recommending an alternative and improved cognition—a mode of understanding that will avoid instrumental or anthropomorphizing appropriations—and is thus far also operating with a notion of "truth" or "authenticity."[5] Whether, then, the advice is "return" to nature, get "closer" to it, "dwell authentically," and so forth, or to be wary of our own too appropriative representations of that "closeness" or "authenticity," the ecocritical task is presented as a matter of correcting our views about nature or exploring texts as guides to a better appreciation.

I myself, however, shall not here be concerned with these questions of representation and ideological distortion, or at least not very directly. This is not said in any strongly critical sense, since it seems difficult to conceive of an ecocriticism that does not in one way or another gesture at how we ought to be more accurately conceptualizing (and thus more properly relating to) nature. It is also true that some rethinking of attitudes to nature is needed, particularly in the affluent nations in view of their special responsibility for securing a more just and ecologically sustainable order, and that cultural works have a significant contribution to make to that transformation. But I am certainly wary of viewing the key to ecological good practice as a matter simply of "getting to the truth" about nonhuman nature, particularly if that means something like "recementing" a lost unity with it, respecting the "otherness" of nature, or "valuing it in itself."

I think we have to be clear that we have no conception of what the "difference" of nature consists in other than in the conceptions we have of its difference. All representations of nature are thus far discursively mediated, and they are all informed to some degree by the ideas we have of human identity. In this sense, there is no escaping conceptual anthropocentricity.

But neither is there anything deplorable about this. The fact, for example, that we cannot interpret the being and needs of nonhuman creatures other than in the light of our own identity is cause neither for distress nor for giving up on the exercise of representation. All it means is that in any understanding we bring to other animals, we need to be aware of the limits of that understanding.

One of my favored expressions of the point is in Derek Mahon's poem *Man and Bird,* where he suggests that to think from the position of the birds is to accept a certain inability to do so. They fly away from him ("The ancient fear is in them still"),[6] making him an "enlightened alien" doomed to parodic whistling. Yet Mahon, one cannot help feeling, does more to illuminate the quality of the "gap" between the "world of nature" and the "world of man" than many who insist either on the difference of the "world of nature" or on our actual or desirable closeness to it. Second, and more important, we should not pretend to a unity or communality with nonhuman nature that could be had only by denying or overlooking our more specifically human needs, concerns, and qualities. We (or at any rate, some Western intellectuals) may suffer at times from what might be called the "envy of immanence"—by which I mean the desire to be like plant and animal life, immersed in nature rather than consciously confronting and representing it. This is the wish, as Rilke puts it, to be admitted to the "Open," becoming one of the "great accustomed" who are by nature "benumbed" and live only in their "dim delight"[7]—and it is a wish or envy that also finds powerful expression in the poetry of Wordsworth, Edward Thomas, and a number of others. But in the final analysis very few of us would opt for immanence were we to be offered the choice, and certainly neither Heidegger nor Rilke nor Wordsworth nor Thomas showed any real interest in renouncing their aspirations to philosophical or poetic transcendence.

I want to argue, furthermore, in this connection, that our current ecological situation is to be illuminated primarily not by reference to the nature of nonhuman nature but through consideration of the fraught nature of our own (distinctively human) condition as creatures who are both a part of nature and apart from it—both members, like other animals, of a natural species and dependent on natural resources for the supply of all our material needs but at the same time quite unlike them in the urge we have to cultural transcendence. Considered very abstractly, we may view the ecological "crisis" faced by humanity as a crisis about these contrary dimensions of human existence and their respective needs and modes of satisfaction. Capitalism, industrialization, Western "civilization"—all this can be viewed in the broadest sense as generated in response to the urge to cultural transcendence (to productivity, innovation, the escape from reproductive and traditional modes of being).

Even Marx, virulent critic though he was of capitalism, recognized its "civilizing influence" in this respect and its dynamic power to break with

all "complacent" and encrusted modes of gratification.[8] Yet the "transcendence" offered through this dynamic of capitalist globalization is extremely
partial, anti-hedonist in many respects, and ultimately disastrous in ecological terms. The question therefore that would seem to be posed in this context is whether a global modus vivendi can be established that is naturally
sustainable, socially just, and humanly rewarding. Can the *ecological* need
for a more cyclical and reproductive (more "natural" or "immanent") mode
of interaction with nature be reconciled with the more distinctively *human*
need for continuous cultural creation and productive innovation (with the
demands of transcendent being)? Can we find ways of living rich, fulfilling, creative, complex, nonrepetitive lives without putting too much stress
on nature? Can we, in short, find more ecologically benign ways of *not*
being natural but remaining assertively and distinctively human?

These are clearly highly abstract and intractable questions, and I shall
not address them here in any direct sense (to attempt do so, in any case,
would be to shift out of an ecocritical mode into something more immediately sociological or political). But it is within the remit of ecocriticism to
concern oneself with their cultural expression, and it is in this role, I suggest, that mythic cognition and narrative have a good deal to offer ecology. To avoid misunderstanding, however, I must make clear in what sense
I intend this claim. For myths have, of course, been made to serve some
repellent agendas, and against the background of their racist and chauvinist
usage one can well understand the resistance to the idea of their having any
positive political force. The tendency of the Left to assimilate mythology
directly to ideology and to dismiss it as a mystifying and reactionary form
of consciousness thus far has my support.[9]

Yet there is a distinction to be made between subscribing to mythic beliefs about nature and a more allegorical or rhetorical use of mythic narratives, and it is clear that myth can be deployed in ecopolitics in a variety
of ways and with differing degrees of solemnity.[10] The piety of the truly
serious nature worshippers is not to be directly assimilated to a more ironic
use of the mythic or magical, and to this mix of modes there corresponds
a mix of responses within the Green movement. In a discussion of the con-
troversies generated by ecofeminism's invocation of Great Goddess mythology and witchcraft imagery, Andrew Ross makes the point that

> the new social movements, after all, are supposed to be the home of diver-
> sity, where politics is infused with more experimental forms of pleasure and
> personality than the older, more austere left was wont to recognize. For Emma
> Goldman, it was all about being allowed to dance. For a Starhawk, it may be
> about being allowed to cast a spell or two. Some see this as innocuous enough,
> others see it as the beginning of the end that Péguy once prophesied: *tout com-*
> *mence en politique, et finit par mystique.* Still others see it as a way of trans-
> forming the style of being political.[11]

Ross is surely right to suggest here that there is a spectrum of positions within the Green movement ranging from those, at one end, who would dismiss any recourse to myth or magic as a capitulation to irrationalism that can only discredit its forms of protest, to those at the other who would insist that is these forms of thinking that offer the most powerful and effective antidote to instrumental rationality. Somewhere in the middle come those, like Ross (and I would include myself here), who would condone a few fictions and fables if they serve to advance a different order of reality.

In any case, what I am concerned to defend and illustrate in this context is not so much reversion to animistic or mystical conceptions of nonhuman nature but the ecological relevance of myth as a story about ourselves—as a cultural register, that is, of what I have termed our "fraught condition" and the tensions between immanence and transcendence, the pull of nature and the pull of culture. Nor am I suggesting that myth in this respect tells us anything that cannot be told in other—more prosaic, objective and scientific—terms, but only that mythic narratives may offer particularly poetic and crystalline insights at this level.

A powerful example here (and in claiming it I am obviously indebted to the presentation of the mythic material by Horkheimer and Adorno in their *Dialectic of Enlightenment*) is that of the Homeric *Odyssey*, specifically the encounters between Odysseus himself, the transcendent, entrepreneurial, protagonist of the story (and representative, if you like, of the Freudian Reality Principle), and the Sirens, Circe, Calypso, the lotus eaters, and other figures registering the compulsion to a more immanent and instinctual mode of being and the enticements of the Pleasure Principle.

Odysseus is the figuration *in* myth of a human, cultural transcendence—an advance beyond a more natural or animal mode of existence (and its animist and mythic modes of belief). In "testing" himself against the various mythic powers, he displays the qualities of a creative and autonomous subjectivity, and the "illusions" of animism (for example, its peopling of the seas with demons and monsters) are exposed as merely "misleading."[12] What is allegorized here is a defiance and mastery of nature's forces in the figure of a "culture hero" who is shown to negotiate and overcome mythic powers by means of a combination of guile and instinctual renunciation.

This cunning is evident, as Horkheimer and Adorno suggest, in Odysseus's dealings with the Sirens, whose fatally alluring song tempts him to give up on ego identity and self-mastery, and to regress to a past forgetfulness and immanence in nature. Fully aware as he is of the seduction of their call but knowing also that he cannot yield to it if he is to remain in his position of power as a master, Odysseus resorts to the device of stopping his men's ears with wax and having them row with all their strength, while he himself, strapped to the mast, listens to the Siren song. Even when he begs to be released, it is to no avail, since his servants, who do not listen, "know only the song's danger but nothing of its beauty, and leave him at the mast in order to save him and themselves."[13] Nature is mastered, the mythic powers quelled, and preservation secured, but only at the cost of self-denial, sensory repression, and the perpetuation of master-slave relations.

The Pleasure versus Reality Principle tensions are also manifest in the encounters with Calypso, Circe, and the lotus eaters, all of whom in their differing ways offer the enticements of self-abandon, absorption in voluptuousness, and/or forgetfulness of toil and removal from the usual spatio-temporal coordinates of mortal life.

Both Calypso and Circe seek to hold Odysseus in a magico-mythical "timelessness" that threatens to undermine his subjective will to make progress and to carry forward the distinctively human endeavor of the *nostos*. Calypso aims to bewitch Odysseus into forgetting his return. She represents the charm of escape from the distinctively human form of memory—together with all the sense of duty, peril, loss, remorse that such a memory preserves. Circe casts his men back into nature through their metamorphosis into swine, and her temptation to Odysseus himself is to return to natural immanence and a more instinctual life and animal order of existence.

So, too, with the lotus eaters (from whom Odysseus forcibly drags his men back weeping to the ships, and straps them in the galleys). Whoever browses on the lotus flower, says Homer, slips into oblivion, surrenders the will to struggle for survival, and has no more thought of returning home. Theirs may be a false and merely vegetative happiness (it is compared by Horkheimer and Adorno to the drug addiction of the victims of modernity, who cannot otherwise endure the unendurable); yet the Odyssean task-master can bring them no genuine happiness either, since he rescues them from narcotic oblivion only to return them to a life of relentless labor.[14]

In all these episodes, then, we are offered some kind of allegory of the tensions between the respective claims of immanence and transcendence, between the impulse to indolence and forgetfulness, on the one hand, and the call to industry and the compulsions of the "work ethic," on the other. The equivocal message of the mythic material should be emphasized in this connection. What we have here is a form of retrospection on, or retrieval of, a precultural past that is at once both nostalgic and menacing. In its nostalgic aspect, it represents various forms of fantastical longing: to "return to the womb"; to forget the ego and human individuality; to live in a world of instantaneous gratifications without the hardship of labor and the deferment of gratification;[15] to be returned to "nature" and relieved of the alienation of being caught up in a normative order of duties, moral laws, punishment, regrets, remorse. It registers, if you like, what I earlier termed the "envy of immanence."

Yet, as we have also seen, in their more menacing aspect all of these mythic images contain their own admonition. Their allurements are in every case tainted with something fearsome, which acts as a warning not to yield. Simultaneously both sinister and seductive, the Sirens, Circe, Calypso, the lotus eaters stand as warnings against the loss of the individuated, self-realized, more distinctively human existence that would be sacrificed in the return to nature, even as they figure the allure of regression to a greater closeness with it. Eros, to employ the Freudian metapsychology, is inextricably intertwined with Thanatos in these mythic episodes, either in the sense (as with the Sirens) that death is the consequence of seduction (and a frightful death at that, an animal's death without the cultural marks of burial or headstone—the Sirens' meadow is an expanse of bleached bones and unburied putrefying corpses); or in the sense of death as a return to quiescence, subsumption in immanence, the return to primitivity and the "savage" state, together with its loss of human subjectivity and individuation.[16] In the case of Calypso's enchantment, moreover, the mythic episode registers the risk of reverting to an animality that is threatened by arrestment within a magical stage of human existence. It figures both the liberation of instinctual energy in the return to Odysseus's men to an "animal nature," and the regression to bestiality (and a swinish bestiality at that) that follows on yielding to that temptation. Horkheimer and Adorno comment on this connection:

> The mythic commandment to which they succumb liberates at the same time the repressed nature in them. What is recalled in their reversion to myth is itself myth. The repression of instinct that makes them individuals—selves—and separates them from the animals, was the introversion of repression in the hopelessly closed cycle of nature, to which—as an older theory has it—the name of Circe alludes. The forceful magic, on the other hand, which recalls them to an idealized prehistory, not only makes them animals, but—like the idyllic interlude of the lotus eaters—brings about, however delusive it may be, the illusion of redemption.[17]

The "return to nature" of those who have once become human is a return not to bliss but to degradation.

Yet the "progress" figured in Odysseus, the "culture hero" has also resulted in its own form of social and ecological degradation. "The curse of irresistible progress," suggest Horkheimer and Adorno, "is irresistible regression."[18] The triumphs of the Enlightenment mastery over nature have been used to perpetuate the toil and duress of pretechnological culture but without gaining any of the gratifications of a life more reconciled with nature and more given over to immediate gratification. Enlightenment, it seems, has served to prolong the negative aspects of the mythic or archaic stage without the compensation of its particular forms of bliss.

In this sense, the *Odyssey* can be read as an allegory of the antitheses between "mythic" (that is, primitive and archaic) and "modern" (that is, industrially developed, Enlightened) modes of interaction with nature and of their respective gains and losses for human happiness and well-being. It is an allegory, that is, of the tension between following the "call to return to nature" (the call to simplicity, immanence, and cyclical reproduction) and the "call to cultural advance" (the call to complexity, transcendence, and ever-expanding productivity).[19] It can be seen as a story that illustrates the tensions of human culturality: of what is given up, and what is gained in its stead, as a consequence of the emergence of industry, symbolic culture, and a distinctively human subjectivity.

Now, I recognize that I am here putting my own particular spin on Horkheimer and Adorno's account in *Dialectic of Enlightenment*, although I think it is an elaboration that has some encouragement in their own discussion, where it is clearly implied at several points that the disastrous "progress" of enlightenment has been achieved only at the cost of repression of natural instinct and hedonist renunciation. The sacrifice of an instinctual "inner" nature—of the gratifications associated with the more archaic, "mythic" stage in human culture—is to that extent viewed as contributing to the more distinctively enlightened (and destructive) forms of interaction with "outer" nature. In their paradoxical interpretation of the entwinement of myth and enlightenment, it is both a "disaster" that Enlightenment has "become" or "reverted" to myth, and a disaster brought about, at least in part, by the advance beyond a mythic immanence in nature and its cyclical and reproductive way of life.

The use of mythic material in *Dialectic of Enlightenment* thus reflects the sites of philosophical and political conflict between Romantic and counter-Romantic responses to Western civilization and its forms of industrialization; in doing so, I suggest, it also figures the tensions with which we have now to come to terms if we are to counter the "self-destruction" of Enlightenment and its ecological consequences. At the socio-economic level, these are tensions between, on the one hand, the modernizing impulse to further the pleasures and forms of enhancement that come with technological development and economic growth, and the pressures, on the other, to protect ourselves from the less welcome effects of industrialization and to conserve the environment and its supply of natural resources. They are the tensions between modernization and the current forms of resistance to it; between the "progress" recommended by the advocates of capitalist globalization, consumerism, and the scientific mastering of "nature" and the "progress" of a sustainable economy and "alternative hedonism" recommended by the Greens. For the challenge of this alterative hedonism is how to conserve the environment and to remain in some kind equilibrium with "nature" while resisting the patriarchal and hierarchical cultural and social divisions that have traditionally always accompanied more reproductive and naturally sustainable societies. Can we find ways of democratizing and *de*-traditionalizing culture—of *not* going back to feudal and patrician social modes—while yet giving up on the more destructive consumerist compulsions associated with modernity? Can we, so to speak, convert to a low-material-consumption, bike-speed, actual pace of life while enjoying an ever more entrancing and exciting mode of being in our erotic relations, friendships, and modes of spiritual engagement?

These questions are at most hinted at in the argument of *Dialectic of Enlightenment*. Indeed, although Horkheimer and Adorno are clearly before their time in offering a dialectical critique of the destructive effects on nature of the process of enlightenment, they are nonetheless writing well before the emergence of the contemporary Green movement and hence without reference to its particular frame of political concerns. Their text is in this sense unconscious of the more specifically ecologically accented tensions that, I am here arguing, are registered in its engagement with mythic materials. But at a more implicit level, it can be read as a text of very considerable relevance, both to the current forms of Green critique of instrumental rationality and to the dilemmas of political ecology at the present time. In its own use of mythic imagery it offers some exemplification of the possible ways of invoking this in illustration of a utopian program to transcend ecological destruction without "returning to nature."

It is worth noting also in this connection that another of the Frankfurt School theorists, Herbert Marcuse, has also drawn extensively on classical myth in his more optimistic projection, in his work *Eros and Civilisation*, of a society that has reconciled Reality Principle and Pleasure Principle, the need to work with the delights of play, the protection of nature with human creativity. Here Prometheus figures as the representative of toil and technological mastery, while Orpheus and Narcissus are invoked as utopian representatives of the relations to nature that might obtain under a nonrepressive civilization.

If Prometheus is the culture-hero of toil, productivity, and progress through repression, then the symbols of another reality principle must be sought at the opposite pole. Orpheus and Narcissus (like Dionysus, to whom they are akin—the antagonist of the god who sanctions the logic of domination, the realm of reason) stand for a very different reality. They have not become the culture-heroes of the Western world: theirs is the image of joy and fulfilment; the voice that does not command but sings; the gesture that offers and receives; the deed that is peace and ends the labor of conquest; the liberation from time that unites man with god, man with nature.[20]

Orpheus and Narcissus figure, says Marcuse, the "Great Refusal" of the Promethean order of the Performance Principle and its culture of repression. As such they are "essentially unreal and unrealistic." They designate an "impossible" existence, in the sense that they explode it, conveying not a mode of life but a commitment to death and the underworld. At best, suggests Marcuse, they are "poetic, something for the soul and heart." Yet at the same time they sustain a reality in breaking with the opposition between humanity and nature, subject and object: "Trees and animals respond to Orpheus's language; and the spring and forest respond to Narcissus's desire. The Orphic and Narcissistic Eros awakens and liberates potentialities that are real in things animate and inanimate, in organic and inorganic nature—real but in the unerotic reality suppressed. These potentialities circumscribe the *telos* inherent in them as: just to 'be what they are,' 'being-there,' existing."[21]

Lastly, let me briefly note, as also relevant to the ecological use and assessment of mythic forms, the more recent argument of the German philosopher Hans Blumenberg, who in his *Work on Myth* has suggested that we should neither dismiss myth as mere irrationalism, on the one hand, nor accept an unqualified Romantic endorsement of it, on the other.[22] If we view myth, he argues, as a primitive and superstitious mode of cognition superseded by science, we cannot explain its perduring hold upon the contemporary imagination and the cultural "work" we continually perform upon it. On the other hand, to endorse it as in some sense more fundamental to human nature than our "surface" rationality would be to legitimate some of the more dangerously fanatical and fascistic use of mythic forms.

Blumenberg's own account of myth views it as a "compound of poetry and terror" that functions as a system to eliminate the generalized dread inspired by the "absolutism of reality"—the name he gives to those situations (he cites as an early instance that encountered by our ancestors on first going bipedal in the open savannah) that provoke a sense of unspecified anxiety, of having little or no control over the conditions of existence. The role of mythic naming and discrimination is to convert or "rationalize" this angst or nonspecific dread into plain *fear* of particular named entities and agencies, personalized powers whom we can address and (to that extent) deal with. That this function remains pertinent in contemporary culture, generating a continuous "work" upon myth is due, he argues, to the facts that our scientific knowledge is itself never more than partial and that we always remain at the mercy of our lack of biological adaptability to the consequences of our technical capacities. If we set this account of mythic function alongside the work of those sociologists, such as Ulrich Beck and Anthony Giddens, who have suggested that what distinguishes modern industrial culture is its exposure to risk and the unpredictable consequences of scientific "advance," certainly we can see that rather than allaying anxiety, our "victories" over nature, whether in the field of nuclear fission, genetic engineering, drug development, or agribusiness, only serve to open up another horizon of danger—a new type of "absolutism of reality" requiring coping strategies that cannot be those of science itself.

To argue this is not to deny the zanier and more problematic elements in Blumenberg's particular approach. Nor am I suggesting here that there are no aspects of the Frankfurt School deployment of mythic forms with which I would want to take issue. What I would endorse is the argument implicit in both these approaches to the effect that myth is to be regarded as an irrational and deluded mode of cognition only from within the perspective of scientific Enlightenment itself, and that insofar as the "reason" associated with the latter has issued in its own forms of ecological lunacy, mythic thought can contribute to a necessary kind of scepticism about the claims of rationality itself.

Indeed, one might claim that there are at least three features that are both distinctive to myth and render it a particularly appropriate resource of ecological campaigning: first, the ambiguity of its epistemological status between scientific and the mystical; second, the powerful and extensive repertoire of images it provides of the nature-culture divide and human relations to the environment; and third, the ease with which it lends itself to the kind of creative recountings that can often bear so strikingly on our modern predicament.

NOTES

1. Richard Kerridge and Neil Sammells, *Writing the Environment: Ecocriticism and Literature* (London: Zed Books, 1998), 5.

2. Cf. Dominic Head's reference to ecocritical calls to "give voice" to nature, and his discussion of Lawrence Buell's "ecocentric" criteria for ecocriticism. See *The Environmental Imagination* (Cambridge, Mass.: Harvard University Press, 1995), and his contribution to Kerridge and Sammells, 27–39, esp. 37.

3. Further quotations from Kerridge and Sammells.

4. Jonathan Bates, "Poetry and Biodiversity," in Kerridge and Sammells, 59.

5. In her critique of the constructivism at work in TV nature programs, for example, Karla Armbruster writes, "Bridging the gap between culture and nature by this kind of excessive (and culturally normative) anthropomorphism ignores the diverse ways in which nonhuman nature is different from humanity. Such strategies are another form of human dominance over the nonhuman: by accepting the absorption of animals, plants and even ecosystems into the sphere of human culture, we participate in the colonizing move of turning what was other into the same, with no respect for its difference from us" (ibid., 231). We might note in this connection the extent to which ecocriticism seems drawn to realism: whereas very few critics have problems with nonrealist representation in respect of other fictional or poetic material (human relations, the built environment, sexuality, etc.), when it comes to nature (wildlife, the unbuilt environment, landscape, wilderness, etc.) the point seems to be to avoid any nonrealist register.

6. Derek Mahon, *Selected Poems* (Harmondsworth: Penguin, 1991), 16.

7. Or in Heidegger's terminology, it is the wish not to have "to go with the venture as one that is represented." See "What are Poets for?" in *Poetry, Language, Thought*, trans. Albert Hofstadter (New York: Harper & Row, 1971), 110. Heidegger himself discusses Rilke and Holderlin in this context.

8. See especially Marx's discussion in the *Grundrisse* (London: Allen Lane, 1973). Cf. my own discussion in *On Human Needs* (Brighton, Sussex: Harvester Press, 1981).

9. Such, for example, is the position represented in a text such as Roland Barthes's *Mythologies*. Marxists have, for the most part, we might note in this connection, subscribed to the standard Enlightenment view of myth as a primitive and irrational mode of cognition superseded by the advent of science.

10. For example, the more ironic or purely rhetorical use of myth—as in the regular references by Green writers to such figures as Prometheus or Demeter—needs to be distinguished from the more studied ecofeminist invocations of fertility symbols and Earth-Mother myths. Both these represent a rather different approach to that involved in the revampings of older legends or historical traditions of protest (as in the use that has been made, for example, of the Robin Hood, Digger, or Luddite identities) or in the invention of quasi-mythic visual and verbal imagery that is characteristic of many of the Green movement's recent campaigns (as instanced, for example, in the inspired naming by Greenpeace of its helicopter *Tweetie* during its harassing of Shell over the disposal of the Brent Spar; or in the awe-inspiring tactics of the encampments resisting road construction in the United Kingdom through which we have become accustomed to silhouetted images in the media of networks of treewalks and treehouses, with their aerial eco-warrior inhabitants improbably suspended from branches and tripods; or in the recent car "trials" mounted by the English neo-Luddites).

11. Andrew Ross, *The Chicago Gangster Theory of Life* (London: Verso 1994), 229.

12. Theodor Adorno and Max Horkheimer, *Dialectic of Enlightenment*, trans. John Cumming (London: Verso, 1979), 46–47.

13. Ibid., 34.

14. Ibid., 62–64.

15. The yearning to live in a golden age before toil and hardship and to escape mortality is a theme endlessly repeated in Arcadian and Paradisial myths, and it is clearly registered in Homer, as we have seen, where the indolence of the lotus eaters and of Calypso is pitted against Odysseus, who represents the industry and deferment of gratification essential to sustaining human culture. Calypso and the Sirens, for their part, both attempt to seduce Odysseus into believing he can cross the boundaries defining human existence and still survive.

16. This death, we might note, is the conception of Thanatos that Freud associates with the merely fantastical gratifications afforded by the Pleasure Principle, and which he contrasts to the real satisfaction that can only be attained through obedience to the Reality Principle: an obedience demanding renunciation of immediate gratification, the deferment of pleasure, and the detour of toil. This is the obedience that alone can secure the goods essential to bodily survival, and whose promise is of a happiness won "against the odds," of something more worthy and genuine than the bliss gained in the arms of Morpheus, and the forgetfulness attendant on the too purely hallucinatory gratifications of the Pleasure Principle. (In his *Interpretation of Dreams*, Freud makes the point that the baby's hunger can only be assuaged through the reality of the actual breast, not through the imaginary perception of the breast, and that in the failure of such nourishment the organism dies: obedience to the Pleasure Principle at the cost of the detour via the real world to real satisfactions adjured by the Reality Principle is literally the "kiss of death.")

17. In this, like Calypso, suggest Horkheimer and Adorno, she too asserts the equivocal erotic attraction of an older, nonmonogamous, prematrimonial life. She is the courtesan, who "assures happiness and destroys the autonomy of the one she makes happy—this is her equivocation." Yet in the encounter with Odysseus her power is weakened as a direct consequence of his self-repression and determination to remain master of the situation. He sleeps with her, but it is on his terms. She subjects herself to the one man who is able to resist her magic, agreeing as she does so to the contractual terms for the release of his men, and thus becomes antithetical yet complementary mistress-whore to the monogamous wife, Penelope, in the patriarchal order of domination. *Dialectic of Enlightenment*, 70.

18. "Mankind, whose versatility and knowledge become differentiated with the division of labor, is at the same time forced back to anthropologically more primitive stages, for with the technical easing of life the persistence of domination brings about a fixation of the instincts by means of heavier repression. . . . The curse of irresistible progress is irresistible regression." *Dialectic of Enlightenment*, 35–36.

19. Odysseus is even presented to us as the typical bourgeois "homo economicus": a "Robinsonade" (the reference is to Marx's dismissal of the "Robinsonade" individualistic illusions of the bourgeois economic theorists in his 1857 introduction to the *Grundrisse*), a capitalist entrepreneur who justifies his "thefts" of the workers' labor time by appeal to the notion of the "risks" he is taking. Comparably to the ways in which the capitalist boss profits from his subtle manipulations of the contractual relations of the wage system, Odysseus can be seen to fulfill his contracts with the gods and mythic figures while always yet deceiving them. In Horkheimer and Adorno's reading the epic thus becomes an allegory of the exploitations of capitalism (at any rate viewed from the Marxist perspective): capitalist exchanges with labor power are always "free and equal," the contract always fulfilled, but the worker nonetheless cheated of the full product of the labor time expended. Their reading also reveals dimensions in which it might be said to "defend" a capitalist work ethic. For example, in Odysseus's encounter with Polyphemus and the Cyclops (depicted as "savages" because they do not till the land, etc.), Homer is interpreted as condemning a mere hand-to-mouth existence as precivilized and lawless: "The civilised accusation of anarchy," write Horkheimer and Adorno, "is almost a denunciation of plenitude" (cf. the same charge made against the "abundant" nature encountered in the South by the first colonizers of America, some of whom saw this as encouraging "sponging," idleness and sloth).

20. Herbert Marcuse, *Eros and Civilisation* (London: Ark, 1987), 120.

21. Ibid., 122.

22. Hans Blumenberg, *Work on Myth*, trans. Robert M. Wallace (Cambridge, Mass.: MIT Press, 1985).

6

The Way of the World: Nature, History, Human Ontology

Joseph Margolis

The early Platonic Dialogues, the so-called elenctic or Socratic dialogues, begin on a subversive note. They make an attempt to discern what, determinately, the mark of a good life is—what, as we might say, directs human conduct to its proper good, its end, insofar as that might be read off from a review of the human condition. These dialogues, including the first two books of the *Republic*,[1] appear to fail, since the discussants, aware enough of the purpose or function of a ship's pilot or a physician or a shepherd to be able to say easily enough what it is to perform such functions well, cannot say what the natural function or corresponding virtue of a human being is, or whether human beings have a "nature" that yields any clue about man's normative mode of functioning. It is true that the *Republic* goes blithely on, in spite of the apparent stalemate, to sketch "the ideal state," in which of course the organizing virtues of personal life and the life of the *polis* are shown, effectively, to be the same: the one writ small, the other writ large. It is clear to everyone present that even Socrates, who "knows that he is ignorant," ventures, ignorantly, to give his impression of the ideal answer—that is, justice: "giving everyone his due."

The early dialogues are notable because everyone who participates in the discussion seems to have a sense of the standard answers and how to test them, without being able to state the proper method of answering or, as already remarked, what the true "good" of human nature is. Furthermore, when, later in his career, Plato composes the *Statesman*,[2] we are explicitly invited to consider how to organize a good state in spite of the fact that we cannot claim to know the Good—that is, the changeless norm, which, if known, would make the task routine. We are invited, accordingly, to sketch a "second-best state," evidently in Socratic ignorance and perhaps in the spirit of an instructive joke. For we need to organize our lives in a reasonable way in spite of the fact that we cannot possibly claim to "know" how to do so "best."

That, I would say, is where we find ourselves still. We cannot pretend that any examination of "human nature" yields a reliable sense of the purpose or function or good of what it is to be a human being, or even whether human beings *have* any essential nature at all. *Homo sapiens* obviously has a characteristic biology. But *homo sapiens* has no inherent purpose or function—or does the baboon have a function? *Human beings,* as we understand ourselves, are hardly to be adequately described in whatever terms serve the usual Darwinian accounts of *homo sapiens.* Darwin, of course, prided himself on having eliminated any purposive or normative teleology from the process of natural selection.[3]

We ourselves are inclined to say that what it is to be a human being cannot be completely understood in biological terms alone; you must take into account, we say, the formative influence of language and culture. But therein lies trouble. There is no generally accepted account of the natural norms of "human nature" analyzed jointly in terms of biology and culture. Furthermore, it seems entirely reasonable to suppose that you cannot really say what human nature *is* (in this more complicated sense) or, indeed, whether there is anything essential or unchanging in merely being human, or whether the "ontology" of the human—human nature, human existence, the human condition, what we believe distinguishes the human from every other life form—can rightly rely on our ordinary attempts at self-description.

Martin Heidegger cleverly converted our sense of puzzlement about our own nature into what he took to be the principal insight about or mode of "Being"—*Dasein,* the mode of being that is uniquely human, according to Heidegger. Humans—or the existing individual beings who are actually human, who manifest *Dasein*'s unique mode of being—he says, are distinguished by their (our) being the only beings *(Seiende)* who have a compelling concern or "care" for Being itself *(Sein),* which of course entails a concern for their own (mode of) being *(Dasein).* Heidegger goes off on his own toot, however, regarding the subtleties of *Sein,* which go well beyond the question of what it is to be or become human.[4]

To be sure, Heidegger correctly forgrounds the fact that human beings—human persons or selves, let us say, anticipating distinctions we shall need to add—are, among living creatures, the only "beings" that are capable of reporting, reflexively, the "content" of their mental states, which, of course, only humans can "understand." That is a breathtaking discovery (hardly Heidegger's, of course), possibly deep enough to pardon Heidegger's own philosophical extravagances. For example, late in his career Heidegger concluded, apparently on the basis of his analysis of *Sein* and *Dasein,* that the whole of Western philosophy and social history involved a "forgetting" of Being, so that all of modern life (before and after the defeat of Nazism) counted as a huge "ontological" mistake—in fact, a disaster that might almost be called a form of original sin.

In spite of this bit of political spleen, Heidegger managed to advance the idea that "being human" constituted a unique kind of "being," the "nature" of which could not be adequately captured by any idea of man's animal nature; being human, the implication warns, is not anything that can be drawn from what is common to humans and animals.[5] For, after all, being human, exhibiting the concerns of *Dasein,* say, appears nowhere else in the world we know. For all its focus, Heidegger's way of putting things is remarkably vague about how to account for the appearance of creatures who "become human," though he is not vague at all about what, once manifest, counts among the distinctions of such beings. He does say, provocatively, that *Dasein*—the mode of being or the individual instantiations of the mode of being (selves, effectively)—is "onto-ontological." But I cannot find any satisfactory analysis in Heidegger himself as to what to understand by the implied contrast; where he offers a clue about the "ontological," he points to the "concern" for Being, which is already too late for explanatory purposes and perhaps too ornate to be of much use.

The "ontic," by contrast, seems to range over everything else that we find in the world that is both intelligible to *Dasein* and not itself a manifestation of *Dasein*'s unique distinction—that is (rather) what, broadly speaking, is no more than the factual world. But then of course we must ask ourselves what distinguishes the human (which participates in the "ontic" or "factical") from all else that is confined to the merely ontic (whatever that may now mean)—that is, belongs to the "ontological." We are told only that it is other than the ontic and is not captured conceptually by the "categories" by which the ontic is itself grasped.

If you read matters this way, you see the important sense in which Heidegger's proposed analysis of the human invites comparison with Immanuel Kant's pivotal discussion of his own idea of the effective rational powers of the human self, who is (as Kant sees matters) also a hybrid being, unique in our world in regard to its highest competence. Heidegger viewed his own effort as a valiant attempt to replace Kant's dualism: the idea of a human being completely subject, on the one hand, to the causal determinism of the natural world and capable of being entirely free, on the other hand, to exercise autonomous reason in taming and directing the forces of the first (in accord with the higher calling of the second).

The trouble is this. Kant was obliged to concede (according to his own lights) that, though we can actually *know* that we are subject to causal determinism, we can only *think* (we cannot know) that we are free rational beings. Hence, as Hegel—Kant's principal "successor"—notes, both in criticism and admiration of Kant's immense accomplishment, we must complete Kant's guess at the analysis of what it is to be human. We may do so,

Hegel openly advises, by formulating an account of human selves as fully integrated, operative agents, even if hybrid beings, who cannot be divided ("ontologically") within or against themselves (within their own "mode of being," so to say) by any disjunction between the "phenomenal" and the "noumenal" (to speak with Kant).

Hegel's criticism of Kant amounts to this, that Kant had no convincing account of the single being that *is* a human being, even though Kant certainly prepared the ground (even the conceptual apparatus) for understanding and assessing whatever a human being might do or think or judge—except that, given his analysis, there remain questions and commitments that Kant's "subject" cannot effectively address, since to do so would require a unity of "being" in existential terms. For example, a rational agent might abstractly judge that private property (as conventionally regarded) should be respected and, also, separately, judge that it would be rational (again, abstractly) to abolish property (on the grounds that it is theft). But it is not clear that a Kantian self could rightly explain why, *given the course of history in which the self exists,* we should favor the one policy over the other. For that, we would need an "ontologically" unified self, free and rational in spite of uniting the empirical and the transcendental in a single form of effective agency—an impossibility, on Kant's reasoning.

This is a fatal weakness in Kant, the result of failing to integrate the two strata of "being" of the human condition, which, then, clearly points to the deficient analysis Heidegger offers in its place. For we do not know clearly enough how Heidegger distinguishes the "ontological" from the "ontic," though, mysteriously, they are apparently inseparable in *Dasein.* In this interesting sense, Hegel stands at the beginning of any adequate account of "human being," though it must be conceded that in his own zeal to complete Kant's project Hegel tries—particularly in his analysis of history (or better, historicity, the idea that human thought—which is a unique talent, remember—is itself, or has, a history, changes under the condition of historical existence)—Hegel tries, I say, to incorporate Kant's conceptual extravagances (or a correction of those extravagances along historicized lines) into his own account. Kant's excesses concern the powers of what he calls the "Transcendental Subject," a form of being (let us say) entirely disjointed from the natural powers of *homo sapiens,* the human animal, but bound, as far as rational understanding, commitment, appreciation, interpretation, and the like are concerned, to exercise its unique competence only on, in, and upon whatever experiential materials the nontranscendental talents of sensory and animal life can provide.

You see, therefore, that there is a remarkably strong tendency in Kant and the post-Kantians to treat the "nature" of the human in bifurcated terms. It is also not strange, therefore, that this same tendency should remind us, by analogies that are hardly strained, of certain aspects of Plato's and Aristotle's ancient accounts—of, say, the separable *psyche* of Plato's *Phaedo* and quasi-divine power of reason posited (but hardly explained) in Aristotle's *De Anima*.[6] It is small wonder that Heidegger's distinction between the ontic and the ontological should seem to be a retrograde step from Hegel's emancipatory insight, in effect something close to a failed effort to escape the Kantian injunction. But then the question nags: Can we do better?

The single clue I find most compelling stems from the remarkable fact that the modern conception of history—really, historicity—makes a sustained appearance for the first time in the West, possibly in the world, about the time of the French Revolution. It may be the one large "ontological" discovery accessible at once to people who are not professional specialists of any kind and that was never featured in any systematic analysis of the human world prior to the latter part of the eighteenth century. Extraordinary. With it comes the idea that human existence, like human thought, is inherently historical—really, historicized, in the sense that our conceptual powers, our interests and commitments, our understanding of our own capacity to understand and act and deliberately transform our own world themselves change and are diverse as a result of the contingent histories of our interacting societies and of our own interventions in those histories.

Insofar as this is true, *we* are, as a consequence, beings that lack a "nature" or have (as our nature) only a history, or a history embedded in the nature of *homo sapiens*—more the historicized potentiality of a longitudinal career within the enabling possibilities of a particular culture than the general possibilities of our merely biological nature. In this sense, *we* are "cultural artifacts," transforms of *homo sapiens*, "second-natured" as a result of successfully internalizing the language and culture of our home society. In the same sense, we are "hybrid" beings, maturing as the newborn offspring of parent members of *homo sapiens*, themselves already successfully second-natured, hence capable of facilitating our own transformation—though how exactly that is accomplished we do not understand well at all.

We have made an "ontological" leap here, though it may not catch the eye at once: not in the way of a discontinuity in nature itself but in the way of fixing the fundamental difference between *homo sapiens* and what it is to be a self or person—which can and must be explained as part of a continuous process that nevertheless issues in the emergence of certain sui generis competences that are clearly different, as "modes of being," from the biological sources from which they first issue. There is, in fact, a profound analogy in the transition from inanimate nature to the contingent emergence of self-replicating DNA. There, as the studies of Jacques Monod and François Jacob confirm,[7] the spontaneous synthesis of amino acids and proteins in accord with the (emergent) algorithmic functioning of codons within the apparently simpler functioning of DNA replication draws attention to a difference that begins to count as an "ontological" difference between inanimate physical things and living creatures.

That selective codons within standard DNA behave algorithmically in certain favorable but contingent chemical environments, and there yield emergent structures essential to the entire evolutionary process (by which more and more complex organisms are generated), shows very clearly the conceptual compatibility of "ontological" emergence and generative continuity. There is no paradox there, nor therefore need there be any paradox in the very different setting that admits the emergence of the cultural and the linguistic (for the first time) from the social and communicative resources of sublinguistic creatures.

Here, you must see that we are on the point of redeeming the contrast between biology and culture that spans the entire tradition of Western philosophy, from Plato and Aristotle to Kant and Hegel, that is so deficiently systematized in, say, Heidegger, as it is also in Kant and Hegel. That is, we are on the point of redeeming the contrast—the "ontological" contrast—without admitting any generative discontinuity of substantive dualism, without exceeding therefore the bounds of nature. The only conceivable way in which that can be done is to describe a process of generally enriching sublinguistic communication among primates and early hominids such that a threshold was probably passed, prehistorically, in which incipient reference and predication (in effect, the beginnings of primitive grammatical functions) emerge from a variety of calls and behavior that have differentiated "messages" (such as those that appear already among the monkeys). One plausible conjecture, associated with the important but not quite adequately developed notion advanced by the American pragmatist George Herbert Mead, identifies the ability of the human subject to take on (or internalize) the "role of the generalized other" (covering, as Mead explains, the linked roles of the "I" and the "me").[8]

My suggestion here is that the acquisition of a first language is the same process by which a member of *homo sapiens* is transformed—second-natured—into a self or person, and that the evolution of language is itself probably the result of a smooth continuum of small incremental gains in sublinguistic communication beyond some putative threshold at which, by alternative but different and differently empowered skills, the human creature acquires the perceived power of self-reference and the ability to apply predicates to itself and other selves and things. Once this threshold is passed, I surmise, the gains that are thereby facilitated, sui generis, accumulate in a startlingly rapid way. The result is the proliferation of historical cultures and the continual transformation of the selves that are the second-natured artifacts of the original process—possibly by means of nothing more than the nurturance of talented infants within a society of already apt selves. But

I cannot see how that original ability can be accounted for on behavioral but nonlinguistic grounds.

There is an essential metaphysical novelty to be acknowledged here. First of all, the power of speech and "enlanguaged" thought is itself a hybrid competence, being emergently embedded, indissolubly, in the biological aptitudes of *homo sapiens,* though not, for that reason, reducible to those original aptitudes. To speak is, normally, to utter words composed in sentences and similarly structured strings that are conveyed as such by, and are "incarnate" in, the physical sounds that we learn to utter in learning to speak—within the vocal resources of the species. What we acquire thereby is an aptitude to share, however idiosyncratically, a common—I would say, a collectively shared—competence that we exercise singly or aggregatively as engaged selves. Herein you glimpse the distinction of the new ontology.

That means, in effect, that there can be no mystery about understanding language; for to be a self *is,* effectively, to understand one's home language and one's home culture. (That, one might reasonably say, is the essential lesson of Wittgenstein's *Philosophical Investigations,* which therefore exhibits a Hegelian turn of mind, without benefit of knowing Hegel's own line of reasoning and without ever explaining its own novelty.)[9] But it also means that to be a self is to function as, or to manifest the skills that define the role of, emergent selves. Hence, to be a self is to be a cultural artifact, a second-natured transform of *homo sapiens,* a hybrid creature that is integrally poised as an effective agent: an agent that can think and speak and report the contents of its mind and plan and act deliberately for intended ends, singly or aggregatively, and can make and do and create whatever it thus "utters" in culturally significant and significative ways—which are open therefore to being interpreted and displaced and surpassed.

But in saying all this, we are in danger of neglecting the underlying "ontological" distinction, the very reason for holding that selves and what they "utter" (language, artworks, deeds, machines, customs and practices, technologies, theories and ideologies, and the like) are sui generis: distinguished in the sense that what marks the culturally emergent dimension of their lives cannot be reduced to, analyzed in terms of, or suitably replaced by whatever, *salve veritate,* we might imagine could approximate to the cultural. If such "naturalizing" maneuvers are impossible—they dominate the strongest currents of Anglo-American analytic philosophy, as in the work of W. V. Quine, Donald Davidson, Wilfred Sellars, D. M. Armstrong, Paul Churchland, and Daniel Dennett—we may reasonably say that we have found an ontologically emergent level of functioning that is "natural but not naturalizable" (not reducible or eliminable along the lines favored by the theorists just mentioned). The question remains of how best to characterize that new "world."

If we can provide an adequate and supple distinction for the entire range of human culture in the spirit, in which, as has been said, the enabling process proves to be entirely natural and continuous within nature and yet issues, contingently, in some incipiently novel structures that may then develop in their own way so as to account for the whole of human history and culture, we will have eclipsed the intimations of all those already mentioned (such as Plato, Aristotle, Kant, and Heidegger), who cannot isolate the distinction needed without falling back to some sort of dualism or mythic or quasi-divine or transcendental or inexplicit contrast that we need to be able to explain directly without assuming any untoward privilege.

The idea is familiar enough but not altogether simple. We are looking for an emergent family of attributes—or of entities and events and processes that can be qualified by such attributes—that seem able to collect everything that distinguishes the cultural from the physical. In particular, we expect these attributes, which we take to qualify the lives of human selves and their characteristic form of "utterance," to be hybrid and incarnate in a way that adequately matches the hybrid and embodied nature of the things of the cultural world. Our account must draw therefore on the analysis of language, art, history, action, practices, institutions, norms and rules, theories, and the like. For example, human thought will be seen to be essentially "enlanguaged," informed by the structure of our home language and by whatever else may inform our language; characterized thus, thought will also be seen to be incarnate neuro-physiologically, or in some way (indissolubly). In analyzing thought, then, we expect to analyze what may be properly reported (by way of language) as the "content" of our thought, whether in dreams or waking reflection.

Hence, the distinctive features of the "content" of our thought are as close as we are likely to get to isolating the attributes of the cultural world. By parity of reasoning, we suppose that we can analyze the "import" or "intended purpose" or the like of our acts and machines and artworks. Here too we are guided by the ideas that we understand ourselves by understanding our utterances and that we understand our acts, works, and creations by understanding our own intentions and mental life, and also that we understand changes in the relationship between these two poles—selves and their characteristic modes of utterance—by reflecting further on historical changes in the larger life of the enabling societies in which we move and pursue our own lives.

There is, therefore, no particularly strenuous difficulty in encompassing the whole of the cultural world. What calls for a finer analysis, however, is what generically distinguishes the cultural from the physical and marks what is common to the multiple manifestations of the cultural world itself. Here, I remind you of a philosophical clue introduced in the second half of the nineteenth century (more accurately, reintroduced from a revival of a medieval distinction) by Franz Brentano and developed in a notably complex way by Edmund Husserl, originally under Brentano's influence. Brentano introduced the idea of the "intentional" as marking the difference between the mental and the physical, but Brentano (also, it seems, Husserl) treated the "intentional" in a methodologically solipsistic way, more keyed to thought than to language and not linked explicitly to the cultural formation of the self. By the intentional, Brentano meant that feature of the mind that addresses the world in such a way that we are said to think "about," or want or remember, this or that, or intend that this or the other should be true, regarding what is actual or not.[10]

Brentano's notion is deficient in a number of ways. But I take up his important clue and offer as a term of art a more inclusive replacement that can easily accommodate whatever Brentano and Husserl (and others influenced by either) might wish to include within the boundaries of the "intentional." Call the replacing notion the "Intentional" (marked by a capital I), according to the formula "the Intentional = the cultural." Then, whatever exhibits "aboutness" (in Brentano's sense) or, more generally, is intrinsically significant or significative in culturally pertinent ways (as in speech, behavior, the creation of artworks, and the like) is, on my account, inherently Intentional. So the cultural world is emergent primarily in the sense in which Intentionally qualified hybrid "things" emerge, in a sui generis way, from the biological and physical world, by dint of the utterances and activity of Intentional apt, "enlanguaged" selves, functioning singly or aggregatively in their cultural milieu.

Let me suggest a series of different kinds of Intentional attributes by which we may begin to collect all of the distinctive features of the cultural world under the generic rubric of the Intentional—for instance, the expressive, the representational, the symbolic, the semiotic, the linguistically meaningful, the signific, the interpretable, the rhetorical, the stylistic, the genre-bound, the intensional (or nonextensional), the historical, the traditional, the institutional, the purposive, the intentional, the rule-like, the normative, the ideological, the practical, the theoretical, the descriptive, the explanatory, the appraisive, the appreciative, the semantic, the grammatical, the pragmatic, the ideal, the cognitive, the doxastic, the mental, the heuristic. It needs to be said that a number of these distinctions may apply to sublinguistic creatures. My own idea is that they are applied in such cases (the mental, for instance) only by anthropomorphizing (or by heuristic) means—meaning by that that we seem able to understand the "minds" of animals only by analogizing, with care, between the human paradigm and suitably diminished applications to the animal world.

Clearly to introduce such a large run of distinctions, under the advice that they cannot be reduced or replaced, salve veritate, by physical (non-Intentional) descriptions, signifies the recognition of a problematic new world not adequately grasped by the terms of the physical sciences alone. For example, there is no known criterial or algorithmic means by which "meanings" or the "intensional aspects" of Intentional life can be rendered in purely physical or "extensional" terms. It is commonly assumed that physical phenomena can be completely analyzed in extensional terms. Hence, the bare admission of the large number of Intentional phenomena (inevitably infected by "intensional" constraints—say, in interpreting the meaning of a remark or the representational import of a sculpture) threatens to subvert the would-be hegemony of physicalist paradigms of both reality and science.

Here, I venture to say only that selves are, as far as we can tell, irreducibly Intentional beings and that whatever counts as a science is the work of such agents. If we grant the point, then, of course, an accurate picture of the way of the world is probably very different from many of the canonical views about the real world and what we know of it.

NOTES

1. Plato, *Republic of Plato*, trans. Francis Macdonald Cornford (Oxford: Clarendon Press, 1961).

2. Plato, *The Statesman*, trans. J. B. Skemp (Indianapolis: Bobbs-Merrill, 1977).

3. See Charles Darwin, *On the Origin of Species* (London and New York: Cambridge University Press, 1975).

4. See Martin Heidegger, *Being and Time*, trans. John Macquarrie and Edward Robinson (Evanston, Ill.: Harper and Row, 1962).

5. See Martin Heidegger, "Letter on Humanism," in *Basic Writings*, ed. David F. Krell (San Francisco, Calif.: HarperSanFrancisco, 1993).

6. Plato, *Phaedo*, trans. David Gallop (Oxford: Clarendon Press, 1975); Aristotle, *De Anima*, trans. Hugh Lawson-Tancred (Harmondsworth: Penguin, 1986).

7. See, for example, Jacques Monod, *Chance and Necessity: An Essay on the Natural Philosophy of Modern Biology*, trans. Austryn Wainhouse (London: Fount, 1978); *Selected Papers on Molecular Biology*, ed. André Lwoff and Agness Ullmann (New York: Academic Press, 1978); François Jacob, *The Logic of Living Systems: A History of Heredity*, trans. Betty E. Spillman (London: Allen Lane, 1974); and *Of Flies, Mice, and Man*, trans. Giselle Weiss (Cambridge, Mass., and London: Harvard University Press, 1998).

8. George Herbert Mead, *Mind, Self, and Society: From the Standpoint of a Social Behaviorist* (Chicago and London: University of Chicago Press, 1962), chap. 22. See also chaps. 25, 27, and 35.

9. Ludwig Wittgenstein, *Philosophical Investigations*, trans. G.E.M. Anscombe (Oxford: Blackwell, 1958).

10. See Franz Brentano, *Psychology from an Empirical Standpoint*, trans. Antos C. Rancurello, D. B. Terrell, and Linda L. McAlister (London: Routledge and Kegan Paul, 1975), and his *Sensory and Noetic Consciousness: Psychology from an Empirical Standpoint III*, trans. Margarete Schättle and Linda L. McAlister (London: Routledge and Kegan Paul, 1981).

Part III

Screen Narratives
of Human Becoming

7

Death Twenty-four Times a Second: The Inorganic Body and the Cinema

Laura Mulvey

This chapter considers the cinema in the light of two aspects of the uncanny, primarily using Freud's 1919 essay in which he tried to establish what it is that makes the human mind, and its body, shudder involuntarily. Freud is, in the first instance, taking issue with Wilhelm Jentsch's 1906 essay "On the Psychology of the Uncanny." He dismisses Jentsch's interest in an uncanny effect that is aroused by the new and the unfamiliar—by automata, for instance. After a long detour, he reflects rather on the uncanny nature of death itself, the living body's passage to an inorganic state. To my mind, there is a significant connection between these two aspects of the uncanny, one acceptable to Freud, one not. Both aspects are relevant to the points I will be making here. For the exact figuration of the human body and its deathly counterpart have the potential to blur the crucial division between animate and inanimate, human and inhuman, organic and inorganic bodies. In one case, the organic body has become inanimate; in the other, the inorganic body takes on the appearance of animation. However, both Jentsch and Freud note that a third phenomenon exists: long-standing human belief has constantly resurrected the body after death into a ghostly apparition, inorganic but animate. This denial of the sovereignty and finality of death unsettles the most fundamental beliefs about human ontology. I want to apply these reflections to the presence of the human body in cinema, showing its equivocal inhabitance of the space between animated human and spectral inhuman.

FREUD'S DEBATE WITH JENTSCH

Jentsch, it seems, is interested in the kind of *trompe-l'oeil* phenomenon that had proliferated with the rise of nineteenth-century optical entertainment and mechanical toys: "The unpleasant impression is well known that readily arises in many people when they visit collections of wax figures, panopticons and panoramas. In the semi-darkness it is often especially difficult to distinguish a life-size wax or similar figure from a human person . . . whether it is animate or not."[1] He goes on to say:

> This peculiar effect makes its appearance even more clearly when imitations of the human form not only reach one's perception, but when on top of everything else they appear to be united with certain bodily or mental functions. For example, life-size automata that perform complicated tasks, blow trumpets, dance and so forth very easily give one a feeling of unease. The finer the mechanism and the truer to nature the formal reproduction, the more strongly will the special effect also make its appearance.

Jentsch associates the "uncanny effect" with doubts, "intellectual uncertainty" about whether "an apparently animate being is really alive or, conversely, whether a lifeless object might not in fact be animate."[2]

Jentsch's subsequent citation of Hoffman's successful use of automata as a psychological artifice provokes Freud's rather convoluted digression in "The Uncanny," where he dwells specifically on Olympia, the beautiful mechanical doll in "The Sandman." He argues that the mechanical doll is irrelevant to the uncanny aspects of the story, which are an effect of castration anxiety. Even if Freud is correct in his analysis, his argument turns radically away from Jentsch's point, away from the doll, and emphasizes instead one of his key theoretical principles—that only "that class of the frightening which leads back to what is known of old and long familiar" can be of interest to psychoanalysis.[3] Anxiety caused by the mechanical doll cannot have its roots in something familiar that has been previously established in the mind, it cannot be a formative influence on the unconscious itself, such as the castration complex. To put it another way—for an emotional effect to have a relation to the unconscious mind, it must have undergone a process of repression from which it may return. From Freud's perspective, it is unlikely that the modern and the newfangled would represent a return of the repressed.

It seems that even in 1906 Jentsch was unaware of the cinema's relevance to his proposition. But his comments on replicas of the human body in precinematic entertainment clearly lead to a consideration of the uncanny aspects of the moving image. Freud's hostile reaction to Jentsch's interest in the "newfangled" chimes with his more general resistance to aspects of the modern world and its manifestations. Stephen Heath, in his article "Cinema and Psychoanalysis," has pointed out that Freud's hostility to the cinema went beyond his reasonable doubt about its ability to express the complexities of psychoanalytic theory. When refusing to collaborate with Hans Sachs on the development of the film that would be G. W. Pabst's *Secrets of a Soul,* the actual terms he uses are, to my mind, relevant. He says: "There can be no avoiding the film, any more than one can avoid the fashion for bobbed hair (*Bubikopf*); I however, will not let my hair be cut and will personally have nothing to do with this film."[4]

The cinema, he implies, is as ephemeral as fashion and, furthermore, through a process of condensation, elides with the feminine. Indeed, the cinema was, at the time, widely understood to be catering to the tastes of a flapper audience, summed up a little later by Kracauer in "Little Shop Girls Go to the Movies." Freud's resistance to the uncanniness of the mechanical doll, Olympia, and his rejection of the mechanical cinema as femininizing suggest, to my mind at least, a link to the robotic, androgynous body of the fashionable "flapper" in the 1920s. These bodies, Freud might imply, are saved from uncanniness and are therefore of no interest to psychoanalysis, because they eviscerate the womb and deny the maternal and abject aspects of the woman's body that he sees as a true site of the uncanny: "It often happens that neurotic men declare that there is something uncanny about the female genital organs. This *unheimlich* place, however, is the entrance to the former *Heim* of all human beings, the place where each one of us lived once upon a time and in the beginning."[5] The mother's body, of course, represents the truly ancient for the human psyche. Not only is it the "first home" itself, but its once-upon-a-time memory of security and totality must become abject for the child to become an independent and autonomous being. It would seem, from Freud's line of argument, that the relation of eviscerated femininity to the uncanny leads only down the road of negation.

However, Freud allows another figuration of the inorganic body to enter his consideration of the uncanny, one that is truly archaic, not in the history of the individual psyche but in the history of human culture and its movement toward rationality and knowledge. That figuration is the persistent belief on the part of "civilized" people in the afterlife (and, ultimately, in resurrection), as well as the residues of archaic belief that the spirits of the dead are present in the world and that nature is, itself, animate. He turns his interest to the "uncanny experience . . . when primitive beliefs which have been surmounted seem once more to be confirmed."[6] Thus, the "repressed," the ancient and the archaic, is represented by animistic beliefs that "civilized people" consciously reject but to which they might suddenly return. The move from "repression" to "surmounting" allows Freud to move from the individual psyche to the world of culture. He makes a distinction between residues of superstition and their use by creative writers, such as Hoffmann, denying that their translation of uncanny material can in fact arouse the uncanny effect. He identifies the living culture of superstition most closely with the feeling, experienced by many people "in relation to death and dead bodies, to the return of the dead, and to spirits and ghosts."[7] Also, he points to the near-universal insistence by both religions and civil governments on the existence of life after death. He writes: "Since almost all of us still think as savages do on this topic, it is no matter for surprise that the primitive fear of the dead is still so strong within us and always ready to come to the surface on any provocation."[8] Further: "Nowadays we no longer believe in [the return of the dead] . . . but we do not feel quite sure of our new beliefs, and the old ones still exist within us ready to seize upon any confirmation. As soon as something *actually happens* in our lives which seems to confirm the old, discarded beliefs we get a feeling of the uncanny."[9] Having dismissed Jentsch's association between the uncanny and intellectual uncertainty in relation to "whether an inanimate object becomes too like an animate one," Freud backtracks slightly: "And are we after all justified in entirely ignoring intellectual uncertainty as a factor [in the uncanny], seeing that we have admitted its importance in relation to death?"[10]

Freud's return to the question of intellectual uncertainty opens a way to return to Jentsch's interest in the "newfangled" uncanny and then suggests two ways in which their differing approaches to the inorganic body might be reconciled. First of all, Jentsch's approach leads to a technological uncanny, to the intellectual uncertainty that can be experienced by the most rational mind when faced with an illusion that is, if only momentarily, inexplicable. As Jentsch puts it, "Even when they know they are being fooled by merely harmless illusions, many people cannot suppress an extremely uncomfortable feeling."[11] This kind of *frisson* can be located in the moment itself, the sudden moment of doubt, an involuntary and bewildered loss of faith in the rational. The whole history of visual illusions is contained in this effect and its investment in that moment. This history is located in that liminal area between the rational knowledge and irrational belief that Freud is attempting to locate in his discussion of animism and its persistence in the human mind. Archaic beliefs and the superstitions are able to return within the popular culture of illusions that depend on exploiting this particular, repressed for their effect.

Throughout the history of magic tricks, the raising of spirits was very often a key item on the illusionist's program so that form, the uncanny effect of the technology, tended to merge with the uncanny content, the return of the living dead. This illusion, the erased space between the animate and the inanimate, the organic and the inorganic body, conflates the "problem" of the illusion posed by the living doll with that posed by the appearance of the living dead. Both have their place in the technology of "uncomfortable" illusions. This line of argument could then lead further and rescue the popular culture of modernity from Freud's rather sanitizing denial of its uncanny properties. It is here, emanating from the technological uncanny, that popular culture has, in some of its manifestations at least, come to inhabit the world abandoned by literal animistic belief. Exploiting the fact that the "civilized" mind still likes to enjoy at least the illusion of irrationality, the cinema gathered together, in the most rational manner, a range of effects that trigger "uncanniness." It concentrates into its mechanisms, and then into storytelling and fiction, "the return of the repressed" of beliefs that should, in Freud's terms, have since been surmounted. In this suspension of disbelief, the operation of fiction and the illusion of cinema work to reinforce each other. Furthermore, the cinema was born into a world in which illusions, from magic tricks to *trompe-l'oeil* to spiritualism, flourished and had become part of popular entertainment.

SPIRITUALISM AND THE TECHNOLOGIES OF ILLUSION

Freud mentions the fashion for spiritualism in his essay on the uncanny: "In our great cities, placards announce lectures that undertake to tell us how to get in touch with the souls of the departed; and it cannot be denied that not a few of our most able and penetrating minds among our men of science have come to the conclusion, especially toward the end of their own lives, that a contact of this kind is not impossible."[12] The essay was written in 1919, and there were, of course, many bereaved who attempted to reach "the other side" after the appalling losses of the war. This was definitely the case after World War I and might also account for the rise in spiritualism in the United States in the aftermath of the Civil War. These phenomena, as well as the feelings aroused more casually by some forms of mass entertainment, indicate how strongly "ancient beliefs" persist.

Recent historians and theorists of cinema have challenged the sense that the literal invention of cinema constituted an abrupt break from its surrounding culture of both illusion and realism. Ian Christie points out that "uncertainty" associated with death was a key factor in the late-nineteenth-century citizen's response to film:

> What did they want to believe? Essentially that death was not final: that communication with "the other side" was possible. . . . So the respectable Victorians threw themselves into spiritualism, seances, tarot cards and magic of any kinds. In this climate it was scarcely surprising that moving pictures seemed supernatural to their first viewers. Both the Paris papers which reported the first Lumière show ended on the same note: "Death will cease to be absolute[;] . . . it will be possible to see our nearest alive again long after they have gone."[13]

Maxim Gorky, in a now famous paragraph, described his experience for a Russian newspaper in 1896: "It is terrifying to watch but it is the movement of shadows, mere shadows. Curses and ghosts, evil spirits that have cast whole cities into eternal sleep come to mind and you feel as though Merlin's vicious trick had been played out before you."[14]

Standing, as Rosalind Krauss once put it, rather strangely at the crossroads of science and the supernatural, still photography had already generated associations with life after death. In France, for instance, the photograph of the recently deceased came to replace the traditional death

mask during the 1860s. Tom Gunning has pointed out, particularly in relation to spiritualism, that the invention of photography created a new field
for inquiry about perception and its relation to knowledge and belief. New
technologies, often at the moment of the appearance outside popular understanding and common sense, can paradoxically enable and revive irrational and superstitious beliefs. A technological uncanny, if only in its very
early days, dovetails with an intellectual uncertainty that continues to haunt
the human mind. The Spiritualist movement related its revelations to new
technologies such as electricity, telegraphy, chemistry, and so on, all of which
seemed to suggest that invisible forces animated the world. The strange-
ness of new technologies could latch on to archaic beliefs in invisible spirits.
Gunning comments:

> It is hardly surprising that Spiritualism would intersect with photography. That
> photography could create a transparent, wraithlike image (if the plate were
> double exposed or if the figure moved before a full exposure had been
> made). . . . That such images could display the iconic accuracy and recogniz-
> ability of photographic likenesses and at the same time the transparency and
> insubstantiality of ghosts seemed to demonstrate the fundamentally uncanny
> quality of photography, its capture of a spectre-like double.[15]

Thus the intrinsic ghostliness of the photograph elided with technological
innovation, the sense that the machine might be able to perceive a presence
invisible to the human eye. But Gunning's key point is that these initial uses
of ghost photography began to creep into the world of popular culture:
"The increasingly spectacular nature of Spiritualism mined a deep fascination in visual events that amazed spectators by defying conventional belief.
The potential entertainment value of such visual attractions was immediately recognised." The visual spectacles were "constructed as entertainment,
manifestations which opened the way for the enjoyment of appearances
whose very fascination came from their impossibility, their apparent severance from the laws of nature."[16]

It was this encounter between "spectacular spiritualism" and the nineteenth-century magic show that led the showmen increasingly to distance
themselves from charlatans who insisted that their tricks came from the supernatural. John Neville Maskelyne, for instance, developed his magic show
without, as he put it, the help of spirits. These were showmen who prided
themselves on their own skill and ability to make an audience gasp, to leave
it on the cusp between credulity and incredulity—"I don't believe it"—while
seeing with its own eyes. Harry Houdini became deeply involved in a campaign to debunk spiritualism, leading to his fraught friendship with Arthur
Conan Doyle, who was convinced that he had reached his son, killed in World
War I, through a medium. Adam Phillips has described Houdini's implacable
hostility to spiritualism as going beyond professionalism to conviction:

Like any successful professional magician—and Houdini was the man who put magic on the map, who took it out of quackery and into mainstream entertainment—Houdini had no appetite for the inexplicable; he wasn't keen to be impressed by it. He didn't claim to understand everything, but what had always fascinated him was people's talent for creating mystery. "Why, Sir Arthur," he once remarked to Doyle, "I have been trained in mystery all my life and once in a while I see something I can't account for." But when this happened he wanted to discover how someone had made it. Mystery, for Houdini, was the great secular commodity.[17]

It should be noted, though, that this urge to debunk claims of supernatural intercession was not new, even in Houdini's day. The tradition goes back to the seventeenth century and Anastasius Kircher, Jesuit and theorist of the magic lantern. Kircher was committed to rationalizing illusion in order to distinguish legitimate Catholic belief from the residues of popular superstition and belief in magic. His work contributed to the process in which religion became, in Freud's term, "civilized," as the Catholic Church of the Counter-Reformation attempted, without going to the lengths of the Protestants, to reduce the irrational to those elements that the Church considered to be essential for dogma. In his book *Ars Magica*, Kircher explained how the lantern worked, as he also did as part of his live demonstrations.

For the showmen, it was essential to purge their magic tricks of any trace of the supernatural in order to open up the space for a different kind of amazement. If the audience believed that a divine power had intervened, they would be indeed awestricken, but the act would be, given the terms of the supernatural, perfectly explicable. The showmen's aim was create a space for doubt and generate the frisson associated with the breakdown of rational understanding that gives rise to a sense of intellectual uncertainty. This is their modernity. They shifted the cultural agenda away from the supernatural toward a kind of super-humanity in which their own transcendent powers were at the center of the stage. While the rigorous materiality of the performance would cause astonishment, their feats would inevitably raise questions about the limits of the human—on the one hand a super-human ability to defy the laws of nature, on the other the ordinary inability of the audience to decipher what it was seeing.

MÉLIÈS, LUMIÈRE, AND THE PRESENCE OF THE PAST

The key figure linking the tradition of the magic showmen to the cinema is, of course, Georges Méliès. Méliès had two moments of epiphany in his life. The first took place at Maskeleyne's permanent magic theater, the Egyptian Hall, in London in 1888, where he fell in love with magic. On his return to Paris, he took over the theater of the famous prestigitator Jean-Eugene Robert-Houdin (after whom Houdini later named himself). The second was at the Lumières' demonstration of the cinematograph in 1895 at the Grand Cafi, when he is said to have exclaimed, "What a great trick! That's for me!" He then created a film studio that fused the new, cinematic potential for trickery with the traditions of the magic theater. Méliès too saw his magic as very much within the materialist tradition, and made fun of the Spiritualists.

In numerous ways, Méliès's cinema is reminiscent of Jentsch's uncanny, exploiting technological novelty as well as the cinema's ability to blur the boundary between the animate and the inanimate. As Paul Hammond describes, "An object can be transformed, either instantaneously or gradually, into another object; an object can grow or diminish before our eyes, while the rest of the image remains a constant size; an object, usually human, can disintegrate into parts, then these can assume a life of their own; an inanimate object can begin to move and an animate one defy the laws of gravity; an object can appear or disappear instantaneously or gradually."[18] He comments particularly on the phenomenon, noted by Jentsch, whereby inanimate images of the human body take on apparently animate properties: "Not only statues but scarecrows, snowmen, dummies, skeletons. Figures in paintings, posters, photographs, playing card and book illustrations all pulsate with life, through the camera's stop-motion capability."[19] Méliès overtly harnessed cinema in the interests of creating the marvelous and the mysterious, overturning the natural order of things with wit and showmanship and confusing the attributes of things. Just as the cinema brought stillness to life, so he gave life to lifeless objects.

These were qualities that appealed to the Surrealists, who in the 1950s drew up a list dividing the history of the cinema into two categories: one list, "Don't See," was headed by the Lumières; the other, "See," was headed by Méliès. This is probably the origin of the great cliché of the cinema that uses these two pioneers to create an arbitrary opposition of value. From the Surrealist perspective, the Lumière brothers stand for the realm of the visible, of literal photographic realism, while Méliès could conjure up a parallel universe of magic and marvelous effects. Looking at the opposition after more than a hundred years have passed, we see that it seems to have almost moved into reverse, that the quality of the uncanny has shifted from the films of Méliès to those of the Lumières. This shift highlights the way that the uncanny is affected by time. While Gorky's initial reaction to the Lumière program was in terms of the ghostly, he was responding to the unfamiliar technology, its animation of the inanimate, its silence, and its lack of color. Quite soon, as time passed, the Lumière films would seem no more threatening than any home movies or technological demonstration. By now, the moment at which they were shot has become the distant past. The figures of ordinary people moving in everyday life are now figures of the dead, not only animated by the mechanism of cinema in projection but the ghostly images of bodies resurrected into the appearance of life.

The Lumières' images have now moved into the threshold where the gap between the presence of life and death become confused. The original uncanny effect, the technological uncanny, returns to merge with the intellectual uncertainty concerning death that Freud finally allowed. The figures on the screen are disturbing in their very literalness—their ordinary lack of significance, their integration into their surrounding world. A minute of film becomes a seamless fragment of time, uncanny because it is the literal imprint of the scene the camera saw and registered on photosensitive material. While Méliès's films retain their beauty and wit, those of the Lumières' have shifted in significance. It is impossible to look at them as the result of a simple demonstration of a machine. Now every gesture, expression, movement of wind or water seems to be touched with mystery. This is not the mystery of the magic trick but the more disturbing sensation of seeing life fossilized.

We can certainly say, with Freud, that we have "surmounted" belief in the return of the dead, of animate forces in nature and even in the afterlife. However, the presence of the past in the cinema is also the presence of the body resurrected, which can trigger, if only by association, reflection on issues that still seem to pose imponderable questions: the nature of time and of death. There is a further poignancy. The cinema is now itself an archaic technology. No longer identified with modernity and the latest fashion, as it seemed to Freud writing in 1919, cinema has the connotation of the old and the familiar that he associated with the truly uncanny return of the repressed. The cinema has become, once again, a site for reflection on the inorganic body, returning by a strange movement to the culture of the ghostly that haunted its origins.

The cinema literally transforms the living human body into its inorganic replica, which in this form is also stilled, preserved as a series of static images that once projected then become animated to create the illusion of the living actions once recorded by the camera. There is, therefore, also another doubling—the recording of life on inanimate celluloid and the illusion of life re-created on the cinema screen. The homologies align inorganic, inanimate, still, and dead with organic, animate, moving, and alive. When blurred, these boundaries start to infect each other with uncanniness. The cinema has, of course, largely worked hard to suppress spectator consciousness of this phenomenon. A sudden sense of the uncanny, the perception of the screen image as a perfectly preserved death mask or veronica, may occur only incidentally, or accidentally, half-glimpsed with a particularly striking close-up or gesture of a favorite star now long dead. Watching these movies now is to feel a more severe reality behind Jean-Luc Godard's answer to the question of what cinema is: "Cinema is truth twenty-four times a second." The truth of the technological uncanny I have described above, and its unsettling confusion of human and inhuman properties, is the ubiquity of death, twenty-four times a second.

NOTES

1. Ernst Jentsch, "On the Psychology of the Uncanny" (1906), *Angelaki* 2, no. 1 (1995), 12.

2. Ibid., 10.

3. Sigmund Freud, "The Uncanny," in *The Standard Edition of the Complete Psychological Works of Sigmund Freud,* vol. 17, trans. and ed. James Strachey (London: Hogarth Press, 1963), 218.

4. Stephen Heath, "Cinema and Psychoanalysis: Parallel Histories," in *Endless Night: Cinema and Psychoanalysis, Parallel Histories,* ed. Janet Bergstrom (Berkeley, London, and Los Angeles: University of California Press, 1999), 27.

5. Freud, 245.

6. Ibid., 249.

7. Ibid., 241.

8. Ibid., 242.

9. Ibid., 247–48.

10. Ibid., 247.

11. Jentsch, 10.

12. Freud, 242.

13. Ian Christie, *The Last Machine: Early Cinema and the Birth of the Modern World* (London: BFI/BBC, 1985), 111.

14. Maxim Gorky, "The Lumière Cinematographe," in Ian Christie and Richard Taylor, eds., *The Film Factory: Russian and Soviet Cinema 1896–1939* (London: Routledge and Kegan Paul, 1988), 25.

15. Tom Gunning, "Phantom Images and Modern Manifestations: Spirit Photography, Magic Theater, Trick Film and the Photograph's Uncanny," in Patrice Petro, ed., *Fugitive Images* (Bloomington: Indiana University Press, 1995), 46.

16. Ibid., 60.

17. Adam Phillips, *Houdini's Box: On the Arts of Escape* (London: Faber and Faber, 2001), 130.

18. Paul Hammond, *Marvelous Méliès* (London: Gordon Fraser, 1974), 89.

19. Ibid., 90.

8

Toward a New Demonology

Steven Connor

We are accustomed to think of what Jean Bodin called the "demonomania" of the sixteenth and seventeenth centuries in Europe as the expression of a wave of irrationality, unleashing itself in the form of a gynocidal frenzy directed at women and various forms of outsider, and legitimating a judicial savagery on a massive scale. I will be saying later that I think it is necessary to find cause to wonder a little more at our credulity regarding the credulity of other epochs and cultures. For the moment, I will content myself with drawing attention to a strikingly persistent subtheme that accompanies writings on witchcraft, demonology, and spirit possession, namely, the difficulty of distinguishing real from pretended effects. It has always been obvious to even the most credulous viewers how easy it is to counterfeit the signs of possession: the roaring, foaming, convulsion, the disgorging of pins, the ventriloquial voices from the belly. Exorcists were thus at pains not only to specify measures for the expulsion of demons but also to distinguish the infallible signs of real as opposed to counterfeited possession—signs that, of course, made the job of the counterfeit much easier and the necessity of testing the reality of the demon all the more imperative.

Why does the demon become powerful at the very moment at which it becomes dubious? Because simulation, counterfeit, doubt, and indeterminacy are at the heart of and of the nature of the demonic. Basing himself on the demonology of the severe second-century Latin Christian Tertullian, who was himself later in his life to embrace the ecstatic doctrines and practices of Montanism, Pierre Klossowski offers a more doctrinally based account of why this should be so. The demon, he says,

> reveals his demonic tendency by his contradictory aspiration to be in order to cease to be, to be in order to be no longer, to be in not being. . . . The demonic spirit must borrow another being than its own, because it disowns

being; being itself pure negation, it needs another existence to exercise its negation. It can do this only with respect to creatures who, without intrinsic being, have received being. The spirit seeks to associate with such creatures in order to experience its own contradictoriness, its own existence in inexistence. . . . This, in broad outline, is the traditional idea of the demon; having no personality of its own, he is without inclination, and can exert influence only by means of a borrowed existence.[1]

The one simulating the signs of demonic possession is hard to distinguish from the real victim of demonic possession because possession is an act of simulation; the one who pretends to have a devil, pretends to have been occupied by a spirit whose nature it is to pretend to existence. This means that even the simulator is genuinely occupied by the spirit of counterfeit. The practice of simulating possession is seen as the work of the devil.

This also explains why it is that Protestant sensibilities in the late sixteenth and early seventeenth centuries are so much more in awe of the demonic than Catholics. On the whole, Protestants like the bishop of London, Samuel Harsnett, who mounted a campaign in the early 1600s to banish the practice of exorcism from the English church as unholy, pagan, and politically subversive, did not attach much credence either to the power of demons or to the pretended power of the priests who claimed to dismiss them. Harsnett published his *Declaration of Egregious Popish Impostures* in 1603 in order to discredit some contemporary Protestant exorcisms by comparing them to some spectacular exorcisms practiced by recusant Catholic priests under the leadership of one William Weston some fifteen years previously.[2] Harsnett's horror at the absurd mummeries of Catholic exorcisms is a horror at the devilishness of demonic pretense. There can be no absolute distinction between real and counterfeit demons when counterfeit itself appears so demonic.

Et quis haec daemon? And who was the devil, the brocher, herald, and perswader of these unutterable treasons, but Weston the Jesuit, the chief plotter and arch-impostor, Dibdale the priest, or Stemp, or all the holy Covey of the twelve devilish comedians in their several turnes? For there was neither devil nor urchin nor Elfe but themselves, who did metamorphoze themselves in every scene into the person eyther of the devil himselfe or of his Interpreter; and made the devils name their Puppet, to squeak, pipe, and fume out what they pleased to inspire. . . . O lamentable desolation! Weston and his twelve Priests doe play the devils themselves, and all to grace from hel (being now forsaken of heaven), their pope, their Masse, their Sacraments, their Medalls, their agnus dei, their charmes, their enchauntments, their conjurations, their reliques, their hellish sorceries.[3]

Much rested on the vexed question of the propriety of what Harsnett called "dialoguizing with the devil." Even Catholics in France were divided over the question of whether, given the reality of a demonic possession, one should allow the demon to speak, and converse with it. The more enthusiastic Catholic exorcists enthusiastically drew or drove the demon into utterance, in order either to score sectarian points (Catholic devils are always boasting of their intimate relations with Huguenots) or to demonstrate the necessity even for demons to acknowledge the apostolic power of the Catholic priest as the representative of Christ or the magical sanctity of the host and other holy objects.

As Michel de Certeau has argued, a place is always prepared for the demon in discourse before it begins to speak.[4] The demon is expelled from discourse precisely by being taken into it—made to speak, and to name itself, before silence can be enjoined upon it. The victims of possession, who sometimes began their episodes claiming to have had a "good" possession, by an angel or the Holy Ghost, knew full well that for their devils to be made to speak was the beginning of the end. For Protestants, the ceding of a voice to the devil was regarded as extremely dangerous; for Catholics, the giving of a voice was the submission of the devil to rule and convention. The *procès-verbal* of exorcism performed on 24 November 1632 during the famous possessions at Loudun records the following:

> M. Barré holds up the Host and asks the devil, *"Quem adoras?"* Answer: *"Jesus Christus."* Whereupon M. Daniel Drouyn, Assessor of the Provost's Office, said in a rather loud voice, "This devil is not congruous." The exorcist then changed his question to, *"Quis est iste quem adoras?"* She answered, *"Jesu Christe."* Upon which several persons remarked, "What bad Latin!" But the exorcist retorted that she had said, *"Adoro te, Jesu Christe."*[5]

The devil is drawn into the human in order to be the more satisfactorily expelled from it. Once the devil has a name and a number (Catholics were keen on multiple possessions and on identifying all the participants in a particular case), its end was near.

If demonic possession shows the extreme vulnerability of the human being to invasion, discourse can enact the capacity of the human being to tolerate and contain this invasion. At one end of this process we might instance the story from Plutarch's *Lives* of the confrontation of Brutus with his demon, a story that Samuel Harsnett retells admiringly in the *Declaration*. Marcus Brutus is in his tent, poring over maps and documents on the night before the battle of Philippi. Suddenly a foul, terrifying being appears before him; when Brutus enquires whether it be god or demon, it replies, *"Sum malus tuus genius,"* I am your evil spirit. The demon threatens, "You will see me tomorrow on the fields of Philippi"—*cras Philippis me videbis*. Brutus looks at the demon, returns the one word—*videbo*, "I will see you"—and falls to his reading with never a goodnight to the discomfited demon.[6] This is not just another proof of the usefulness of a bit of sprightly

Latin in cutting demons down to size. Brutus does not merely deny the demon but defers his encounter with him. To borrow the demon's words is to acknowledge the demon, acknowledging that he is indeed the form of Brutus's fear and shame; but it is also to be able to keep him at a distance, an internal distance. In returning the word *videbis* in the form *videbo,* Brutus turns a necessity into an act of personal decision: "You will have no choice but to see me" becomes "I will consent to see you, but not now." Discourse allows the appalled and fascinating inundation of seeing to be broken up, to be articulated: the word *videbo* is accompanied by a looking away, and names a way of looking that is not seeing. For Brutus, and for Harsnett, the devil is not purely endogenous, not merely the projection of Brutus's fears and rage, but an outside that is kept at bay by being taken inside, by a self that is determinately divided, that includes and contains its self-divisions.

Catholic exorcists attempted to drive the devil out. Protestants, fearing that driving the devil out only succeeded in summoning it up, attempted to exorcise exorcism. In the long run, they would both succeed. Inexorably, demons lost their power to enact the invasion of the human by the nonhuman, or the power of the human to be the vehicle or scene of the nonhuman. The rituals of exorcism remained—most particularly, as Monique Schneider has argued, in psychoanalysis[7]—but the possessing agency became less and less inhuman. The difference between archaic and modern conceptions of the demon lies not so much in where demons are supposed to have come from—from outside or inside the nature of the human, from hell or from the mind—as in where they are supposed to go. Archaic demons are spewed out, exiting spectacularly from the nose, mouth, ears, or fundament, and cast into outer darkness, thus acting out the establishment of a bracing boundary between the human and the inhuman; modern demons are acknowledged, incorporated, ingested—rehabilitated.

In the Judeo-Christian adoption of demons, the human surges up out of its encounter with the nonhuman. The development of procedures for disposing of devils is only the first step in a process that will be further refined and diversified, and will involve first of all distinctions between the human and the animal, the human and the mechanical, and the human and the divine, and then distinctions between the human and the less-than-human within human beings themselves—the mad, the monstrous, the evil, the infantile. In all of these distinctions, the demonic will have its place. For only the demon will be capable of sustaining the idea of transcendence or otherness passing as, and passing into, the human; because it operates in and on the human, the demonic cannot fail to become human. Aldous Huxley suggests that the experience of possession is explained at different moments by different identifications of the possessing agency:

[N]eurotics who, at an earlier epoch, would have attributed their malady to devils, were inclined, after the rise of the Fox Sisters, to lay the blame on the discarnate souls of evil men and women. With the recent advances in technology, the notion of possession has taken a new form. Neurotic patients often complain that they are being influenced, against their will, by some kind of radio messages transmitted by their enemies. The Malicious Animal Magnetism which haunted poor Mrs Eddy's imagination for so many years has now been transformed into Malicious Electronics.[8]

If we extend Huxley's series backward to include the experience of Old Testament prophets who heard the voices of God and of angels, and forward to include the contemporary craze for alien abduction, its declensive logic becomes clearer: Gods beget devils, who beget spirits, who beget aliens. At each stage, it appears, the agency of the possession becomes less and less exalted, more and more materialized. At each stage the invasive but intensely desired otherness becomes more vulgarized and materialized, and more humanized. The end of this process of incorporation of the inhuman is a habilitation of the demon, the creation of the veritable "familiar spirit," who speaks *in propria persona* and in his own voice, in Anne Rice's *Interview with the Vampire*.

The freeing of human reason from the threat of the devil on the outside identifies an even more dangerous threat to reason and sanity on the inside, in the endogenous tendency of the human mind to entangle itself in fantasy, imposture, and illusion. Already, for Samuel Harsnett, our power to delude ourselves by simulating devils, conjuring them out of nothing, is even more dangerous than the alleged powers of the devil itself. The devil can no longer be lodged in and chased around the body, locked up in the toe, or driven out through the nostrils or anus. In later periods, we will find that where discourse was previously the means employed to substantiate, identify, and dismiss the demon from the body, the demon begins to take up residence in the body of discourse itself, as it circulates between the subject of possession, the exorcist, and the historian of the possession. When devils become merely figurative, figurativeness can start to seem demonic. Rather than devils being drawn into dialogue, dialogue itself starts to have a devilish aspect. As the power of the demon is both driven out and driven farther in, the demon is not an outlaw but a virus. All of this occurs within the sphere of the human, which prides itself on the fact that it contains its own borderlines, is capable of ingesting its own unthought. Nothing inhuman, we might say, varying the ditty of Terence, is foreign to me.

Our predicament, the predicament that both instances and calls for the new demonology of my title, is one in which the demonic has become a general principle of human being and definition but will not consent to be named and held in place. We have become in the West a society of ecstatic submission to powers, presences, influences, and fascinations, whose names are Legion, and all of which act as guarantees of the capacity at once to be exposed to and to be able to hold together in the face of that which exceeds and besieges us. The more familiar these alien powers and fascinations become, the more indistinguishable from our own impulses and susceptibilities, the more they must be demonized. Inexorably, as one demon is named and tamed (let us say, homosexuality), another must be produced to take its place: cultism, conspiracy, terrorism, addiction, fanaticism, superstition.

I suggested that Harsnett finds demonic power not in demons themselves, in whom he can scarcely bring himself to believe, but in the credulity of others regarding the demon. We may have grown so desperately numb in the face of the dwindling of hysterical display, in the habituation of hysteria, that we need to produce the fantasy of the other who is subject to the power of possession, to secure the possibility of demonic danger to us. Whenever our military leaders are looking for a reason to send the bombers in, we are sure to see the image of chanting, frenzied crowds. We may confusedly think we are securing ourselves against that demon, or even perhaps in the long run rescuing *them* from it; in fact, we are securing ourselves through the possibility of the demonic that they enact. Our magical need to believe in the belief in magic is too intense to be given up. In the waning of the belief in our capacity to be threatened by the demon, it may be enough to conjure up the possibility that there are others who are thus threatened. This has an historical dimension, too; we speak of our own longing for possession through our contemporary fascination with the lure of possession and the demonic in other periods. The flood of narratives of possession, from *Invasion of the Body Snatchers* onward through the *Omen* films, the *Friday the 13th* sequence, to the stories of alien abduction, is accompanied by representations of the Victorian supernatural, from the fairies of Conan Doyle to the fascination with mesmerism in novels like *Alias Grace* and *Jack Maggs,* along with the revival of interest in séances and spiritualism. The haunting is, we might say, transactive rather than transitive: it is we who are haunted or obsessed with the belief that others might have been haunted and obsessed.

In all this the demon threatens to lose his name and shape, precisely through being generalized and familiarized. In philosophical thinking, the demon becomes associated with impersonal forces that haunt and thwart the power of rational self-determination: with illusion and error in Descartes; with the operations of chance in Maxwell's demon, with will and power in Schopenhauer and Nietzsche, and with sexuality in popular Freudianism; and finally, perhaps, with Serres's parasite. Where previously it had been the demon that interfered with the system, now it is the human that represents the principle of noise, disruption, or interference. Where previously the role of the demon was to mark the outside, or the limits of the human—for Origen, the very air, the space between earth and heaven, swarmed with demons and other invisible entities—suddenly the human has become identified with the human. The human is now the counterfeiter, the defector, the riddling exception. But the more we become the demon, the less use the demon is in guaranteeing the human.

Thus we arrive at a situation in which the desire for the charism of possession is generalized, in which the human borrows its power to be from the power of being borrowed. Our problem is a problem of names. Ours are immanent and ubiquitous demons, which we fear may no longer submit themselves to be named and personified. The evidence of this problem is to be found precisely in its insufficient solution, in the multiplication of powerful names, or names of power. I might focus on any one of the names that have been given to the demon in the human—sexuality, language, technology, desire, DNA, the "evil demon of images"—all of those "inhuman" forces that are said to undermine or surpass the human, and in doing so, secure it.

I want to focus on one of those names of power in particular—power itself, the Beelzebub of inhuman agencies. Of course, the operation of the demonic always focuses on questions of power. In asking what the demon is or means, we are asking what its power over us may be, as well as what the power for us may be of the conception of the demon. In fact, of course, the approved contemporary manner of interpreting the history of possession, demonic magic, bewitchment, and exorcism is precisely in terms of the operations of power. Just as the demon must be compelled to cough up its name, so historical analysis compels the stories of possession and witchcraft to yield up their implications in terms of power. Possession trials are shown to be nothing more, and nothing less, than power plays—displays of power that are at once dumb show and reality, playacting that leads to the noose and the stake. The same goes for nineteenth-century stagings of hysteria, whether in the Sâlpetrière or University College London, or in the consulting rooms of Freud and Breuer.

In previous eras, it was believed that the powerful name of Jesus Christ was enough to compel submission on the part of the demon, submission to the holy name, and submission to its own name. What if the demon were not so easily to be dispelled in the name of power? What, in short, if power were itself demonic in its structure—that is to say, dependent on the paradoxical intercourse of being and nonbeing, counterfeit and reality, that defines the demon or is the demon's trace? Just as for a former age it was possible neither to entertain a coherent notion of what the devil was nor to do without the idea of the devil, so for our age it is impossible to entertain a coherent notion of what power is or to abandon the notion that there must, at all costs, always be power. Now, our desire for there to be power is demonic, in two senses: first of all in the form that we imagine that power takes; and second, in the demonic form of our imagining. We think of power as a pure, agentless, inhuman force, a force exercised upon and through the human, but not as in itself human. Power must therefore be curbed, controlled, channeled, made visible and answerable. Power must be given a substantial and punctual form, and concentrated in certain places and persons. But the reason for this is precisely the growing unavailability of power in the archaic, infantile, magical form in which we need it to exist. We need there to be power, which is to say, the prosopopoeia of power. Just as in the sixteenth and seventeenth centuries it was necessary for there to be persons in the power of the devil in order that the power over the devil be demonstrable, so we need there to be persons who are more and more undeniably and more and more visibly in what we beautifully call "in power," or "in positions of power."

Demonic possession is a curious way of proving power by its inversion, a way of claiming or confirming the charism of power in submission to a greater force; think of the fascinating acts of public abasement, ridiculous and daring at once, of figures who have claimed power in powerlessness— Princess Diana, President Clinton. Or think also of the curiously relieved participation of male feminists in the ritual abasement and demonization of masculinity, the group in society who can receive the rage that has been politely withheld from previously softer targets like Jews, women, cripples, and ugly people. One female columnist in a recent mainstream newspaper remarked casually that she had no difficulty in dealing with men as long as she remembered to bring her hammer. (The motif of the hammer neatly joins the fifteenth-century *Malleus Maleficarum* to the demonic demon seeker Peter Sutcliffe.) Men are, I think, much less worried by losing power than by losing the chance of being "in power": by denying power, by embracing the voluptuous condition of powerlessness and hurt, one remains the vehicle or instance of power. It does not matter who has the phallus— another eminently demonological conception—as long as somebody does, or somebody once did. The loss of power is the best proof that it must once have existed and must still exist somewhere else. What matters is not that anyone has power but that there *is* power. What matters is not that there are subjects and objects of power but that there be bearers of power.

And yet, just as for Harsnett and those who unwittingly inaugurated the new regime of the demon, the power of the demon is the power of human reason to make itself powerless before counterfeits of its own making, so the power of the idea of power consists in the acts of representation that act as a magical prophylactic against the fear that power may be dissipated by those very acts of representation. Or, in short—we need human bearers of the inhuman force of power, lest the bracing force of the inhuman vanish altogether.

All that remains is for me to define a new demonology in the exposure and denunciation of this new demonism, to call for an end, like Samuel Harsnett, to this infantile mummery, this submission of our human reason and responsibility to fantasms of inhuman powers that are powerful in proportion to their unreality. To exorcise the demon of dependence upon demons, dispel the magical power of the stubborn need for magic. *Wo es war, soll ich gewesen*—where the it was, there shall I be. Where demons seemed to swarm, there shall we come into our own. Only by first looking the seeming inhuman full in the face will we be able at last to avert our eyes from its fascination, so that tomorrow we can become human. We will see.

(And yet isn't that . . . ? Wasn't that . . . ? Oh, nothing.)

NOTES

1. Pierre Klossowski, "Gide, du Bos et le démon," in *Un si funeste désir* (Paris: Gallimard, 1994), 39–40 (my translation).

2. The complex relations between Harsnett's text and the disputes about exorcism in England during the late 1590s and early 1600s are discussed in Corinne Holt Rickert, *The Case of John Darrell: Minister and Exorcist* (Gainesville: University of Florida Press, 1962); D. P. Walker, *Unclean Spirits: Possession and Exorcism in France and England in the Late Sixteenth and Early Seventeenth Centuries* (London: Scolar Press, 1981), and Stephen Greenblatt, "Shakespeare and the Exorcists," in *After Strange Texts: The Role of Theory in the Study of Literature*, ed. Gregory S. Jay and David L. Miller (Tuscaloosa: University of Alabama Press, 1985), 101–23, and "London and Loudun," *Critical Inquiry* 12 (1986), 326–46. I discuss the dislocations and locations of voice in these and other contemporary possession cases in my *Dumbstruck: A Cultural History of Ventriloquism* (Oxford: Oxford University Press, 2000).

3. Samuel Harsnett, *A Declaration of egregious popish impostures, to with-draw the harts of her Majesties subjects from their alleagance and from the truth of Christian religion professed in England, under the pretence of casting out devils* (London: printed by James Roberts, 1603), reprinted in F. W. Brownlow, *Shakespeare, Harsnett, and the Devils of Denham* (Newark: University of Delaware Press; London and Toronto: Associated University Presses, 1996), 322, 333. Harsnett found the story in Plutarch's *Life of Marcus Brutus*, chap. 16; see *Makers of Rome: Nine Lives by Plutarch*, trans. Ian Scott-Kilvert (Harmondsworth: Penguin, 1965), 254–55.

4. Michel de Certeau, "Discourse Disturbed," *The Writing of History*, trans. Tom Conley (New York: Columbia University Press, 1988), 244–68.

5. Aldous Huxley, *The Devils of Loudun* (Harmondsworth: Penguin, 1971).

6. Harsnett, *Declaration*, 306.

7. Monique Schneider, *De l'exorcisme à la psychanalyse: le féminine expurgé* (Paris: Retz, 1979).

8. Huxley, *Devils of Loudun*, 173.

9

Rights of Sacrifice

Richard Kearney

There is, in our contemporary popular unconscious, an intertwining of monsters and scapegoats. The two are codependent, in the sense that the pervasive obsession with the monstrous in our culture is symptomatic of the enduring role of sacrificial scapegoats.[1] This double helix of monster/scapegoat might be seen as an archetypal means of safeguarding human ways of being from those inhuman infiltrators that serve to undermine such ways of being. Yet if this safeguarding means the adoption of "inhuman" behavior, then any simple separation of human and inhuman becomes greatly complicated, as does the cluster of humanist beliefs that supports and maintains this separation. To understand further the complications involved, and to try to make sense of them, I propose to look at some dramatic reapparitions of the sacrificial demon in recent cinema: first, the extraterrestrial monster of the *Alien* series, and then the figure of Kurtz in *Apocalypse Now Redux*.

THE *ALIEN* SERIES: ON BEING NOT AT HOME

> My mummy always said that there were no monsters, no real ones—
> but there are.
> —First words of Agent Ripley in *Alien Resurrection,* echoing her
> adopted girl, Newt, in *Alien 3.*

The *Alien* series consists of four films directed by Ridley Scott, James Cameron, David Fincher, and Jean-Pierre Jeunet over the two decades leading up to the third millennium. One of the most intriguing features of the quadrology is that it not only screens alien monsters but actually reflects the very process by which such screening takes place. This self-reflexive gesture is accentuated by the fact that the four directors quote each other's works—held together by the same, self-replicating protagonist (Ellen Ripley, played by Sigourney Weaver). But this mirror play recurs *within* the films themselves, as well as between them, to the extent that various exchanges between the characters focus on the *monstration* of sacrificial scapegoating, thereby exposing the ways in which our most feared monsters can serve as uncanny doubles for our all too human selves. The series has already been critically analyzed in my own *On Stories* and, more extensively, in Stephen's Mulhall's *On Film*,[2] so I confine myself here to a few remarks that I consider especially relevant to my present argument.

I think it telling that throughout the series allusions are made to the interchangeability of human and extraterrestrial aliens. Human space travelers actually find themselves playing "host" to the hostile monster from space, thus discovering (to their horror) that the monster is not just "out there" but "in here." The dragon-shaped alien, recalling portraits of the satanic beast of the Apocalypse, is capable of invading our most intimate being. Thus the thing these human astronauts consider most foreign is in fact the most familiar.[3] What really terrifies them is the alien *within,* already there in the homely situation but such that it cannot be integrated or named. The extraterrestrials in the series thus serve, I am suggesting, as imaginary personifications of our inner alienation, reminding us that we are not at home with ourselves, even at home. They are, we might say, postmodern replicas of the old religious demons—figures of chaos and disorientation within order and orientation.[4]

Stephen Mulhall argues convincingly that the monsters symbolize our fear of our own carnality—e.g., sexual difference, phallic penetration, genital violation, pregnancy, generativity, reproduction, labor, birth-death. The alien, he writes, "represents the return of the repressed human body, of our ineluctable participation in the realm of nature—of life."[5] More specifically, for the androgynous Lieutenant Ripley, maternal fecundity represents her "monstrous other." But the monstrosity of the alien represents more than just life. It stems also from a deeper fear that nature may itself be reduced to the out-of-control and invasive culture of biotechnology. The alien's body, as Mulhall notes, *is* its technology, an unnerving phenomenon that suggests that science is amoral and inhuman, and terrifyingly "sublime." Indeed in the last film in the series, *Alien Resurrection,* Ripley herself is replicated as a cloned, posthumous hybrid who behaves like an android but possesses the racial memory and flair of the alien who invaded her. Here Ripley embodies the saint and the stranger in one!

The sentiment that the monstrous nature of the alien is not in fact so alien to humanity at all is vividly captured in the scene in Ridley Scott's *Alien* (the opening film in the series) where the android Ash describes the monster-foetus that has exploded through Kane's chest as "Kane's son"— an allusion to the evil inherited from the original Cain of Genesis. Even

Agent Ripley comes to resemble the alien in terms of physiognomic features by *Alien 3,* and at one point she finds herself impregnated by the extra-terrestrial beast whose offspring bursts through her torso in the final sequence. What most deeply defines Ripley is that she is so irrevocably obsessed by the Alien that she becomes incapable of recalling almost anything else.[6] In this sense, Ripley is not just one of the alien family—"she *is* the alien; it incarnates the nightmare that makes her who she is, and that she has been incubating." On this reading, Ripley's encounter with the impregnating alien is paralleled by her sexual intercourse with Clemens, marking the decisive point where she overcomes her deep antipathy toward human embodiedness. For Ripley, "the sexual body is ultimately the long repressed and sublimated *das Ding* from which she has sought to flee."[7] Mulhall offers this reading of the final graphic scene: "As she descends into the flames, the alien queen bursts out; Ripley holds it gently in her cupped hands, and lays its crowned head on her breast, as if to suckle it. The logic of the Alien universe, and of Ripley's own nature, is here finally consummated. Since the alien itself originates from within her, since it is an incarnate projection of her deepest fears, she can succeed in eliminating it only by eliminating herself."[8]

This uneasy sense that we humans are in fact the *real* aliens—or at least just as alien as the "others somewhere out there"—is further reinforced by a number of revealing puns and allusions. One of the Hispanic women officers preparing to do battle with the monsters in the first sequel refers to herself as an "illegal alien." The heinous criminals exiled in the space prison, Fiorina 161, in *Alien 3* are themselves so alienated from all humanity that some try to rape Ripley (just as the monster does). They can be saved only by following their Christian-apocalyptic leader, Dillon, into the ultimate sacrificial encounter with their own "in-human" double, the face-hugging, chest-bursting monster itself. Moreover, the suggestion of collusion between robotic clones and galactic aliens in the first film of the series—where the android Ash is conspiring with *Nostromo*'s central computer, Mother, to divert the ship to the alien-infested planet—is cleverly transposed in the second and third movies into a realization that the worst monsters are not: (a) the extraterrestrials, who are simply following their nature (like their Alien Queen protecting her nursery); nor are they (b) the robotic clones and androids (Bishop actually saves Agent Ripley and her adopted daughter, Newt, from the exploding planet). The ultimate monsters turn out, in the final analysis, to be the all too *terrestrial* humans of "the Company," who have employed Ripley to hunt the space monster with a view to bringing it back to earth as a deadly addition to their bio-weapons program.

This reversibility between human and inhuman orders of monstrosity is underlined by James Cameron's own avowal that his depiction of the Marine mission to LV 426 is a replay of the Vietnam War. In short, while the alien movie series could be said to dramatize the rite of scapegoating, there is a radical religious inversion of this mechanism when Ripley finally chooses to transcend the mimetic order of sacrificial violence and offer herself up for the sake of the human race. In the final scene of *Alien 3*, Ripley defies the company's plans to extract the monster-foetus from her womb, falling in cruciform position into a pit of molten lead.[9] Only, of course, to be miraculously reborn in the next sequel, *Alien Resurrection*!

This final reversal is, I think, key to the message of the series regarding the sacrificial phenomenon. For while ostensibly scapegoating monsters from other planets, the series actually suggests that the primary source of death and destruction is to be found in humanity's own will-to-power. The real culprits of the piece are the *human* manipulators of war technology and biogenetic engineering back on earth. In sum, the most alien-ating and alien-making forces of all are shown to reside not out there in intergalactic space but within the human species itself. Left alone, the aliens would have just done their own survival thing—reproduce their biological species in their "natural" way. It is humanity's tampering with this different order of being that causes havoc and carnage. It is *we* who have turned these strangers into scapegoats.

There is, one might say, nothing particularly new about this. Human interference with monsters goes back to Greeks myths of the Minotaur, Kabbalistic stories of golems and gothic tales of vampires, ghouls, and Frankensteins. Indeed, Dr. Pretorius sounds the typically apocalyptic note on this score when he makes his famous toast in *The Bride of Frankenstein*: "To a new world of gods and monsters!" But what sets the *Alien* series off from such prototypical versions of the human-inhuman monster is the fact that today we actually possess technology that can travel into space and bring the *imaginary* world of aliens into contact with the *real* earth. The boundary separating science from science fiction has become blurred—hence the inflation of our horror before the undecidability of the monstrous. As Stanley Cavell so astutely reasons, "Isn't it the case that not the human horrifies me, but the inhuman, the monstrous? Very well. But only what is human can be inhuman.—Can only the human be monstrous? If something is monstrous, and we do not believe that there are monsters, then only the human is a candidate for the monstrous." Horror, Cavell deduces, is the name we give to the experience of the "precariousness of human identity, to the perception that it may be lost or invaded, that we may be, or may become, something other than we are, or take ourselves for; that our origins as human beings need accounting for, and are unaccountable."[10] Though he is not speaking of the *Alien* series as such, Cavell's deduction bears directly on our thesis. We will return to it in our conclusion.

APOCALYPSE NOW REDUX: IDENTIFYING (WITH) THE MONSTER

> Horror may have a face, and you must make a friend of horror. Horror and moral terror are your friends. If they are not then they are an enemy to be feared.
>
> —Colonel Kurtz

"The Horror, the Horror"—a phrase made immortal by Conrad's *Heart of Darkness* and given contemporary celebrity by Coppola's film version, *Apocalypse Now Redux.* By way of offering an alternative look at the theme of strangers and scapegoats, I propose to end this chapter with a brief account of this film.

Apocalypse Now transposes the characters of *Heart of Darkness* to Vietnam. It tells the story of a U.S. Special Forces officer, Lieutenant Willard, sent up the rivers of North Vietnam in search of a renegade colonel, Walter Kurtz. Kurtz has gone AWOL after returning to Vietnam. He has forfeited a high-ranking job in the Joint Chiefs of Staff in Washington to counter a threat by double agents endangering the lives of hundreds of American soldiers. Operating deep within Cambodian territory—then legally off limits to U.S. troops—Kurtz disobeys orders and eliminates the threat. Faced with disciplinary action, he escapes deeper into the jungle and starts carrying out indiscriminate raids against military stations and villages. His methods are ruthless and utterly effective. But the U.S. command judges that he has gone too far. Willard is called in to terminate Kurtz's command, and to do so "with extreme prejudice."

This summary expression betrays how U.S. war policy mirrors the "illegal" activities of Kurtz. The mirroring becomes more and more alarming as the film unfolds, charting Willard's journey toward the heart of darkness that is Kurtz's hideout. The parallel between righteous executioner and evil criminal is signposted from the opening scene of the film: Willard admits that his narrative and Kurtz's are inextricably bound up with each other. "There is really no way of telling his story without telling mine," says Willard. "If his is a confession, then so is mine." As he leafs further through Kurtz's dossier, Willard discovers that Kurtz was once just like him. He reads one of Kurtz's letters to his son in which Kurtz claims that the charges leveled against him by the high command are "quite simply insane" (the very term used by the high command to describe Kurtz's behavior). In this same letter, Kurtz explains to his son that he is beyond the army's "lying timid morality"—a morality that Willard has plenty of opportunity to realize is only skin deep. The photograph in the dossier is a shadowy silhouette marked "Believed to be Col. Walter Kurtz"—a signal that as we approach the heart of darkness the Minotaur lurking in wait becomes more undecidable. The question of whether we are dealing with a neo-

Nietzschean hero or a psychopathic monster grows problematic. "Who is the real demon?" we find ourselves asking—this out-of-bounds, unknown reprobate or his sanctimonious accusers back in Washington and Saigon? Should Willard embrace this estranged being or execute him? How, in short, is he to make the right call? How, in this night of fear and trembling, is he to *judge?*

The narrator's odyssey to the heart of the labyrinthine jungle retraces Kurtz's own itinerary. From the sententious briefing with top brass at home base, to the various detours through one horrifying U.S. Army outpost after the next, Willard begins to realize that Kurtz's horrific acts are no more than efficient enactments of "legitimate" military behavior. Kurtz, he finally acknowledges, is playing the role of a sacrificial scapegoat as the high command keeps its hands clean. The final scene, in which the execution of Kurtz is juxtaposed with graphic shots of animal sacrifice (a caribou cleft in two by a sword), aptly captures this.

Several premonitory scenes anticipate this sacrificial denouement. Already at the opening military briefing, Willard is told by his senior officer that Kurtz has crossed the line between "us" and "them." The general describes Kurtz as being "out there . . . with the natives . . . operating beyond the pale of any human decency." He tells how Kurtz, once a prized, top-rated colonel, has supped with the devil and has gone beyond the point of return, traversing the border between civilians and barbarians. Kurtz has broken with the norms of civilized, reasonable behavior. He has gone "insane," ultimately yielding to the temptation "to be a god." He has become the Other, the Monster, one of the pure who has passed over to the Hades of the impure—a friend turned enemy. He is damned.

The irony of these demonizing sentiments is breathtaking, of course, in light of what we soon discover the "civilized, reasonable behavior" of the officially approved U.S. troops to be. But the discovery is gradual, as Willard steers his gunboat up the river leading from North Vietnam to Cambodia. His nightmare encounter with two military commands says it all. The first of these is led by Colonel Kilgore, a cavalry officer who has the same rank as Kurtz but seems more brutal in his bloodlust. He distributes "death cards" to his victims, orders his troops to surf on the river during military maneuvers, and plays Wagner—the chosen music of Nazi machismo and *Birth of a Nation* suprematism—to accompany his helicopter gunship missions. In contradistinction to Kurtz's crystalline logic of terminating the war by whatever means, Kilgore just wants to keep it going for the heck of it. The banality of evil could hardly be more graphically illustrated than in these surreal scenes of gratuitous violence. If we are talking "insanity," this is it—though Kilgore is considered "legitimate" while Kurtz is not. Compared to this hellish mayhem, Kurtz's description of his incisive actions as "moments of clarity" begin to sound more convincing than the army's dismissal of them as "unsound methods" (as if the actual *aim* of "exterminating the brutes" is quite acceptable!) The army objects to the means, not the end.

The confusion of friend and foe, ally and alien, is compounded as Willard visits the U.S. frontier outposts. At the first we see GIs debauching themselves at an officially sponsored show of Playboy bunnies, while the second displays an inferno of military inefficiency, cowardice, and drug abuse. The U.S. myth of the noble frontiersman takes a last dive here as one of Kilgore's super-surfers collapses in a hail of shrapnel. Could Kurtz possibly be worse than this?

As Willard arrives at his final destination—Kurtz's hideout—the enigma deepens further. Willard is met by an American photographer who proclaims Kurtz to be a "poet warrior." He hails Kurtz as the prophet of a new "dialectic" that, far from making him mad, brings him beyond conventional categories of good and evil. "No maybes, no supposes, no fractions." Willard appears to vacillate yet one more time. He eventually meets Kurtz himself and is invited into his den.

So the pursuer confronts the monster. They talk for days without guard. Kurtz expounds his reasoning. He recounts how he learned from the Vietcong "enemy" the uncompromising logic of war. He tells the story of how he and his troops had vaccinated children in a certain village only to discover that, after they had left, the Vietcong had returned and cut off each inoculated arm. This enemy act struck Kurtz "like a diamond bullet through his forehead," revealing to him the inner truth of military action—pure will to power, without judgment. These were "not monsters but men," he learned. These were "geniuses . . . perfect, genuine, complete, crystalline, pure of act." These were men who could both love and kill—love their own families with total passion and kill their enemies "without passion . . . without judgment. Because it is judgment that defeats us." Kurtz ultimately confesses to Willard that if he had ten divisions of men like that he could have dispensed with all hypocrisy and terminated the war "in no time." Even the corpses strewn on Kurtz's compound serve a specific purpose— to instill enough horror to bring the war to an end. What looks like madness is in fact a (perverse) obsession with peace, the desire to win the war as effectively and rapidly as possible. Here we have a morality of immorality.[11] Kurtz's speech culminates with the observation, "You can kill me but you cannot judge me."

Having listened to Kurtz's razor-sharp reasoning and witnessed the result of his new im/morality—a camp inhabited by crazed warriors and strewn with body parts and decapitated heads—Willard *does* eventually judge. He kills Kurtz. Coppola does not explain what criteria Willard deploys to differentiate between Kurtz the neo-Nietzschean hero and Kurtz the manic monster. We are not told how Willard decides, or how we might judge his decision in turn. Coppola, after all, is a moviemaker, not a philosopher. It is his business to screen this age-old conundrum, not to solve it. But in dramatizing this fundamental question of discernment for a contemporary audience, Coppola has performed a great intellectual service.

From the perspective of our scapegoating thesis, this film raises key questions. Among these are: How do we judge the horror? How do we distinguish between one kind of monstrosity and another? How does one differentiate between "normal" and "abnormal" actions, especially in a war like Vietnam, where, in Willard's words, "charging a man with murder here was like handing out speeding tickets at the Indy 500"? How is Willard to know who is on the "right" side in a war where even the Americans have changed sides, as he learns from French colonials on a lost plantation (where he also learns from a French widow that "men love and kill")? If it is true that Kurtz has welcomed his potential executioner, Willard, in an act of unconditional hospitality, has Willard been entirely just in responding to this hospitality with an act of summary execution? (It is an execution without trial, to boot, in seeming defiance of Willard's own prolonged scruples about high command's order to "terminate—with extreme prejudice.")

Moreover, the fact that his host, Kurtz, hangs out in a Buddhist temple and is an avid reader of Eliot's *Hollow Men*—not to mention Frazer's *The Golden Bough* and the Bible—sharpens the enigma by suggesting how deeply resolved Kurtz is to prosecute the chilling logic of war, even if it means succumbing to its "horror." "After such knowledge what forgiveness?" as Eliot says. So, even if the demands of absolute hospitality seem impossible here, one is left wondering if the only alternative is the sacrificial killing of the monster at the heart of the labyrinth. Willard obeys his command. Theseus rules, OK. But does it have to be like this?

Two key scenes toward the close of the film put these questions into sharp relief. The first shows one of Willard's troops, Chef, being terrified by a tiger as they patrol the jungle. They are on the lookout for the "enemy." But what actually surprises them is an animal, who is perfectly at home in his local environment. Because they are estranged from this "foreign" place the U.S. Marines mistake one "monster" for another, confusing human and animal adversaries. At least one implication of this scene is that the "monster" Kurtz, who has gone over to the other side and assumed the mores of the natives, who revere him, may also be a case of mistaken identity. This suspicion is deepened by the fact that when Kurtz and Willard eventually encounter each other at the heart of darkness, their seminaked, sleek-headed figures have become almost indistinguishable. The question of who is the hunter and who the hunted accentuates the problem of prejudice and judgment.

The second image, also at the film's finale, shows a Buddha in Kurtz's Cambodian hideaway just before the latter's execution. We see the veiled statue facing Kurtz as he recites his terminal reflections on war onto a tape recorder. (He is railing against the hypocrisy of the U.S. Army that trains troops to drop napalm on innocents but refuses to allow the word "fuck" to be painted on its planes.) In the preceding scene Kurtz was seen entering the doorway of the Buddhist temple as a caribou passes him on its way to its own ritual sacrifice. Both will be offered as scapegoats to purge the community. It is significant that the twin sacrificial rites that follow—the slaughtering of the caribou juxtaposed with the killing of Kurtz, in graphic montage—give rise to a scene where the "purged" Willard reemerges through the same temple door. His bare, dark figure is almost identical to Kurtz's, but with this difference: it is Willard who now wields the executioner's axe and possesses the manuscript (Kurtz's memoirs).

So here again the question is raised as to whether one is justified in executing an enemy deemed inhuman. With Kurtz's closing statement to Willard—"You have a right to kill me but not to judge me"—still ringing in our ears, the calm visage of the bald Buddha that closes the film gives us pause. This is all the more the case if one is mindful of the Buddhist doctrine of nonjudgment. Could Willard have executed Kurtz had he heeded this ancient Buddhist prayer?

> When I encounter beings of wicked nature
> Overwhelmed by violent negative actions and suffering,
> I shall hold such rare ones dear,
> As if I had found a precious treasure.
> When someone gives me terrible harm
> I shall regard him as my holy spiritual friend.[12]

What, in short, if Willard had forgiven Kurtz and tried to save him from this inferno, acknowledging that Kurtz was not only the ultimate expression of U.S. military involvement in Vietnam but also a scapegoat serving to maintain the illusion of a clean conscience? A man who, for all his *killing,* was still capable of *loving* (his wife and son, and even Willard, arguably, whom he refuses to slay). A man who, in his own words, hated the "stench of lies."

Yet there is one mitigating factor in Willard's role—the confessional narrative of these events. These events are related *retrospectively,* to be sure, but they are no less cathartic for that. In acknowledging that (a) there was no way to "tell his (Kurtz's) story without telling my own" and (b) that "if his (Kurtz's) story is really a confession, then so is mine," Willard admits to a deep identification with the monster he has slain. He openly acknowledges his role as testimonial witness to Kurtz's life, before the world but most especially before Kurtz's son. "It was no accident that I got to be the caretaker of Colonel Walter E. Kurtz's memory," he concedes. Both Willard and Kurtz expose the mendacities of U.S. military practice in Vietnam. Willard does so by telling the whole story in direct response to Kurtz's final request: "I worry that my son might not understand what I have tried to be. I want someone to tell him everything. . . . There is nothing that I hate more than lies. . . . If you understand me, you'll do this for me."

These are hardly the words of an irredeemable monster. They are those of someone who was ultimately subsumed by the horror. Someone for whom the truth of war won out over the truth of poetry. Someone who could not survive to tell the tale. In this he differs from Willard, who in spite of his collusion with sacrificial killing, manages to transcend the logic of scapegoating in favor of narrative testimony and wisdom. He tells the story of Kurtz that he carries in his hand as he exits the temple and merges finally with the face of the Buddha.

Willard refuses to be divinized by Kurtz's followers after he has killed the demon. As the throngs of warriors kneel before him in their bandoleers and bloodied loincloths, Willard passes through them to his waiting boat. Having defeated the Minotaur, Theseus declines the sacrificial role of replacement deity. He escapes the cycle of bloodletting. In resisting the lure of false gods, he appears to choose the option of poetic catharsis so well described by Eliot himself: "[The storyteller] is haunted by a demon against which he feels powerless, because in its first manifestation it has no face, no name, nothing; and the words, the poem he makes, are a kind of form of exorcism of this demon."[13] *Apocalypse Now Redux* is such a poem, as was *Heart of Darkness* and *The Hollow Men* before it.

Yet the tragedy for Kurtz himself is that redemption comes, if it comes at all, *posthumously,* through the confessional voice of the film's narrator. The catharsis by pity and fear comes to Willard the narrator, and perhaps also to us viewers, but not it seems to the crazed colonial. Willard's narrative testifies to the hidden root of the alienation in Kurtz that, it transpires, is symptomatic of the war itself. When Willard finally departs from the heart of darkness, refusing the nihilism of the "Horror," he takes Kurtz's story back with him. He carries the typed pages of testimony in his trembling hand. In the retelling that is *Apocalypse Now Redux* the Horror becomes that bit less horrible, the monster that bit less monstrous.

CONCLUSION: THE STRANGER WITHIN

If it is the sleep of Reason that produces Monsters, as Goya says, it is, I would suggest, the perversion of Reason carried out in a certain sacrificial mood. If we are to put an end to the cycle of scapegoating, might we not begin by trying to understand our own monsters? In so doing, might we not transform some of them into creatures of passionate peace? Might we not even (who knows?) help one or two of those real persons who behave monstrously "out there"—tyrants, torturers, rapists, murderers—to come to terms with their own internal monsters and thereby put an end to homicidal and genocidal practices of scapegoating, as Willard almost does in the final confrontation with Kurtz? Or as Ellen Ripley and the prisoners of Fiorina do at the end of *Alien 3*? Indeed, is this not the very meaning of Ripley's crucificial act as she cradles her alien offspring and holds it to her breast? But we do not have to send our Ripleys and Willards to the darkest reaches of Asia or space to find our monsters. They are lurking within our midst here at home—often in the depths of our own selves.

The notion of the stranger within is as old as civilization itself. Almost every wisdom tradition attests to it. We find it in the story of Jacob struggling with his dark double through the night before transmuting his monster into an angel of God. We see it in the testimony of Jesus confronting his demons in the desert before giving himself, in an act of ultimate *caritas*. We encounter a similar lesson being offered by the Buddha when he takes the monster of violent hatred to his heart and meditates on it for so many years that it eventually mutates into compassionate calm. A disciple of the Tibetan Buddhist school, Milarepa, learned this truth the hard way when one day he discovered his cave taken over by a demon. After fighting with the beast for many years to no avail, he finally put himself into its jaws, saying, "Eat me if you want to." It was only then the demon left.[14] When violent fears go, so do monsters. Love is the casting out of fear.

The key, perhaps, is not to kill our monsters but to learn to live with them. For that way there is hope that monsters may eventually learn to live with themselves and cease to scapegoat others. As Nietzsche put it in his own aphoristic way, "Whoever fights monsters should see to it that in the process he does not become a monster."[15] Agreed. Yet at the same time, embracing monsters does not mean you have to invite them to dinner—or set up house. Some monsters need to be welcomed, others struggled with. The important thing is to try to tell the difference.

NOTES

1. See Richard Kearney, *On Stories* (London and New York: Routledge, 2001), especially part 3.
2. Stephen Mulhall, *On Film* (London and New York: Routledge, 2002).
3. This is another way of describing what Heidegger and Freud identify, in their different ways, as the "uncanny" (*das Unheimlich*): that which "invades one's sense of personal, social or cosmic security—the feeling of being at home in oneself" (Timothy K. Beal, *Religion and Its Monsters* [New York and London: Routledge, 2002]).
4. Ibid.
5. Mulhall, chap. 1.
6. Ibid.
7. Ibid.
8. Ibid.
9. Ibid.
10. Stanley Cavell, *The Claim of Reason* (Oxford: Oxford University Press,

1979), 418–19. I am grateful to Stephen Mulhall's *On Film* for this quotation and several others.

11. "In his turn, Kurtz the man, became a monster. He fused the moral and the immoral. Action, pure action, is the aim of any warrior for Kurtz. War is about action without thought, without hesitation and that is the new morality. Kurtz has, in a way, embraced the Nietzschean Will to Power in its most horrific form" (Anthony Sculimbrini, "Invitations to the Monstrous," graduate paper, Boston College, unpublished, 2001, 9f.). I am also grateful to Joshua McKimber and Joshua Mills-Knutsen, two other graduate students in my BC graduate seminar, "Strangers, Gods and Monsters," for their presentations on the subject.

12. The Dalai Lama, *The Good Heart* (London: Rider, 1996), 88, 98. Would Theseus (Willard) have slain the Minotaur (Kurtz) if he had observed this verse? Or taken this more explicit Buddhist tale to heart: "When one is thinking about devils, it is important not to have a notion of some independent, autonomous external force 'out there' existing as a kind of absolute negative force. The term should be related more to the negative tendencies and impulses that lie within each of us" (40)? One finds similar teachings on the nonjudgmental attitude to evil and the need to embrace negative energies in Thich Nhat Hanh, *Essential Writings* (New York: Riverhead Books, 2000), and *Bouddha et Jesus* (France: Le Relié, 2001), 136 ff. See also *Benedict's Dharma: Buddhists Reflect on the Rule of Saint Benedict*, ed. Patrick Henry (New York: Riverhead Books, 2001), e.g., the section "Freedom in the Mind's Mirror," which suggests how "our enemy teaches us patience and is therefore someone to be greatly valued"(15). I am grateful to Peggy McLoughlin, Emma Fitzpatrick, Sally Kearney, and James and Patricia Leydon-Mahony for bringing these texts to my attention.

13. T. S. Eliot, *The Three Voices of Poetry* (Cambridge: Cambridge University Press, 1943). See the fascinating discussion of this passage by Denis Donoghue in *Words Alone: The Poet T. S. Eliot* (New Haven, Conn.: Yale University Press, 2000), 27 ff., and Mark P. Hederman, *The Haunted Inkwell* (Dublin: Columba Press, 2001), 14.

14. See Pema Chodron, *Start Where You Are* (Boston and London: Shambhala Books, 1994).

15. Friedrich Nietzsche, *Beyond Good and Evil* (New York: Random House, 1966), sec. 146. I am grateful to Timothy Beal for bringing this quotation to my attention.

PART IV
Politics of Human Becoming

10

The Project of Humanity

Zygmunt Bauman

"Humanism" is a philosophical gloss on the politics of humanity.

As a philosophical issue, humanism is an ethical discourse—though more often than not it appears in ontological disguise. Ostensibly it is about "human nature" and human beings' natural endowments. However, defining human nature also means drawing a boundary around the "human," to make sense of the already drawn, or intended to be drawn, political boundary separating "human" from "inhuman" (or more to the point, from "inept at being human," "undeserving to be human," or "bound to be humanized").

Politics of humanity is the practice of projecting and shifting such boundaries—the very practice on which humanism offers a philosophical gloss. It is concerned with the management of the ethical: mapping the "universe of moral obligation" and drawing its outer limits. Whoever seeks an insight into the close affinity between philosophical humanism and the politics of humanity could do worse than (re)read Anatole France's *Penguins' Island* or Vercors's *Zoo ou l'assassin philathrope*.

Philosophy may deal with timeless truths (or render them timeless by dealing with them), but at each stage of its continuous effort to make sense of human experience it reflects the "topical relevances" of the time. A sociologically informed history of philosophy would thus be a record of changing relevances, themselves of mostly political provenance. It is no wonder, then, that the topics that tend nowadays to be classified under the rubric of "humanism" have come into the focus of philosophical debates time and again, only to sink once more into the unthematized background. Each time they surface, they emerge from somewhat different topical concerns and carry the stamps of their distinct origins.

The successive resurrections of humanist "topics" nevertheless shared one feature: they were prompted by the changing political agenda of the era. It was mostly the emergence of new political problems and ambitions that made imperative another renegotiation of the issues of "human nature" and of the boundaries of humanity.

One has come to see the current round of the "humanist debate" as no exception. Like earlier rounds, it recycles age-old philosophical concerns so they can be mapped onto the grid of new topical relevances, shaped by the political concerns of our time. Though this round draws deeply on re-reading the lore of previous (mostly classical and Renaissance) rounds, it reads into them new queries prompted by political imperatives of very recent origin.

It is on these new political imperatives that I wish to concentrate in this essay, referring only marginally to the ongoing philosophical *querelle* and even less to its prehistory. My argument is intended as an exercise in socio-logical hermeneutics; it attempts to render the present-day resurgence of the "humanist" debate intelligible by referring it to the social realities of the time, reflected in the life-worlds of selected categories of human beings and in political strategies responding to that experience.

CONTRARIETIES OF GLOBALIZATION

That globalization is a blatantly one-sided process, or at best a cluster of developments of grossly uneven pace, is self-evident for some analysts (myself included), though hotly contested by others. There is ample evidence to support the assertion that what is globalizing—and at an accelerating speed—is the network of *dependencies* (Norbert Elias's figuration) and that its globalization is far from being matched by similar transformations in other spheres—social, political, or cultural. Dependencies are indeed global; whatever is done locally may have global repercussions, and precious little of what is being undertaken locally can claim independence from global pressures. Contrary to the modern expectation, the gap between what needs to be done and the ability to do it keeps widening. The conditions under which "humans make their history" have become fully and truly globally operated, without history-makers having been asked to make a choice, while the tools human beings use are as they were before, of local reach only; if they are global, then it is solely in their unanticipated consequences. As far as extant political institutions, the inherited instruments of servicing social conditions and the orthodox means of cultural integration go, the forces that spawn global networks of interdependencies could as well be located in outer space.

Being swept and buffeted by forces residing in mysterious and impen-etrable "faraway" places, resolutely unpredictable and out of control, is for the modern mind a novel experience. Modernity, after all, meant life con-ducted under the aegis of man-made order as well as progressive taming and rational management of human conditions. Globalization ushers in a world that modern human beings have not as yet visited. As Ulrich Beck poignantly put it, "[T]he very idea of controllability, certainty and security—which is so fundamental in the first modernity—collapses. . . . [T]he basis of established risk-logic has whittled away, and . . . hard-to-manage dangers prevail instead of quantifiable risks."[1]

After several centuries during which "society"—the abstract entity above and behind scattered, apparently random, individual pursuits—was imagined in the form of a collective brain, boardroom, or controlling tower, came the time when the realities in question were visualized as a late-medieval God constructed by the Franciscans (particularly the *Fraticelli,* the "Minor Brothers" faction) and the Nominalists (most famously, William of Ockham). In Michael Allan Gillespie's apt summary, that Franciscan/ Nominalist God was "capricious in His power, unknowable, unpredictable, unconstrained by nature and reason and indifferent to good and evil."[2] Above all, he stayed steadfastly beyond the reach of human intellectual powers and pragmatic know-how. Nothing could be gained by human beings in their efforts to force God's hand. Since all attempts to do so were bound to remain ineffective, bearing merely further testimony to human vanity and conceit, they were as condemnable as they were unworthy of trying. God owed nothing to human beings. Having put them on their feet and told them to seek their own ways, He retreated and retired, leaving them to their own devices. If they wanted a controlling tower that would attend to ordering the randomness of their existence, they would have to put it together by their own effort (though the story of Babel warned them of the futility and gruesome consequences of trying).

It is society's turn now to follow the example of the Franciscan/ Nominalist God and retire. In keeping with the spirit of the age, Peter Drucker summed up the new wisdom in a pithy sound bite: "No more salvation by society." It is now up to human individuals to make their cases, to prove those cases and to defend them against the promoters of contrary cases. There is no point in invoking the verdicts of society (to which, a few centuries ago, the powers left unattended by *Deus absconditus* had been transferred) in order to support one's case. First, invocation will not be believed, since whoever keeps the bank in "outer space" plays the cards, in the Franciscan/Nominalist God's fashion, close to his chest, and so the verdicts—if there are any—are unknown and bound to remain so. Second, one thing known for sure about society's verdicts is that they would never hold for long and that there is no knowing which way they would turn next. Third, like God of the late medieval times, society seems to be "indifferent to good and evil"; at least the new totality occupying the place once taken by society does not pronounce unanimous judgment on such matters.

To sum up: the emergent worldwide figuration is by all traditional standards of social "systemic totalities" sorely distorted, one-sided, incomplete, and ailing, as a consequence of blatantly uneven development. Overgrown networks of economic dependencies are not monitored—let alone con-strained, controlled, or held in place—by parallel political and cultural grids. To put it in a nutshell, democratic institutions of self-government that de-veloped in the two hundred years of modern history stay local, while powers that define the limits of their ambition and their capacity to act have turned global and circulate far beyond their reach. The leap from the classical in-ternational law of states to a cosmopolitan law of a "global civil society," which Jürgen Habermas—reflecting on the traumatic experience of the 1999 NATO campaign against Yugoslavia—posited as both imperative and im-minent, has not yet occurred.[3] Neither is the "global civil society," the nec-essary catapult for the adumbrated "leap," much in sight. Even by the most optimistic accounts, its birth seems to proceed at a much slower pace than the entrenchment of "global capitalism." Compared to the sequence re-corded in the birth story of modern nation-states, formation of "totalities" seems to proceed now in reverse order.

It is in the virgin space between the increasingly coordinated global capi-tal-and-market forces and blatantly *under*-coordinated political (by and large) localized forces that the major contest of the present-day stage of globalization is being conducted. Between these two kinds of forces extends an institutional void—a vast expanse of trial-and-error initiatives and partially successful or failed experiments in collaboration or resistance. It is in the same space that the renegotiation and recasting of the meaning of "humanity" would need to be undertaken. In such a badly under-institutionalized space, the problems of "what to do" and "where to aim for" take second place to the big question of "who can do it." The pro-cess of globalization puts at the top of the agenda the issue of *collective agency*.

DECOMPOSING SOVEREIGNTY

Like a game with rules too unstable to be learned and memorized, or an airborne plane whose pilot's cabin is empty, the present situation is one in which the most awesome powers exceed those known agencies of col-lective control and management, the political institutions invented and con-solidated in the two centuries of modern democracy.

When speaking of global trade, global finances, global capital, and even of global economy, we refer to entities that have passed all the tests set by Émile Durkheim for "tough reality." But phrases like "global government," "global law," "global society," "global culture" or "global community" represent mere postulates, if not deceptive illusions. They derive an appear-ance of meaning from logically erroneous yet psychologically plausible ideas of "similarity," following the pattern of "5 P.M. on the sun"—a locution Ludwig Wittgenstein chose as an example of comparisons as persuasive as they are meaningless. If there is to be a global society, it will not be "similar" to the society we came to know, a society tantamount to the "nation-state" able to coordinate economic, military, and cultural autarchies and resting its sovereignty on that triad of powers. It will not be "the same, only bigger."

Of the present degree of uncoordination of powers, Eric Hobsbawm had the following to say:

> What we have today is . . . a dual system, the unofficial one of the "national economies" of states, and the real but largely unofficial one of transnational units and institutions. . . . [U]nlike the state with its territory and power, other elements of the "nation" can be and easily are overridden by the globalization of the economy. Ethnicity and language are the two obvious ones. Take away state power and coercive force, and their relative insignificance is clear.[4]

"State power and coercive force" is indeed, increasingly, "take[n] away." The modern nation-state has grown, or was cultivated, under the aegis of the principle that, as Christian Delacampagne recently put it, "there is on earth no power superior to that of the State."[5] Such power meant *sovereignty*, defined in 1576, on the threshold of the modern era, by Jean Bodin (in chapter 8 of the first of *Les Six Livres de la Republique*) as "absolute and perpetual power," a power without any limits imposed on either its prerogatives or its duration. Such sovereignty of nation-states had been entrenched throughout the modern era, in the course of which it was conducted on two fronts: against the right to rebellion inside, and the right to interference from the outside. Conducting such a war with any degree of success would have been unthinkable if not for the triad of economic, military, and cultural autarchies. There is no nation-state without that triad, but the triad itself becomes dispensable once sovereignty, at least in Bodin's sense, no longer "belongs to" the nation-state; nor is its exercise the nation-state's task.

Sovereignty of the nation-state erodes as rapidly from outside as from inside, but by itself this erosion does not necessarily invalidate the principle that "there is no power on earth superior to that of the state." The sovereignty of nation-states may crumble without anything tangible being put in its place. The power void left in the wake of erosion is made all the more conspicuous by the fact that, and looks all the more abysmal because, the ability to put together the triad of autarchies has ceased to be a *conditio sine qua non* of statehood.

Making the test for statehood easier to pass leads to an accelerating "balkanization" of the globe. With questions about self-sufficiency and ability to balance the books no longer asked, the fragmentation of powers is set irrevocably in motion and acquires more momentum by the year. Apart from the contrary interests of neighbors and the might that can be summoned to promote them, there are no grounds on which the pretensions of a locality, clamoring for its share of whatever remains of once all-embracing sovereignty, could be rejected. There can be more states, therefore, but being a state counts for less; the sum-total of the new microstates' "capacity for getting things done" comes nowhere near the capacity of the big state, whose territory they have jointly filled.

An unspoken assumption that, misleadingly, gives talk of "global society" an air of credibility is that of the "time lag." It is tacitly assumed, if not spelled out in so many words, that the world system is presently in the state of transformation. The potential problem is that *all* transformations are bound to throw the extant system (albeit temporarily) out of balance; some aspects change faster than others, thereby undermining the established equilibrium. More often than not, however, systems emerge from the time of trouble not only "alive" but reinvigorated and fitter, having found a new and on the whole higher level of equilibrium. The lagging sectors sooner or later "catch up" with those ahead, and mutual accommodation is reached through trial and error, infighting, reflection, and self-reflexive adjustment. Consequently, the present one-sidedness of globalizing trends is a transient, and probably short-lived, irritant. Political institutions of the day stuck in their disempowering territoriality can either follow the economic forces into the new ex-territorial space or be replaced by other arrangements, more nimble and swift, hence better fitted to the new game, which requires precisely such qualities. Economy might have escaped the net of political control, but a *new* net is bound to be constructed and fastened, made to the measure of economic globality.

This may be the case, although it is far from certain. The credibility of the "time lag" hypothesis would be much more solidly grounded were we sure that the first assumption—that the global system will be "like" the nation-state society, only bigger—held true; that assumption, however, cannot be tested, given the haziness of the "likeness" idea. Another equally tenable hypothesis is that the conjunction and coordination of the economic, military, and cultural aspects of systems under the aegis of political power, far from being the systems' "natural state" and the outcome of "equilibration," was itself a temporary expedient. This classic-modern solution to the problems of systemic self-perpetuation is not the only one conceivable, let alone final and irrevocable. Political control, without which the modern capitalist economy would never have taken off, could have by now served its purpose—much like the political management of culture that outlived its utility (indeed, its need) once the task of social integration-through-ideological-mobilization had been elbowed out by the massive coordination of conduct by market-guided seduction. It could be that the sovereign political agency, a necessary condition of systemic coordination at the nation-state level, has been cast as "dysfunctional" by the emergent global system. As a matter of fact, this hypothesis seems already to underlie much common thinking on the subject. We can recognize its presence whenever political leaders advise citizens to follow the example of stock shares and currencies and seek "their own level" at labor exchanges and to imitate the globe-trotting capital in sitting on their bikes, never going out without mobile telephones in their pockets.

Hobsbawm suggests one possible link between globalization of capital and political fragmentation of the globe: "the smaller the state, the weaker it is . . . [and] the less money it takes to buy a government." That small and weak states will not be in a position to resist, let alone stem, the erratic movements of capital is obvious—but not necessarily because of the corruption of ministers that Hobsbawm singles out. In fact, there is no evidence to suggest that the politicians of weak countries are less immune to corrupting temptations than are political figures of stronger countries. For capitalist globalization has radically changed the nature of the game. More often than not, it is not capitalists who need to bribe governments to let them enter countries they administer but governments that are obliged to bribe *them,* as an incentive to come and stay. It is the turn now of the "local administrators" to compete with each other in currying favors with nomadic capital by pump priming, subsidizing risky ventures, keeping the population under their rules submissive and meek, and being ready to clean the mess of ecological and social devastation left in peregrinating capital's wake. Local administrators must above all ingratiate themselves in the eyes of itinerant capital brokers, by vowing to suspend their traditional prerogatives and pursuing unswervingly the policy of "deregulation," thereby manifesting their determination to refrain from looking too closely into the ways business is conducted.

In his latest study David Cohen, Sorbonne economist, suggests that the relation between labor and "labor force" described a century and a half ago by Karl Marx has since been reversed.[6] In Marx's time capitalists paid their employees no more than the cost of "labor force," or the sum necessary to keep workers able to work another day and make the next generation of laborers fit for employment. In paying this sum, though, capitalists pushed to the limit the time and intensity of labor that employees were required to perform on the factory floor. Nowadays, companies pay employees the price of their work "in company time"—while making that time as "flexible" as possible—but require in exchange total individual dedication, scrapping the distinction between "private" and "company" time. This is, though, but the actuarial gloss on a profound departure in power relations.

What has actually happened is that the burden of "bringing results" has been shifted from the management of companies to the employees, who now must compete among themselves in proving to the company that they can do the job better than whoever might replace them. "It is no more the job of the company to monitor its workers. It is now up to each worker to convince the company that he does the job well," says Cohen—and not just well, I might add, but better than others who might take his place. It is now the perpetual insecurity, the permanently uninsured future that keeps employees in line and renders meticulous surveillance and fine-tuned normative regulation redundant. It is now the freezing winds of "perform or perish" competition that keeps them exercising—running the company's track twenty-four hours a day, seven days a week—thus making ideological indoctrination and old-fashioned supervision supererogatory.

The orthodox "Fordist factory," the panopticon-like style of domination, put the burden of "whipping employees into submission" on the managers. The latter prompted those on the receiving end to close ranks so that better conditions could be collectively negotiated or enforced. With flagellation replaced by self-flagellation, however, managerial exertions are less necessary, while "joining forces" and "standing arm to arm" in resisting managers' commands lose their force and purpose. As Alain Ehrenberg found out in his study of workplace psychology, the traditional anxieties caused by fear of authority figures have largely been replaced by depression prompted by the fear of missing the action, performing poorly, and finding oneself considered not "up to the challenge."[7]

What Cohen and Ehrenberg discovered while studying these rapidly changing labor relations has wider ramifications. Similar processes occur on every level and in every section of the social system, most notably in the relations between the local (fixed and stationary) authorities and global (unbridled and mobile) powers. These days, all domination tends to be a function of the freedom to move—above all, the freedom to move *on*. The centuries-old trend of the power of the "sedentary" over the "nomadic" has thus been reversed. It is now the lightly traveling and fast-moving nomads who are in command, and not just due to their hit-and-run capability. The dominated are kept in line not by fear of reprisals but by consternation that their masters may cut their losses, wind up operations, and move elsewhere. When faced with expertly mobile masters, unhampered by any of their material resources, the dominated have no other choice than to implore them to stay and continue operations. Workers must earn their bosses' favor by repetitive demonstrations of consent and obedience.

The ex-territoriality of globalized capital and trade is an instrument of domination, inasmuch as potential forces of resistance remain steadfastly *territorial*. The principal strategy of contemporary domination is the capacity (hence the threat) of *disengagement*. Houdini has taken the place of Big Brother. As long as the dominated remain divided (or even better, at each other's throats), there is little they can do to call the bluff of "escape threats," and even less to prevent another vanishing act. As Richard Rorty has put it, as long as "the bottom 95 per cent of the world's population" are kept "busy with ethnic and religious hostilities" and "distracted from their own despair[,] . . . the super-rich will have little to fear."[8]

Thus there are valid reasons to suppose that the coupling of the political, cultural, ethnic, and religious fragmentation of the world with the progressive globalization of economics is not, in fact, the outcome of uneven development. Nor is it a symptom of that temporary disequilibrium that, given the "inner logic" of self-equilibrating systems, is bound to be rectified sooner or later—principally, by politics and culture joining capital and commodities on their worldwide circuit, thanks to Internet and cellular-telephone linkups and the standardization of consumed objects and ways of consuming them. On the contrary, the coupling of fragmentation with globalization is a constitutive, organic feature of the emergent world system. Thus, far from rectifying the present political divisions, globalization in its current form may multiply and exacerbate them, making them more vigorous. As world capital and world trade go, politics and culture being out of step with economic power is perfectly "systemic-functional." Were Talcott Parsons to witness present change, he would no doubt list that disjunction among the principal "functional prerequisites" of the brave new world system.

It is clear that those who address the globalization of the "politics of humanity" cannot confine themselves to watching and recording "the developments," counting on history being "on their side," and hoping that despite the occasional stumbles a desirable outcome will eventuate of its own volition. To the contrary, they will have a fight on their hands, and the conditions under which this fight will take place do not augur well for the outcome.

Globalization of humanity is thus neither a "given" nor the impending product of historical or any other kind of inevitability—technological, informational, or "process-civilizational." It is a task to be undertaken and, given current global conditions, an imperative.

MULTICULTURALISM, OR THE IDEOLOGY OF FLAWED GLOBALIZATION

In a climate of uncertainty, the questions of which values are worthy of preservation and cultivation and in which direction they are to be pursued are constantly being posed. Nowadays, the most common answer offered by the learned and opinion-making classes is: those values and routes that promote multiculturalism. The same answer has become synonymous with political correctness; it requires no further justification. Indeed, it has become a kind of axiom, a prolegomena to all further deliberation, a cornerstone of *doxa*.

To put it in a nutshell: when the learned classes, those contemporary incarnations of modern intellectuals, invoke "multiculturalism," the subtext is: *Sorry, we cannot bail you out from the mess you are in.* Yes, we understand that there is some confusion about values, about the meaning(s) of "being human," and about the best ways of harmonious cohabitation; but it is up to you to sort it out in your own fashion and to bear the consequences, even if you are unhappy about what they might be. Yes, there is a babble of voices, and no tune is likely to be sung in unison, but do not worry; no tune is necessarily better than another, and even if it were, there would be no way of knowing. So feel free to sing—or compose, if you can—your own tune. It is unlikely that you will make the cacophony, which is already deafening, any more unbearable than it already is.

To his trenchant statement about the fatuity of the multiculturalist creed, Russell Jacoby gave the title "The End of Utopia."[9] There is a message in that title—our "learned classes" have no comprehensive or coherent vision of what the human condition should entail. For this reason they seek escape in multiculturalism or that "ideology of the end of ideology." To say "Multiculturalism Rules OK" is to avoid the question that one has neither the will nor the ability to answer.

Standing up to the status quo demands courage, given the awesome forces that prop it up. Yet courage is the very quality that intellectuals, once famous for their breadth of vision, yearning for transcendence and vociferously radical, have lost. Instead, they have adopted new roles as "niche" experts, academic boffins, and media celebrities. It would be tempting to take this updated *trahison des clercs* as an explanation of the learned classes' new meekness, resignation, and indifference.

Such a temptation needs to be resisted, however. More deep-seated reasons than the cold feet of the learned elite lie behind the latter's arrival at their present-day equanimity. Moreover, they have not made that journey alone; a similar disposition characterizes the ex-territorial economic powers, propounded by a society that encourages its members to be consumers rather than producers in an increasingly fluid, "liquidized," and "deregulated" modernity. Thus, in the course of their journey the learned classes have undergone transformations similar to those afflicting their fellow travelers. What they all shared was a tendency toward disengagement, the new strategy of power and domination standing out as a plausible explanation for the spectacular success of the "ideology of the end of ideology."

The modern intellectual was, traditionally, a man with a mission. His vocation was to assist in the "rerooting of the uprooted" (or, in present-day sociological parlance, the re-embedding of the disembedded). The process of achieving this end was split into two tasks.

The first task was to "enlighten the people." That meant fitting the disoriented and perplexed men and women, plucked out from the monotonous routine of the islands they inhabited from cradle to grave, with axiological gyroscopes and looking-glasses that enabled them to navigate the unfamiliar and turbulent waters of "great society." This demanded life skills of a kind they had never needed before, and had never had the chance to learn. "Enlightenment" involved sketching new itineraries and marking new orientation points; suggesting new life purposes, new loyalties and new standards of conformity; and forcing the abandonment of those standards provided by localities and groups to which the inexperienced navigators used to belong, and in which their lives used to be inscribed, until they came to be defunct, ceased to be held firmly enough, or otherwise fell into disuse.

The other task was to assist the job undertaken by the legislators. This meant the design and construction of well-built and well-mapped settings to make navigation possible and effective, as well as purposive. This would then confer shape on the temporarily amorphous "mass" and bring about "social order"—or, more precisely, an "orderly society."

Both tasks derived from the same major undertaking of modern revolution—construction of the state-and-nation, or rather nation-state, an imagined but nonetheless tightly integrated society. What the two tasks also have in common was that they both required a direct, face-to-face confrontation of all its agents with the bodies and souls of the objects of the great transformation taking place. Both required a panopticon-style closeness of supervisor and supervised, guide and guided—the first as unfree to move as the second, and neither able to turn its back on the other.

Indeed, building modern industry came down to the challenge of transplanting producers from the traditional family, parish, or guild-bound routine into a different one, designed and administered by factory owners and their hired supervisors. Building the modern state consisted in replacing the old loyalties held for people nearby and close at hand with the new, citizen-style loyalties to the abstract and distant totality of the nation and the laws of the land. These new loyalties, unlike the old, obsolete ones, could not rely on spontaneous and matter-of-fact mechanisms of self-reproduction; they had to be carefully designed and painstakingly instilled through the process of organized mass education. Constructing and servicing the modern order thus required managers and teachers. The era of state and nation building had to be, and was, a time of direct engagement between rulers and ruled.

As I have argued before, this is no longer the case, or at least it is much less so. Ours is a time of disengagement. The traditional model of domination, with its ubiquitous point-blank surveillance and hour-by-hour monitoring and manipulation of conduct, is being rapidly dismantled and replaced by self-surveillance and self-monitoring of the dominated—as effective in eliciting the "right" (system-functional) type of behavior as the old strategy of direct domination, and considerably less costly.

I suggest that the multiculturalists' "ideology of the end of ideology" can best be interpreted as an intellectual gloss on the human condition, shaped under the impact of the new system of domination and operated by the new style of power-through-disengagement. Multiculturalism is a way for the learning classes to adjust their roles to these new realities. It is a manifesto

of reconciliation, of surrendering to the new realities rather than challeng-
ing or contesting them. It amounts to letting "things"—human subjects,
their choices, and the fate that follows them—"take their own course." It
is also a product of mimicry. The world where disengagement is the principal strategy of power is replicated in the withdrawal of previous arbiters
of value from the messy battleground of value contestation. If these new
realities are not questioned and are assumed to permit no alternative, such
replication comes easy; it is the "natural" thing to do, drawing support from
both rationality and common sense. It is only when such an attitude is taken
that multiculturalism holds water.

Indeed, if society has no preference apart from the preference that human beings, either individually or collectively, make their own preferences,
then there is no way of knowing whether one preference is better than another. Commenting on Charles Taylor's call to accept and respect the differences of communally chosen cultures, Fred Constant observed that
pursuing such a call has a two-pronged effect: the right to be different is
acknowledged, together with the right to *indifference*.[10] Let me add that
while the right to difference is conceded to others, as a rule those granting
such entitlement claim for themselves the right to stay indifferent—to ab-
stain from judgment. When mutual tolerance is coupled with indifference,
divergent forms of life are called to live alongside each other but not to talk,
lest the debate degenerate into a quarrel. But forms of life unused to de-
bating tend to use the barrel of a gun instead of a telephone, and so the
warning becomes a self-fulfilling prophecy. Different forms of life may co-
exist in the world of multiculturalism, but this does not necessarily mean
they will benefit from any shared life.

Constant asks the crucial question: is cultural pluralism a value in its own
right, or does its value derive from the suggestion (and hope) that it may
improve the quality of shared existence? It is not immediately clear which
of the two the multiculturalist program prefers. The question is far from
rhetorical and does not determine the choice between answers, unless it can
be determined what is actually meant by the "right to difference." There
are two possible interpretations, with starkly different consequences.

One interpretation implies the solidarity of the explorers. While we have
all, singly or collectively, embarked on the search for the best form of humanity—of which we hope to avail ourselves, eventually—each of us explores a different avenue and obtains from that exploration different
discoveries. None of the discoveries can be a priori declared worthless; no
genuine, earnest effort to find the best shape of common humanity can be
dismissed in advance as misguided and undeserving of sympathetic attention. On the contrary, the variety of findings increases the chance that fewer
human possibilities will be overlooked and remain untried. Each finding
may benefit all explorers, whatever roads they have chosen for themselves.
It does not mean, however, that all findings are of equal value; what value

each of them contains can be established only through a long dialogue, in which all voices are allowed to be heard and bona fide, well-intentioned comparisons can be made. In other words, admitting cultural variety is the *beginning,* not the end. It is but a starting point to the political process, one that promises to be long and tortuous but that has the potential, finally, to be beneficial to all.

This dilemma is secreted within another hugely popular notion—human rights, widely understood as the natural and indispensable accompaniment to the multiculturalist program. It is the nature of "human rights" that although they are meant to be exercised *separately*—in the sense of the entitlement to have one's own difference recognized, without fear of reprimand or punishment—they must be fought for, and can only be granted, *collectively.* Hence the zeal for "boundary erecting": in order to become a "right," difference must be shared by a group or a category of individuals, who then have a stake in collective vindications. The struggle for and the apportioning of individual rights result in intense community building—in digging trenches, and training and arming assault units. Being different becomes a value in its own right, a quality worth fighting for and preserving at all cost. It is also a clarion call to close ranks, stand firm, or march in step. First, however, the difference must be *recognized*—that is, a difference must be found or construed that is fit to be acknowledged as an entitlement to claims under the "human rights" rubric. It is clear, then, that the principle of "human rights" is a catalyst for the production and self-perpetuation of difference.

Like the multiculturalist program, the principle of human rights makes apparent a political dilemma. Genuine political process—dialogue and negotiation, aimed at a predetermined resolution—would be preempted and rendered all but unfeasible if the superiority of some contenders and the inferiority of others were assumed from the start. But it would also grind to a premature halt if the *other* interpretation of cultural plurality were to prevail—namely, the assumption that the multiculturalist program holds, either overtly or tacitly, that each extant difference is worthy of perpetuation just by dint of its being a difference.

Charles Taylor rightly rejects that second interpretation: "[A] proper respect for equality requires more than a presumption that further study will make us see things this way, but actual judgments of equal worth applied to the customs and creations of these different cultures. . . . In this form, the demand for equal recognition is unacceptable." But then Taylor makes his refusal contingent on the assertion that the question of the relative worth of cultural choices is a matter for scientific experts and needs to be left to *further study:* "The last thing one wants at this stage from Eurocentered intellectuals is positive judgments of the worth of cultures that they have not intensively studied." Recognition of value stays firmly with the intellectuals, notwithstanding their present refusal to bother with this kind of task. True to the nature of academic professions, it would be as wrong as it is bizarre to expect a considered judgment without a "study project," first designed and then seen through *sine ira et studio*. "On examination, either we will find something of great value in culture C, or we will not." It is "we," however, the incumbents of academic offices, who are entitled to call a finding a finding. Taylor reproaches the advocates of the "anything goes" kind of multiculturalism for betraying their academic vocation, whereas he would be more to the point to censure them for shirking the duties of *homo politicus*—the member of the polity that fast becomes global, turning its members into potential *Weltbürger*.

Taylor goes on to suggest that in case we do not know (or do not believe we know) that a certain cultural form is worthy in and of itself, hence worthy of perpetuation, no doubt should remain that the difference needs to be maintained and preserved for the future; thus the rights of living individuals, who are able to make such choices as might jeopardize the future of that difference, need to be restrained. By obliging its residents to send children to francophone schools, Quebec—not at all an exotic or mysterious case but "thoroughly studied and known"—provides Taylor with the pattern for what can (or should) be done in such a case:

> It is not just the matter of having the French language available to those who might choose it. . . . [I]t also involves making sure that there is a community of people here in the future that will want to avail itself of the opportunity to use the French language. Policies aimed at survival actively seek to *create* members of the community, for instance, in their assuring that future generations continue to identify as French speakers.[11]

Quebec is a "soft" (some might say innocuous) case, which makes the supposition of its propriety that much easier to accept. The validity of the case would be more difficult to sustain were another example of cultural distinction-cum-separation invoked, one that unlike the French (or any other) language, we "Eurocentered intellectuals" could more readily despise and keep at arm's length, hiding behind the insufficient funding of research projects. The legitimacy of generalization seems much less convincing when we recall that the French language in the Quebecois case is just one of a whole series of claims, and a particularly benign one at that. Other, more malignant measures tend to be used by communities all over the world to keep their memberships high and to maintain their separateness from other communities; they range from female circumcision to ritual headdress for schoolchildren. Recalling this, we may be more ready to accept that even as we resent past state-administered assimilatory or community-pulverizing pressures and cultural crusades, and respect the right of communities to protect themselves from such forces, we must also recognize the right of the individual to protect against choice-preventing or choice-denying communal pressures. The two rights are notoriously difficult even to reconcile, let alone address simultaneously. The question that confronts us, and that we must deal with on a daily basis, is how to proceed when these two rights clash. Which of the two rights is strong enough to prevail, to annul or set aside the demands of the other?

Replying to Charles Taylor's interpretation of the right to recognition, Jürgen Habermas brings into the debate another value, the "democratic constitutional state," which is largely absent from Taylor's argument. If we agree that the recognition of cultural variety is the right and proper starting point for all sensible discussion of the shared meaning of humanity, we should also agree that the "constitutional state" is the sole framework in which such a debate can be conducted.

To make clearer what is involved in the notion, I would prefer to replace the phrase "constitutional state" with that of "republic," or better still, that of "autonomous society" (following Cornelius Castoriadis). Autonomous society is inconceivable without the autonomy of its members; a republic is inconceivable without the well-entrenched rights of the individual citizen. This consideration does not necessarily resolve the issue of conflicting communal and individual rights, but it does make it clear that without the democratic practice of free-to-self-assert individuals, that issue cannot be addressed with any degree of justice, let alone resolved. Protection of the individual from demands to conform, voiced in a community name, may not be a task "naturally" superior to that of the community's bid for survival in its separate identity. But the protection of the individual/citizen of the republic from both anticommunal *and* communal pressures is the preliminary condition for performing any one of these antithetical yet complementary tasks.

As Habermas puts it:

> A correctly understood theory of rights requires a politics of recognition that protects the integrity of the individual in the life contexts in which his or her identity is formed. . . . All that is required is the consistent actualization of the system of rights. There would be little likelihood of this, of course, without social movements and political struggles. . . . [T]he process of actualizing rights is indeed embedded in contexts that require such discourses as an important component of politics—discussion about a shared conception of the good and a desired form of life that is acknowledged to be authentic.[12]

Universality of citizenship is the preliminary condition for any meaningful "politics of recognition." Let me add that universality of humanity is the horizon by which all politics of recognition, to be meaningful, needs to orient itself. Universality of humanity does not stand in opposition to the pluralism of different forms of human life, but the test of a truly universal humanity is the ability to accommodate pluralism and make it serve the cause of humanity—to enable and encourage an ongoing discussion about the shared conception of the good. As Jeffrey Weeks poignantly puts it, the argument about common values that we seek requires "the enhancement of life-chances, and the maximization of human freedom": "There is no privileged social agent to attain the ends: merely the multiplicity of local struggles against the burden of history and the various forms of domination and subordination. Contingency, not determinism, underlies our complex present."[13]

The vision of indeterminacy is doubtlessly daunting, but it can also mobilize forces to a greater effort. One possible response to it is "ideology of the end of ideology" and the practice of disengagement. Another response, equally reasonable but much more promising, is the assumption that at no other time has the keen search for common humanity, and the practice that follows such an assumption, been as urgent and imperative as it is now.

But what might such "practice that follows the assumption of common humanity" actually look like? Indeed, what would a practice that *results in* common humanity consist in?

THE STRATEGY OF HUMANITY BUILDING

Fred Constant quotes Amin Maalouf, a Franco-Lebanese writer settled in France, on the subject of the reactions of "ethnic minorities" or immigrants to the crisscrossing cultural pressures to which they are exposed in their countries of arrival. Maalouf's conclusion is that the more immigrants feel that their original cultural lore is respected in their new home, and the less they feel resented, threatened, or otherwise discriminated against for their different identity, the more willingly they will open themselves to cultural offers of the new country and be inclined to relinquish their own separate ways.

For the prospects of cross-cultural dialogue, this is a crucial insight. It points once more to the close relation between, on the one hand, the degree of security enjoyed and, on the other, the "defusion" of the issue of cultural plurality, the overcoming of cultural separation and willing participation in the search for common humanity. It brings us face to face with the issue of "recognition," another problematic concept at the center of the multiculturalist vision. In its popular guise, the concept glosses over the politically crucial opposition between what might be called "positive" and "negative" recognition (parallels might be seen in the opposition between solidarity and tolerance, or even that between engagement and disengagement).

Negative recognition consists in, and usually stops at, the "let it be" stance: you are given the right to be what you are, free of any pressure to "acculturate" or "assimilate." In stark opposition to the nation-state building era of "solid" modernity, there are no cultural crusades or missionaries, and no demands are made for conversion. Negative recognition by itself comes down to tolerance of otherness. It is a stance of indifference and detachment rather than sympathetic benevolence: let them be, let them bear the consequences of who they are. The small print is that anyone who demands recognition should calculate the risks; insisting on difference and refusing to compromise may have to be paid for with distributive drawbacks. In the competition for resources and rewards, "being different" may well prove to be a liability, even if discrimination is formally outlawed.

If this does not make negative recognition seem unappealing, there is another, more compelling reason why groups or categories demanding acknowledgement of their separate identity would not settle for such recognition: just "being tolerated" does not endow the identity being proclaimed with the comforting and healing faculties desired for it. The cognitive frame in which tolerance is granted is utterly at odds with the frame in which it is sought and received. Tolerance is granted in the spirit—joyfully or resignedly embraced, as the case may be—of *relativism*. Those who grant tolerance for a way of life different from their own do not consider it important enough to wage a war over, or they suspect that the war is either lost before it starts or is too costly to undertake. For one reason or another, they "agree to disagree." Yet their agreement more often than not is unilateral—a contradiction in terms, as agreements go—and so the truce is likely to be observed by one side only. The act of tolerance diminishes, rather than magnifies, the identity's importance. For those fighting for recognition, this importance is the most precious and avidly desired part of the struggle, indeed, the prime cause of going to war. As Nicholas Lobkowitz has convincingly argued, since the tolerant are relativists, whether overtly or implicitly, the gift they offer to the seekers of recognition is always tainted. It is something unattractive, and hence unwanted.[14]

Unlike the tolerance givers, the seekers of recognition are essentialists or fundamentalists. Whatever formula they might use to match the prevailing mood, the better to serve their cause (e.g., paying lip service to the principle of equality), the difference for which they seek recognition is not one of many, equal among equals. It is a quality not just precious in its own right but endowed with a unique value lacking in other forms of life. Perhaps it is even *superior* to other such forms as could be adopted without concern for their recognition, which would not even raise the issue of recognition were the possessors of difference permitted, and were willing and able, to practice it in matter-of-fact ways. Only a difference endowed with a unique status would meet the bill issued to the postulated identity.

Thus it is *positive* recognition that is on a par with the purpose of war. Such recognition ensures those who seek it against the unduly high costs of staying different endorses the intrinsic value of difference and sustains the dignity that it bestows on its bearers. Positive recognition is expected to fulfill all these ends (and converts liabilities into assets) by tying the postulate of recognition to *distributive* justice. "Positive recognition," unlike its negative counterpart, prepares the way for "positive discrimination" and "affirmative action," and subsidizes the cultivation of identity. It augurs, in short, an entitlement to preferential treatment and to winning extra points on the ground of being different from the rest. Distributive justice is thus the natural sequel to the war of recognition; the latter is incomplete until it finds fulfillment in the former.

Nancy Fraser was right, therefore, when she complained about the "widespread decoupling of the cultural politics of difference from the social politics of equality," insisting instead that "justice today requires *both* redistribution *and* recognition": "It is unjust that some individuals and groups are denied the status of full partners in social interaction simply as a consequence of institutionalized patterns of cultural value in whose construction they have not equally participated and which disparage their distinctive characteristics or the distinctive characteristics assigned to them."[15]

I have indicated before that the logic of the war of recognition presses the combatants to absolutize the difference; there is a difficult-to-eradicate fundamentalist streak in any recognition claim, which makes its demands (in Fraser's terminology) "sectarian." Shifting the question of recognition from a context of "self-realization" to one of social justice has a detoxifying effect: the poison of sectarianism, with its consequences of social separation, communication breakdown and self-perpetuating hostilities, is extracted from the sting of recognition claims. The recognition of difference is stopped short, on the verge of the relativist precipice. If recognition is defined as the right to equal participation in social interaction, and if that right is conceived in its turn as a matter of social justice, it does not follow (quoting Fraser once again) that "everyone has an equal right to social esteem" (i.e., all values are equal and each difference is worthy just by being different) but only that "everybody has an equal right to pursue social esteem under fair conditions of equal opportunity." Cast in the framework of self-assertion and "self-realization," recognition wars lay bare their agnostic (and, as recent experience has shown, ultimately genocidal) potential; returned to the problematics of social justice, where they belong, recognition claims and policies become a recipe for dialogue and democratic participation.

All this is not, I suggest, a question of philosophical hair-splitting, nor is it just philosophical elegance or theoretical convenience that is at stake. The blend of distributive justice with the policy of recognition is, one might say, a natural sequel to the modern promise of social justice under conditions of "liquid modernity," or, as Jonathan Friedman aptly put it, "modernity without modernism." This era, says Bruno Latour, indicates reconciliation to the prospect of perpetual coexistence—hence it is a condition that meets, more than anything else, the art of peaceful and humane cohabitation, an era that can no longer entertain (or wish to entertain) the hope of a radical, one-fell-swoop eradication of human misery, followed by a conflict-and-suffering-free human condition. If the idea of the "good society" is to retain any meaning in the liquid-modernity setting, it may only be to allude, first, to a society able to "give everyone a chance"; and second, to remove, one by one, all obstacles preventing chances from being taken up, as successive impediments become known and are brought to attention by successive recognition claims. Not every difference has the same value, and some ways of life and of living together are superior to others—but there is no way of finding out which is which, unless each one is given equal opportunity to argue its case.

The politically uncontrolled globalization of dependencies does not bring this condition anywhere near fulfilment. In fact, it actually *undermines* the chance of its being fulfilled, by setting in motion a global process of unprecedented polarization of living conditions that deprives a large and growing section of humanity of the prospect of transforming their individuality de jure (individuality as necessity to self-assert) into individuality de facto (individuality as capacity for self-assertion). Arresting and reversing the process of polarization requires more than recognition of difference; talk of dignity is empty unless it is takes into consideration the conditions under which human choices are made, or are prevented from being made. Richard Rorty hits the nail on the head when he castigates the "culturalist left" for shunning all talk about money and income inequalities. The most passionate debates about difference-recognition will not advance the cause of humanity a single inch if, as Loïc Wacquant calculates, the incomes of company directors that, ten years ago, were forty-two times bigger than those of blue-collar workers are today 419 times bigger, and if 95 percent of the $1.1 trillion surplus generated between 1977 and 1996 has been appropriated by the top 5 percent richest Americans.[16]

In the era of globalization, the politics of humanity and the cause of humanism face the most fateful steps they have made in their long history. If those steps are to be taken, the ancient issues of human equality and social justice need to be raised to unprecedented new heights, instead of being declared null and void, obsolete, or "counterproductive." The latter charges have been made by the theory and practice of market liberalism, which jointly service the present-day separation of power from politics and the new structure of world domination, construed and perpetrated by the strategy of disengagement. Recognition of human rights and equality of conditions under which those rights are acted upon are inseparable.

No one has done better than Richard Rorty in sketching out the road that needs to be taken, and cannot but be taken, if the cause of humanity is to meet the challenge (and take up the chance) of the era of globalization:

> We should raise our children to find it intolerable that we who sit behind desks and punch keyboards are paid ten times as much as people who get their hands dirty cleaning our toilets, and a hundred times as much as those who fabricate our keyboards in the Third World. We should ensure that they worry about the fact that the countries that have industrialized first have a hundred times the wealth of those that have not yet industrialized. Our children need to learn, early on, to see the inequalities between their own fortunes and those of other children as neither the Will of God nor the necessary price for economic efficiency, but as an inevitable tragedy. They should start thinking, as early as possible, about how the world might be changed so as to ensure that no one goes hungry while others have a surfeit.[17]

NOTES

1. Ulrich Beck, *World Risk Society* (Cambridge: Polity Press, 1999), 3, 36.

2. Michael Allan Gillespie, "The Theological Origins of Modernity," *Critical Review* 13, nos. 1, 2 (1999), 1–30.

3. See Jürgen Habermas, "Bestialität und Humanität: Ein Krieg in der Grenze zwischen Recht und Moral," in *Die Zeit,* 29 April 1999. Translated by Stephen Maver and William E. Scheuerman as "Bestiality and Humanity: A War on the Border between Legality and Morality," *Constellations* (September 1999), 263–72.

4. Eric Hobsbawm, "The Nation and Globalization," *Constellations* (March 1998), 4–5.

5. Christian Delacampagne, *La philosophie politique aujourd'hui* (Paris: Seuil, 2000), 165.

6. Daniel Cohen, *Nos temps modernes* (Paris: Flammarion, 1999), 60.

7. Alain Ehrenberg, *La fatigue d'être soi* (Paris: Odile Jacob, 1998).

8. Richard Rorty, *Achieving Our Country* (Cambridge, Mass.: Harvard University Press, 1998), 88.

9. See Russell Jacoby, *The End of Utopia: Politics and Culture in an Age of Apathy* (New York: Basic Books, 1999).

10. Fred Constant, *Levinas multiculturalisme* (Paris: Flammarion 2000), 89–94.

11. Charles Taylor, "The Policy of Recognition," in *Multiculturalism,* ed. Amy Gutman (Princeton, N.J.: Princeton University Press, 1994), 88–89, 98–99.

12. Jürgen Habermas, "Struggles for Recognition in the Democratic Constitutional Regime," in *Multiculturalism,* ed. Gutman, 113, 125.

13. Jeffrey Weeks, "Rediscovering Values," in *Principled Positions,* ed. Judith Squires (London: Lawrence and Wishart, 1993), 208–9.

14. According to Lobkowitz, the question of "how to be tolerant without succumbing to relativism" is nowadays the most daunting issue democracy has confronted. See Nicholas Lobkowitz, "Remarks on Tolerance," in *The Crossroads of European Culture 1999: Responsibilities and Hopes,* ed. JiY´i Fuka´, Zden´k Chlup, Alena Mizerova, and Alena Schauerova (Brno: Vitium Press, 1999), 173–77.

15. Nancy Fraser, "Social Justice in the Age of Identity Politics: Redistribution, Recognition, and Participation," in *Kritische Theorie der Gegenwart,* ed. Detlev Claussen and Michael Werz (Hannover, Ger.: Institut für Soziologie an der Universität Hannover, 1999), 37–60.

16. Loïc Wacquant, *Les prisons de la misère* (Paris: Raisons d'Agir, 1999), 69–70.

17. Richard Rorty, "Failed Prophecies, Glorious Hopes," in *Philosophy and Social Hope* (Harmondsworth: Penguin, 1999), 203–4.

11

Value, Justice, and the Wilderness Ideal

John O'Neill

Environmentalism, especially as it has developed in the new world contexts of the United States and Australia, often centers on a defense of "wilderness" and "nature," understood as that which is untouched by human interference. Our environmental crisis is presented as one of "the end of nature," understood as the disappearance of a world that is not affected by human intention. "An idea, a relationship, can go extinct just like an animal or a plant. The idea in this case is 'nature,' the separate and wild province, the world apart from man to which he has adapted, under whose rules he was born and died."[1] For the deep Green movement, "nature" and "wilderness" are the central normative categories of the environmental movement.

These attitudes are not confined to explicitly deep Green radicals. Something of them pervades the nature conservation movement. Natural landscapes, pristine and untouched by the marks of human beings, form the primary objects of appreciation. This is sometimes expressed in quasi-scientific terms—for example, in references to landscapes that exhibit "ecological integrity," characterized by states that show only minimal human intervention. It is also expressed in aesthetic and moral terms by reference to the experience of wilderness. Correspondingly, "cultural landscapes," particularly those transformed by human labor, are characterized as second-best landscapes that have environmental value only to the extent to which they approximate "the real thing." Thus one finds talk of "semi-natural" landscapes as landscapes of particular value. One does not find reference to "semicultural" landscapes. Where cultural landscapes are introduced they are often taken to have value for more humanistic reasons that do not properly fall under an environmental or nature conservation ethic—say, to do with reasons of cultural identity.

This attitude is often accompanied among European conservationists by something of an inferiority complex—there is very little, if any, "wilderness" in Europe. It is often accompanied, for the visiting deep ecologist, by incredulity at the ways in which landscapes in Europe are managed. Here, for example, is a comment from Richard Sylvan on his visit to the Three Peaks area of the Yorkshire Dales in the United Kingdom:

> [T]he Three Peaks district is now prized for its recreational values, it is prized for its *comparative remoteness and wilderness,* its fewness of people and absence of industry, for the walks and wild meadows it offers. But it is a landscape far removed from its *pre-agricultural original.* It has been almost totally *stripped of its native vegetation,* and most habitats and much of *its ecology destroyed, the remainder substantially modified,* in the former quest . . . for agricultural advantage and optimal, or often excessive, grazing usage. The district remains starkly treeless. . . . But woods, formerly with different wildlife, there formerly were, as a tiny protected strip at Colt Park pleasantly testifies. Most of the district still remains overrun by, and severely eroded by, sheep, which none but subsidized and distorted market system would support. Remarkably, however, there appears little pressure for economic adjustment and ecological restoration, for removal of some sheep and return of more woods. Many recreationalists appear to prefer impoverished grasslands, treelessness. Even environmental organisations like English Nature own sheep and lease out lands for sheep grazing.[2]

What is notable here, as the passages I have emphasized here indicate, is that the ideal by which landscapes are to be judged is the unmodified "pre-agricultural original." It is an ideal of nature independent of human intervention that forms the standard from which others are judged.

Two lines of criticism are often offered in response to this line of argument. The first is from a variety of constructivists who deny there is something called "nature" to be defended. To take a few examples:

"Nature per se does not exist. . . . Nature is only the name given to a certain contemporary state of science."[3]

"It is fair to say that before the word was invented, there was no nature."[4]

"We have no basis for distinguishing between Nature and our own changing historically produced representations of nature. . . . Nature is a cultural product."[5]

"There is nothing outside the text."[6]

This constructivist line has often been used against appeals to nature and wilderness by environmentalists.[7] The second line of criticism is that developed in the environmental justice movement and concerns the role of appeals to "nature" and "wilderness" in the appropriation of land of often socially marginal populations, in particular their control and exclusion for the creation of "nature parks."[8]

These two lines of argument, from constructivism and from justice, are often found together. They are, however, logically independent. My own view is that the second line of argument is broadly right, and my main purpose in this chapter will be to contribute to it by placing recent appeals to "wilderness" in the context of a longer history of use of wilderness to justify the appropriation of land. However, the first line of argument has, I think, more problems. While there may be good reasons for believing we should start with cultural rather than natural landscapes in environmental valuation, I do not think that strong forms of constructivism of the kind expressed in the passages above are defensible. In developing those doubts I examine what survives of modern environmentalism after proper criticism of the wilderness ideal.

WILDERNESS PROTECTION: POLITICAL PROBLEMS

The appeal to wilderness to appropriate land is not new to political argument. It has a long history in social and political thought. Indeed, that history points to part of the problem with the wilderness ideal in deep Green environmentalism. Two initial points need to be made here. First, the image of much of the "new world" as wilderness relies upon a colonial perception of European colonial settlers of an unspoiled pristine terrain dramatically different from the domesticated environments of Europe. Second, this image was associated with claims that were made for the justifiable appropriation of that land from its native population. Both points are illustrated well in the work of Locke and the characterization of America as wilderness.

Consider Locke's comparisons of the "wild woods and uncultivated waste of America left to Nature without any improvement, tillage or husbandry"[9] with the improved and cultivated lands of the Britain and his corresponding account of the original appropriation of land:

> Whatsoever he tilled and reaped, laid up and made use of, before it spoiled, that was his particular Right; the Cattle, and Product was also his. But if either the Grass of his Inclosure rotted on the Ground, or the Fruit of his planting perished without gathering, and laying up, this part of the Earth, notwithstanding his Inclosure, was still to be looked on as Waste, and might be the Possession of any other.[10]

Locke's references to the "wild woods and uncultivated waste of America left to Nature without any improvement, tillage or husbandry" needs to be read in its historical context. It formed part of the denial of rights in land to the Aboriginal population.

Locke, through the patronage of the earl of Shaftesbury, was the secretary to the Lord Proprietors of Carolina and the Council of Trade and Plantations.

Locke's theory of property was shaped by the arguments of colonialists for an ethical justification to appropriate the land of the Native American population, particularly a justification that appealed to the rational use of land that had remained wild and unimproved. Subsequently appeal was made to Locke's arguments to justify further appropriation of native land.[11] Locke's justification of private property in land, given the Christian premise of original common ownership, is voiced in terms of appropriation through cultivation and enclosure.[12]

> God, who hath given the world to men in common, hath also given them reason to make use of it to the best advantage of Life, and convenience. . . . And though all the Fruits it naturally produces, and Beasts it feeds, belong to Mankind in common, . . . yet being given for the use of Men, there must of necessity be a means *to appropriate* them some way or other before they can be of any use, or at all beneficial, to any particular Man. The Fruit or Venison which nourishes the wild *Indian,* who knows no Inclosure, and is still a Tenant in common, must be his.[13]

To claim that the "wild *Indian* who knows no Inclosure" is still a tenant of the common is to deny his claims to the land. Indigenous populations had rights only to what they had appropriated through their labor, and given the European image of them as hunters and gatherers that Locke reiterates here, appropriation extended only to what they caught and collected. The land being "a wilderness," uncultivated and unenclosed, the "vacant places of *America*" could be rightfully settled by Europeans without the consent of previous inhabitants or with their having "reasons to complain"—"God gave the World to Men in Common, but . . . it cannot be supposed He meant it should always remain common and uncultivated. He gave it to the use of the Industrious and Rational (and *Labour* was to be *his Title* to it)."[14]

The right to the original acquisition of land is subject in Locke's theory to two well-known limiting provisos, that its produce not spoil and that there be good enough left for others. Both provisos are overcome through the introduction of money, which can be hoarded without spoiling, and which, through commerce, serves to foster the improvement of agriculture and hence "to increase the common stock of mankind."[15] The appropriation of America is justified by its being brought into the world of commerce and hence cultivation. It is the absence of money and commerce that explains the lack of productive appropriation of the land in America:

> What would a Man value Ten Thousand, or an Hundred Thousand Acres of excellent *Land* . . . in the middle of the in-land Parts of *America*, where he had no hopes of Commerce with other Parts of the World, to draw *Money* to him by the Sale of the Product? It would not be worth the Inclosing, and we should see him give up again to the wild Common of Nature, whatever was more

than would supply the Conveniences of Life, to be had there for him and his
Family. . . . Thus, in the beginning, all the World was *America*, and more so
than that is now; for no such thing as Money was anywhere known.[16]

By being brought into the world of commerce the wild common of
America, uncultivated by the indigenous population is turned into a productive resource cultivated by the industrious and rational.

The Lockean account of the "vast wilderness" of America as land uncultivated and unshaped by the pastoral activities of the indigenous population formed part of the justification for the appropriation of native land.
It is also false. The land had been shaped by its native populations. However, it is a myth that has survived and has led to conservation management
policies that ignore the impact of indigenous pastoral and agricultural activities. The problems are evident in the well-discussed problems in the history of the management of one of the great symbols of American wilderness,
Yosemite National Park. In their influential report *Wildlife Management
in the National Parks,* the Leopold Committee recommended that the goal
of management be to maintain or recreate the biotic associations "as nearly
as possible in the condition that prevailed when the area was first visited
by the white man. A national park should represent a vignette of primitive
America."[17]

What was that "primitive" condition? Here is their report of the first
white visitors to the area: "When the forty niners poured over the Sierra
Nevada into California, those who kept diaries spoke almost to a man of
the wide-space columns of mature trees that grew on the lower western
slope in gigantic magnificence. The ground was a grass parkland, in spring-
time carpeted with wildflowers. Deer and bears were abundant."[18] However, the "grass parkland" was in part the result of the pastoral practices
of the indigenous people, who had used fire to promote pastures for game
and black oak for acorn. After the Ahwahneechee Indians were driven from
their lands in 1851, "Indian style" burning techniques were discontinued
and fire-suppression controls introduced. The consequence was the decline
in meadowlands under increasing areas of bush. When the Totuya, the
granddaughter of chief Tenaya and survivor of the Ahwahneechee Indians
who had been evicted from the valley, returned in 1929, she remarked on
the landscape she found—"Too dirty; too much bushy." Moreover, in the
giant sequoia groves the growth of litter on the forest floor and competi-
tive vegetation inhibited the growth of new sequoia and threatened more
destructive fires. Following the Leopold report, both cutting and burning
were used to "restore" Yosemite to its "primitive" state.

The shift from the land management policies embodied in the Leopold
report and those found in the work of Locke reflects a change in attitudes
to wilderness. The wilderness ideal is historically a local one. It is uncultivated land that the environmentalist now attempts to protect, not the

cultivated landscapes that Locke praises. The dominant perceptions of land and landscapes have shifted. Recent environmental thought has echoed Mill's Romanticist-influenced observation about the limits of agricultural expansion.

> It is not good for man to be kept perforce at all times in the presence of his species. A world from which solitude is extirpated is a very poor ideal. Solitude, in the sense of being often alone, is essential to any depth of meditation or of character; and solitude in the presence of natural beauty and grandeur is the cradle of thoughts and aspirations which are not only good for the individual, but which society could ill do without. Nor is there much satisfaction in contemplating the world with nothing left to the spontaneous activity of nature; with every rood of land brought into cultivation, which is capable of growing food for human beings; every flowery waste or natural pasture ploughed up, all quadrupeds or birds which are not domesticated for man's use exterminated as his rivals for food, every hedgerow or superfluous tree rooted out, and scarcely a place left where a wild shrub or flower could grow without being eradicated as a weed in the name of improved agriculture.[19]

It is something like Mill's post-Romantic vision that informs the modern environmental movement.

The problem with this wilderness ideal is that it is not just an historically local perception that was associated with the appropriation of land. It is also socially and geographically local as well, and it retains its link with appropriation. However, the appropriation is now made in the name of wilderness rather than cultivation. It is invoked in the creation of "nature parks" for the new eco-tourism, at home and abroad, which is premised on the assumption that nature requires at least the absence of human activity and at best the absence of people. It has led to policies of exclusion and control of the indigenous human populations on grounds that they do cultivate and shape the land—thus the development of conservation parks in the third world through the eviction of the indigenous populations that had previously lived there. In Africa, consider the fate of some of the Masai, who have been excluded from national parks across Kenya and Tanzania.[20] Attempts to evict indigenous populations from the Kalahari reveal the influence of the same wilderness model: "Under Botswana land use plans, all national parks have to be free of human and domestic animals."[21]

The history of exclusion is illustrated in the conflicts surrounding the Batwa in Uganda. "Officially" excluded from forest reserves during the British colonial period of the 1930s, in practice they continued to use forests as a means to livelihood. Since the establishment of national parks in 1991, their exclusion was made effective, which has led to continuing conflicts.[22] Similar stories are to be found in Asia, where the alliance of local elites and international conservation bodies has led to similar pressures to evict indigenous populations from their traditional lands. In India, the development of wildlife parks has led to a series of conflicts with indigenous populations; there has been a series of much discussed evictions and resettlements of local populations in the creation of parks and sanctuaries. Consider for example the resettlements of Maldheris in the Gir National Park,[23] the proposed and actual exclusions of local populations in the Melghat Tiger Reserve and Koyna Sanctuary in Maharashtra, and the conflicts around the Nagarhole National Park, where there have been moves from the Karnataka Forest Department to remove six thousand tribal people from their forests on the grounds that they compete with tigers for game.[24] The moves are supported by international conservation bodies. Hence the remark of one of the experts for the Wildlife Conservation Society in the Nagarhole case: "Relocating tribal or traditional people who live in these protected area is the single most important step towards conservation."[25]

The control and exclusion of populations is a theme that runs through much anthropological work on the environment. Consider the comment from a person in the Makala-Barun National Park and Conservation Area in Nepal reported by Ben Campbell: "This park is no good. They don't let you cut wood, they don't allow you to make spaces for paddy seed-beds, they don't permit doing *khoriya* [a form of slash-and-burn agriculture]."[26] The wilderness model fails to acknowledge the ways parks act not as wilderness but as home for native inhabitants, the degree to which the landscapes and ecology of the "wilderness" were themselves the result of human pastoral and agricultural activity, and the cultural significance of particular landscapes, flora, and fauna to the local populations. Insofar as the indigenous populations are recognized, they are often themselves treated as a kind of exotic fauna, a part of nature, rather than fellow humans who also transformed their landscapes.

The conflicts between the attempts to create nature parks that embody the wilderness and the local, often marginalized, populations who have lived and worked in that wilderness are not confined to the third world. Consider, for example, the following comments of an individual living near the natural park of Sierra Nevada and Alpujurra, granted biosphere status by UNESCO and natural park status by the government of Andalusia:

[Miguel] pointed out the stonework he had done on the floor and lower parts of the wall which were all made from flat stones found in the Sierra. I asked him if he had done this all by himself and he said "Yes, and look, this is nature" *(Si, y mira, esto es la naturaleza)*, and he pointed firmly at the stone carved wall, and he repeated this action by pointing first in the direction of the Sierra [national park] before pointing at the wall again. Then, stressed his point by saying: "This is not nature, it is artificial (the Sierra) this (the wall) is nature" *(Eso no es la naturaleza, es artificial* [the Sierra] *esto* [the wall] *es la naturaleza).*[27]

Finally, in the United Kingdom consider the Yorkshire Dales, of which Richard Sylvan expressed his criticisms. There is a real conflict in the perceptions of the landscapes between farmers and conservationists.[28] Farmers, on the one hand, and landscape planners and conservationists, on the other, have different perceptions of what constitutes a good environment, of which some are self-conscious. Farmers' perceptions are often husbandry based. Hence the comment of a farmer in the Yorkshire Dales: "A farmer will look at someone else's farm and could tell whether it was well farmed or not. They wouldn't look at the view and think 'What a good view!'"[29] Given that perspective, the wildness loved by the conservationist can be seen as a defect. "If a piece of land's conserved, it tends to get overgrown, it gets brown. I suppose people from off will tend to look at that and admire its tones, an autumn sort of thing. Or golden spring, or whatever. But a farmer will look at it and think—it's overgrown."[30] The farmer will sometimes look upon the land in a way that is different from both the nature conservationist and the visitor admiring the landscape. Attempts to fence off nature and allow it to grow wild are met with disapproval; it represents a "mess."[31]

Hence the resistance felt by some farmers to the authorities who represent conservationists and landscapers—outsiders who aim to mold the environment in ways that are alien to their own husbandry-based conceptions. Correspondingly, there is the articulated threat that a community founded upon farming will be transformed into a museum exhibit to conform to some idealized Romantic image of how the countryside should look: "National Parks, English Nature, they'll finish up with all the farmers running about in smocks, like museum curators. That's not a community. We have a community which is a working community."[32] The worry here is that a particular conception of the way nature and landscape ought to be is being imposed from the outside on those who live and work in an environment, for whom nature is not primarily an object of scientific interest or aesthetic contemplation but something with which one has a working relationship.

WHAT'S LEFT OF THE WILDERNESS?

Thus goes the case for the prosecution against the wilderness ideal. It is a historically and socially local vision, historically implicated in the colonial appropriation of land, and currently implicated in the exclusion or control of often poor and powerless groups that live on lands too marginal to sustain intensive agricultural activity. The case against the wilderness model in this context is, I think, powerful, and it is one with which I broadly concur. It also suggests, as I noted earlier, that perhaps we should reverse the order of primacy between natural and cultural landscapes. For it might be argued that the natural landscape itself is just a particular cultural landscape, one that has a particular social and cultural history. Landscapes themselves, like that in the Yorkshire Dales or Yosemite, are managed so that they might be molded to expected patterns. Even where landscapes are not directly managed, the perception of the landscape as "natural" or "wilderness" is itself a culturally specific achievement. The conflicts outlined in the previous section are conflicts between different cultural landscapes. These can be direct material conflicts on how landscapes themselves should be transformed by human activity. However, they can also be conflicts in ways of seeing landscapes—consider the comments of the farmers above. Conflicts about appropriation can likewise be conflicts about who has legitimate powers to determine the material future of landscapes, who has property rights and economic and political power to shape a landscape.[33] However, conflicts about appropriation can also have a cultural and symbolic dimension, as to which perceptions and understandings of environments predominate.[34] The conflicts between the farmers and the conservationists in the Yorkshire Dales, or between Miguel and the park authorities in Andalusia, or between the peasants and park authorities in Nepal all have both dimensions. They are in part about who has rights to direct and control the land, but they are also about how the land is to be described and perceived. On this view, then, environmental conflicts are conflicts between different cultural landscapes. Natural landscapes are cultural landscapes that dare not speak their name. Pushing the line of argument further, it is sometimes argued that we should drop the notion of nature altogether from environmental discussion.[35]

There is, I think, much in that line of argument. However, the final conclusion, that nature should disappear altogether from discussion, is mistaken. Neither would I want to reject the environmentalist's view as simply internally incoherent. Indeed, I think there is much to the environmentalist's position that can be rescued from the wilderness. An initial point to be made here is that even appeal to "wilderness" itself has a more ambivalent role in the politics of nature than my discussion this far might suggest. Wilderness, in particular in the Romantic celebration of it, has sometimes been appealed to in order to justify public access to what is common, against the privatization of land. Consider, for example, Mill's comments on access to uncultivated land:

[T]he exclusive right to the land for purposes of cultivation does not imply an exclusive right to it for purposes of access; and no such right ought to be recognized, except to the extent necessary to protect the produce against damage, and the owner's privacy against invasion. The pretension of two Dukes to shut up a part of the Highlands, and exclude the rest of mankind from many square miles of mountain scenery to prevent disturbance to wild animals, is an abuse; it exceeds the legitimate bounds of the right of landed property. When land is not intended to be cultivated, no good reason can in general be given for its being private property at all; and if any one is permitted to call it his, he ought to know that he holds it by sufferance of the community, and on an implied condition that his ownership, since it cannot possibly do them any good, at least shall not deprive them of any, which could have derived from the land if it had been unappropriated.[36]

The appeal to wilderness in this context forms part of an assertion of rights to common access for common enjoyment.[37] Such appeals were central, for example, to the struggles in the United Kingdom for access to mountains and moorland by the urban working class in the nineteenth and twentieth centuries, culminating in the mass trespass movement. It still animates parts of current nature conservation, which appeal to the need to maintain boundaries around land, to protect it from privatization and commercialization. Hence one of the worries of defenders of wilderness is that its critics remove constraints on the commercial development of currently protected areas. For the reasons outlined earlier, I do not believe that the concept of wilderness in the sense of places relatively untouched by human intervention is the appropriate one to use in this context. There is little if any wilderness in this sense. Neither am I convinced that employing the concept in its older sense of "uncultivated land" fares particularly better. However, the defense of particular places and the maintenance of boundaries against commerce are entirely proper—and there are good reasons to hold that this should include places in which the (albeit culturally specific) experience of wildness is possible.

Moreover, much of the ethical vocabulary that environmentalists call upon to criticize features of some of our contemporary relations to the nonhuman world survives the rejection of the wilderness model. Examples are references to the cruelty inflicted on fellow creatures, to the failure of care involved in the wanton destruction of places rich in wildlife and beauty, to the pride and hubris exhibited in the belief that the world can be mastered and humanized, to our lack of a sense of humility in the midst of a natural world that came before and will continue beyond us. Nor do I think there are reasons to deny that both arts and sciences have developed the human senses, in ways that allow humans to respond to the qualities that objects possess—in a disinterested fashion toward those objects—and that in doing so they have developed a human excellence.[38] What is, I think, true is that they have a particular local cultural origin.[39]

Does the fact that they have a particular cultural origin matter? There are certainly occasions when it appears to matter. Consider the following incident. Returning from a winter climbing trip in Glencoe in Scotland, two friends and myself were passing Loch Lomond. It was a day of bright sunshine and without wind. There was not a ripple on the loch, and the mountains were reflected without flaw on the water. Two of us made the kind of comments full of expletives you'd expect on such occasions. The third, who had a training in the history of art, then began an account of the development during the eighteenth and nineteenth centuries of the aesthetic responses to the landscape that we had just exhibited. And it completely ruined the moment. Should his comments have undermined our appreciation? Does knowledge of the cultural origins of our responses to the natural world destroy those responses? Clearly such histories can have that effect. It is the source of the power of genealogical criticisms of social practices and attitudes; the history of the use of the concept of wilderness outlined earlier is perhaps an example. Or to take another, once one has read the story of the Highland clearances in Scotland, it is difficult not to see a depopulated landscape rather than a pristine wilderness. However, the cultural self-understanding of our attitudes, understanding, and perceptions of nonhuman nature need not undermine it. They can be seen as cultural *achievements*.

Ernest Gellner comments that anthropologists sometimes tend to be liberals at home and conservatives abroad.[40] The comment is not facetious. It raises important methodological issues for anthropology—most notably whether the suspension of criticism of those with whom one is engaged is a condition of understanding, and if not, what the principles of interpretation ought to be.[41] I leave these methodological issues aside here, however. I want to add a variant to the point that sometimes perhaps they may also have a tendency to be celebratory abroad and deflationary at home. Even if the responses to landscapes have historically and socially local origins, they are ones that can have their own virtues, that make contributions to a wider conversation about values.

Two final points need to be made in this regard. First, the cultural sources of our responses need to be distinguished from the objects of our responses. The point is one that needs to be stressed against certain strong forms of constructivism. For the strong constructivist, once we are made aware of the cultural origins of our responses we realize that there is no "nature" there, that we are surrounded by a world of cultural objects. That strong constructivism is mistaken. There is a clear distinction to be drawn between the *sources* of our attitudes, which are economic, political, and cultural, and the *objects* of our attitudes, which can still remain noncultural. That our capacity to appreciate and respond to the nonhuman natural world in a certain way is a cultural achievement, the outcome of social and cultural processes, does not entail that the object of our attitudes is a cultural object. This is not to deny that many landscapes that are presented as "natural" are cultural in a real, material sense—they are the result of human activity. Hence, the proper redescriptions of wilderness outlined earlier. However, it would simply be false to hold that at the level of geology, for example, *all* is a human product; it has a history before us. More generally, the world in which we live is the result of an interplay of human and nonhuman history. At the level of processes rather than objects or end-states, we live in a world of unintentional nonhuman natural processes that proceed regardless of human intentions and that, indeed, often thwart them.

This is a source of both human sorrow—for example, of life and land lost in a flood—but also of human delight, for example, at the plant or bird that arrives unexpectedly in an industrial wasteland. It is possible for culture to foster appreciation of nonhuman objects that themselves are not cultural—to maintain a sense of the otherness of nonhuman nature and our place within it. The picture of a world in which humans can see nothing but the reflections of themselves is itself a peculiar modern human conceit that our constructivist times tend to encourage. There is a core of environmentalism that is properly critical of that conceit. We live in a larger world of which human life is just a part.[42]

Second, the particular local cultural origins of responses and vocabulary with which particular groups approach the natural world do not require that they cannot belong to a wider conversation. All knowledge and value assertions have a local origin—they could have no other. That is consistent with some claims made on a wider audience. However, the possibility and nature of that wider conversation raises some important tensions between the universalizing tendencies of philosophical arguments and the more culturally local concerns that are represented, most notably, in anthropological perspectives.[43]

NOTES

1. B. McKibben, *The End of Nature* (Harmondsworth: Penguin, 1990), 43–44.

2. R. Sylvan, "Dominant British Ideology," unpublished manuscript. Richard Sylvan wrote the paper after a seminar on his work held near Colt Park in the Yorkshire Dales. My criticism of his comments here continues a discussion he provoked on that occasion. It was a discussion that was sadly cut short by his death.

3. C. Larrere, "Ethics, Politics, Science, and the Environment: Concerning the Natural Contract," in *Earth Summit Ethics: Toward a Reconstructive Postmodern Philosophy of Environmental Education*, ed. J. Baird Callicott and F. de Rocha (Albany: State University of New York Press, 1996), 122.

4. N. Evernden, *The Social Creation of Nature* (Baltimore: Johns Hopkins University Press, 1992), 89.

5. D. Cupitt, "Nature and Culture," in *Humanity, Environment and God*, ed. N. Spurway (Oxford: Blackwell, 1993), 35.

6. J. Derrida, *Of Grammatology*, trans. Gayatri Chakravorty Spivak (Baltimore and London: Johns Hopkins University Press, 1976), 158.

7. See, for example, S. Vogel, *Against Nature* (Albany, NY: State University of New York Press, 1996). For a view from the wilderness side see Holmes Rolston III, "Nature for Real: Is Nature a Social Construct?" in *Respecting Nature: Environmental Thinking in the Light of Philosophical Theory*, ed. T.D.J. Chappell (Edinburgh: University of Edinburgh Press, 1997).

8. For the debates about wilderness see J. Baird-Callicott and M. Nelson, eds., *The Great Wilderness Debate* (Athens: University of Georgia Press, 1998), and W. Cronon, ed., *Uncommon Ground* (New York: Norton, 1995). On exclusions see

R. Guha, "The Authoritarian Biologist and the Arrogance of Anti-Humanism," *Ecologist* 27, no. 1 (1997).

9. J. Locke, *Two Treatises of Government*, ed. Peter Laslett (Cambridge: Cambridge University Press, 1988), 2.37.

10. Ibid., 2.38.

11. For a detailed examination of the relation between Locke's theory of property and justification of colonial expansion see: B. Arneil, "The Wild Indian's Venison: Locke's Theory of Property and English Colonialism in America," *Political Studies* 44 (1996), 60–74; J. Tully, "Placing the 'Two Treatises,'" in *Political Discourse in Early Modern Britain*, ed. N. Phillipson and Q. Skinner (Cambridge: Cambridge University Press, 1993), and Tully, *An Approach to Political Philosophy: Locke in Contexts* (Cambridge: Cambridge University Press, 1993), chap. 5. The influence of the Lockean view is evident not only in appeal to it in subsequent legal claims but also in economic theory. Consider for example the following from Smith:

> The whole of the savage nations which subsist by flocks have no notion of cultivating the ground. The only instance what has the appearance of an objection to this rule is the state of the North American Indians. They, tho they have no conception of flocks and herds, have nevertheless some notion of agriculture. Their women plant a few stalks of Indian corn at the back of their huts. But this can hardly be called agriculture. This corn does not make any considerable part of their food; it serves only as a seasoning or something to give a relish to their common food; the flesh of those animals they have caught in the chase. . . . [I]n North America, again, where the age of hunters subsists, theft is not much regarded. As there is no property amongst them, the only injury that can be done is the depriving them of their game (A. Smith, *Lectures on Jurisprudence* [Liberty Press: Indianapolis, 1982], i.29, i.33, 15–16).

12. The claims that cultivation gives *a* title to land is already in Aquinas, who appeals in turn to Aristotle. "If a particular piece of land be considered absolutely, it contains no reason why it should belong to one man more than to another, but if it be considered in respect of its adaptability to cultivation, and the unmolested use of the land, it has a certain commensuration to be the property of one and not of another man, as the Philosopher shows (Polit. ii, 2)." (Aquinas, *Summa Theologica* II.57.3). In Locke it becomes *the* title.

13. J. Locke, *Two Treatises of Government*, 2.26.

14. Ibid., 2.36, 2.34.

15. Ibid., 2.37.

16. Ibid., 2.48–49.

17. A. S. Leopold et al., *Wildlife Management in the National Parks*, Report to the Secretary, (Washington, D.C.: U.S. Department of the Interior, Advisory Board on Wildlife Management, March 4, 1963), 4. Cited in A. Runte, *National Parks: The American Experience*, 2d ed. (Lincoln: University of Nebraska Press, 1987), 198–99.

18. Ibid., 6 (Leopold), 205 (Runte).

19. J. S. Mill, *Principles of Political Economy* (Oxford: Oxford University Press, 1994), book IV, chap. 6, sec. 2.

20. See G. Monbiot, *No Man's Land* (London: Macmillan, 1994), chaps. 4 and 5. Consider, for example the Masai suffering from malnutrition and disease on scrub land bordering the Mkomazi Game Reserve, from which they were forcibly evicted from land in 1988. (*The Observer*, 6 April 1997, 12).

21. *Times* (London), 5 April 1996, 11.

22. See T. Griffiths and M. Colchester, *Indigenous Peoples, Forests and the World Bank: Policies and Practice* (Washington, D.C.: Forest Peoples Program, 2000).

23. K. Choudhary, "Development Dilemma: The Resettlement of Gir Maldheris," *Economic and Political Weekly* 35, no. 30 (22–28 July 2000), 2662–68.

24. For discussions see N. G. Jayal, "Balancing Ecological and Political Values," in *Political Theory and Environment,* ed. M. Humphrey (London: Frank Cass, 2001); Guha, "Authoritarian Biologist"; and Griffiths and Colchester, *Indigenous Peoples, Forests and the World Bank.*

25. Cited in Guha, "Authoritarian Biologist," 17.

26. B. Campbell, "Nature and Its Discontents in Nepal," paper presented in workshop "Contesting Nature: Anthropology and Environmental Protection," Manchester University, 21 September 1998.

27. K. Lund, "What Would We Do without Biodiversity?" paper presented in workshop "Contesting Nature: Anthropology and Environmental Protection," Manchester University, 21 September 1998.

28. I draw here on M. Walsh, S. Shackley, and R. Grove-White, *Fields Apart? What Farmers Think of Nature Conservation in the Yorkshire Dales,* Report for English Nature and the Yorkshire Dales National Park Authority (Lancaster: Centre of the Study of Environmental Change, 1996). For discussions see J. O'Neill and M. Walsh, "Landscape Conflicts: Preferences, Identities and Rights," *Landscape Ecology* 15 (2000), 281–89.

29. Walsh, Shackley, and Grove-White, *Fields Apart,* 22. Compare the remarks of farmers on conservation on Pevensey Levels in J. Burgess, J. Clark, and C. Harrison, *Valuing Nature: What Lies behind Responses to Contingent Valuation Surveys?* (London: UCL, 1995).

30. Walsh, Shackley, and Grove-White, *Fields Apart,* 22.

31. Ibid., 23.

32. Ibid., 44.

33. J. O'Neill "Property, Care and Environment," in *Environmental Planning C: Government and Policy*, forthcoming.

34. My thanks to Jacques Weber for making this point to me.

35. This line is developed in Vogel, *Against Nature.*

36. Mill, *Principles of Political Economy,* book II, chap. 2, sec. 6. The passages come in the context of Mill's rejection of certain landed rights:

> When the "sacredness of property" is talked of, it should always be remembered that any such sacredness does not belong in the same degree to landed property. No man made the land. It is the original inheritance of the whole species. Its appropriation is wholly a question of general expediency. When private property in land is not expedient, it is unjust. It is no hardship to any one, to be excluded from what others have produced: they were not bound to produce it for his use, and he loses noth-

ing by not sharing in what otherwise would not have existed at all. But it is some hardship to be born into the world and to find all nature's gifts previously engrossed, and no place left for the newcomer. To reconcile people to this, after they have once admitted into their minds the idea that any moral rights belong to them as human beings, it will always be necessary to convince them that the exclusive appropriation is good for mankind on the whole, themselves included. (Ibid.)

37. It is echoed, for example, in the failed attempts to introduce rights of access in the late nineteenth and early twentieth centuries: "[N]o owner or occupier of uncultivated mountain or moor lands in Scotland shall be entitled to exclude any person from walking on such lands for the purposes of recreation or scientific or artistic study, or to molest him in so walking" (Clause 2, Access to Mountains [Scotland] Bill 1884).

38. J. O'Neill, "Science, Wonder and the Lust of Eyes," *Journal of Applied Philosophy* 10, (1993), 139–46.

39. Compare Bernard Williams's comments: "[A] self-conscious concern for preserving nature is not itself a piece of nature: it is an expression of culture, indeed of a very local culture (though that of course does not mean it is not important)" (B. Williams, "Must a Concern for the Environment Be Centred on Human Beings?" in *Making Sense of Humanity* [Cambridge: Cambridge University Press, 1995], 237.)

40. E. Gellner, *Cause and Meaning in the Social Sciences* (London: Routledge and Kegan Paul, 1973), 29.

41. Ibid., 38ff.

42. See Robert E. Goodin, *Green Political Theory* (Cambridge: Polity Press, 1992), chap. 2.

43. An earlier version of this chapter was read to a workshop on "Humans in Nature: The Ethics and Aesthetics of Cultural Landscapes," in Norway, March 2000. It also owes a great deal to my involvement in the seminar workshop "Contesting Nature: Anthropology and Environmental Protection," held in Manchester on 21 September 1998. My thanks for the comments and conversations made on both occasions.

12

On Critical Humility

Thomas Docherty

In 1941–42, Wallace Stevens addressed an audience in Princeton, as part of a series of lectures by diverse speakers on "The Language of Poetry." Toward the end of his lecture, entitled "The Noble Rider and the Sound of Words," he offered an idea of the function of the poet:

> What is his function? Certainly it is not to lead people out of the confusion in which they find themselves. Nor is it, I think, to comfort them while they follow their readers to and fro. I think that his function is to make his imagination theirs and that he fulfils himself only as he sees his imagination become the light in the minds of others. His role, in short, is to help people to live their lives.[1]

This much is probably relatively uncontroversial. Written at the time when the United States was entering the Second World War, the passage sustains the always ongoing argument in Stevens regarding the proximity of the imagination with reality, the intimacy of aesthetics with materiality. As he glosses the argument further, he turns to the question of the audience for poetry, for what Milton had thought of as the predicament in which he faced a requirement to write for a "fit audience, though few." Here is Stevens from the same lecture:

> Time and again it has been said that he [the poet] may not address himself to an elite. I think he may. There is not a poet whom we prize living today that does not address himself to an elite. The poet will continue to do this: to address himself to an elite even in a classless society. . . . And that elite, if it responds, not out of complaisance, but because the poet has quickened it, because he has educed from it that for which it was searching in itself and in the life around it and which it had not yet quite found, will thereafter do for the poet what he cannot do for himself, that is to say, receive his poetry.[2]

It is clear that such an argument, concerned so visibly with the "elite" condition of an audience, makes for less easily acceptable reading today. While it may be relatively uncontroversial (even if contestable) to advance the view that it is the function of the poet to help people to live their lives, it is certainly provocative (even if arguable) to advance the view that poetry is in some sense addressed primarily to an elite.

Yet it is important here to be precise. Stevens is not so much concerned simply with the idea that poetry is a rather exclusivist coterie activity, pursued among an "elect" group; rather, he is more concerned with the *availability* of poetry, with how it might be *received*. That is to say, his focus most certainly is on the audience, but on the audience that is characterized precisely by the receptivity required to make poetry heard at all, the audience equipped with the sensorium needed to allow poetry to be read—"received," as he puts it.

What might it mean to "receive" poetry? The point that Stevens makes here is that the poet makes her or his own audience, "quickens" an audience into being, but that she or he makes it in the abstract form of a receptivity, as if the task of the poet was to make poetry (her own poems, and also poetry as such) *available* to an audience, to allow an audience to avail of it and, in that availing, to become precisely the fit audience, though few, that is required to make the act that is poetry (an act of making, of *poiesis*) happen. The "quickening" in question here means that the poet brings an audience into a potential being: that is to say, the audience for the poet is one that is endowed with the status of "becoming an audience," and the poet, through the poetry, realizes that becoming, bringing it into material being.[3] It is the process of enacting the "receipt" of poetry—for which we might now read all art, or all aesthetic activity—that rouses me into becoming an audience; my receptivity is central to the establishment of relatedness between poet and reader, and it is in that relatedness that we can "live our lives" or become properly human.

This is a useful starting place for the present enquiry, for what I wish to explore in this paper is what I shall refer to as "critical humility," by which I mean to signal the kind of receptivity in the critic that Stevens sees here as being necessary to the survival of poetry, and with it the survival of humanity, too. That receptivity can be characterized as a kind of "passivity," or, much better, as a "passion" (and the link I shall forge here—relating both words to the notions of waiting, suffering, undergoing—is more than etymological). The dominant critical ideologies of our day—Marxist, feminist, postcolonial, a politically inflected deconstruction, ethical criticism, even the residua of reader-response criticisms—are all concerned with the *agency* of the critic. My argument will be that such an agency is possible only if it is grounded in the *passion* of the critic, and further, that such passion (or even passivity) is the very ground of the humanity of the critic herself or himself.

In the first section of what follows, I examine the idea of the human as the laughing animal, and consider the relation of humor to the kind of humility that I am advocating. This leads me to a consideration, in the second part, of autonomy and its relation to a specific kind of failure—the failure not only to hear poetry but also the failure to achieve the freedom that is associated with modernist autonomy. Finally, the third section turns to explore the relation of this passionate humility to love, via a consideration of the idea of reading as a "bearing witness" to passion; it argues further for an understanding of the "becoming-human animal" as the loving animal.

THE HUMILITY OF OUR HUMOR

In the wake of the Cuban missile crisis of 1962, some twenty years after Stevens's lecture referred to above—twenty years that marked a significant increase in the possibility of total human self-destruction—Kenneth Burke offered one of the first pieces of what has now come to be called "nuclear criticism," when he advanced a "definition of man." In passing in the definition, he attended briefly to Aristotle's *Parts of Animals,* chapter 10, where Aristotle considers the well-rehearsed idea of the defining characteristic of man as "the laughing animal" to be inadequate. In a footnote following this, Burke suggests that a cult of comedy is "man's only hope," given the readiness with which a cult of tragedy is only too ready, as it seemed to Burke and others in 1963, to "help out with the holocaust."[4] Here, Burke is advocating a *cultivation,* even a *culture* of comedy; he does so in the face of the enormity of the possibility of nuclear devastation. If the definition of man, as advanced here, is one that finds some solace in the idea of humanity as the animal that laughs, that is also a definition that has a pragmatic and directive purpose, being more than merely descriptive. Its purpose is "to help people to live their lives" in the very basic sense that its aim is to sustain life, to keep us living on: its aim is survival. Laughter, in this mode of thinking, is a promise of futurity, a deferral of death; it is to this extent that laughter and the culture of comedy can become part of the definition of what it means to become fully human.

In this, the human is considered in a quasi-Heideggerian, quasi-Sartrean fashion: the human is a "project," a throwing forward in time—even, eventually, a throwing forward toward death, but a death that is there always as potential and always therefore deferred. Death, in this view, is an asymptotic instant that can never be reached; it is, as Wittgenstein noted, "not an event in life."[5] Poetry, established as a humanizing activity insofar as it is intimately linked to a cult of comedy in these ways, helps sustain us precisely through an apotropaic warding-off of death, through a laughter that is evoked in the face of death itself, a death the very possibility of which becomes, through this attitude, an impossibility.[6] Poetry, for the human who is human insofar as she or he laughs in this way, engages this paradoxical but oddly logical impossible possibility (or possible impossibility) of death.

When Hobbes considered laughter in both the *Elements of Law* and in *Leviathan,* of course, he saw it as an element in the interminable struggle between humans, a struggle to the death that for Hobbes is concerned not so much with the articulation of an autonomous being as with the simple possibility of staying alive. Laughter is nothing but "sudden glory," arising, as Hobbes puts it, "from the sudden conception of some eminency in ourselves, by comparison with the infirmities of others, or with our own formerly."[7] Glossing this further, he goes on to describe sudden glory as "the passion which maketh those *grimaces* called LAUGHTER."[8] The important thing to note here is that in Hobbes laughter is the result of a play of forces. It is not willed (and therefore not a sign of autonomy), even if it is, in the terms that Burke would use, "motivated."[9] However, it is motivated by something beyond itself and is therefore neither entirely autonomous nor entirely a marker of the autonomous freedom of the individual who laughs, even if it is a marker of her or his felt superiority over others.

We could say that laughter is something that visits us, that inhabits us, that possesses us; for Hobbes, indeed, it is important that we actively resist any such total possession. Laughter, he claims, happens most to those who are least aware of their own shortcomings, and who need to reassure themselves of their own superiority by concentrating intently on the infirmities of others in relation to whom they can feel superior: "And therefore much laughter at the defects of others is a sign of pusillanimity."[10] Laughter, then, is a force to be resisted if we are to become "great minds," as Hobbes puts it, meaning minds that are capable of encountering alterity.

Hobbes is writing, of course, at a historical moment when the very word "humor" is undergoing a semantic shift. On one hand, it is related directly to a discourse of medicine, in which "the humours" determine, through the play of their mutual forces, the physical condition of the individual, their possibilities for staying alive; yet on the other, humor is also coming to mean what we now know as the condition provoking laughter, concerned thus with the relations between or among individuals and not, in the first instance, a purely physical matter.[11]

In seeing laughter in the way that he does, Hobbes allows us to realize that laughter is passionate, certainly. But it is passionate precisely insofar as its passion is determined by something else that predetermines it; in a particular sense, it marks our passivity and helplessness. It is thus not a marker of human autonomy or freedom, not a marker of our capacity to become fully human. In being passionate in this sense, it draws attention precisely to our passivity or receptivity, rather than to our capacity for agency; it marks not so much *spontaneity* (an acting *sua sponte*) as *responsibility* (an acting, or reacting, that responds to something that precedes it or even "pre-vents" it).[12] In the case of Hobbes, the proper action to be undertaken in the face of the force of laughter that moves us to feel our superiority is, rather, the suppression of laughter. It is only in fighting back against the spirit of comedy, a spirit that is thus all the more vital and fundamental to our becoming human, that we can become properly human at all, in his view.

Interestingly, this overlaps with a fragment in which Derrida considers the nature of passion itself, and specifically the nature of a passion of and for literature. In *Demeure,* he outlines seven "trajectories" of passion; and, in the seventh of these, he writes that

> "passion" implies the endurance of an indeterminate or undecidable limit where something, some X—for example, literature—must bear or tolerate everything, *suffer everything precisely because it is not itself,* because it has no essence but only functions. . . . The same exposition may be taken to be literary here, in one situation or according to given conventions, and nonliterary there. This is the sign that literarity is not an intrinsic property of this or that discursive event. Even where it seems to *reside* [demeurer], literature remains an unstable function, and it depends on a precarious juridical status. Its passion consists in this—that it receives its determination from something other than itself.[13]

Literature cannot define itself as such; it is precisely in this condition, this state of affairs in which its autonomy is heavily circumscribed, that it finds itself to be the site of passion, even of passivity. In short, literature requires us—its audience—to "quicken" it into becoming literature as such. In the terms proposed by Stevens, it makes us, its "impassioned" or passionate victims, into the elite that it requires for its (and our) survival.

Might we say the same of human becoming, or of our becoming human, as we say here of literature? If so, then we might describe laughter not merely as a response to something other than itself, implying that laughter is a responsibility of becoming human; also we might describe it as a receptivity, a "passivity" in the face of agency from elsewhere, from another determination of ourselves. We might accept, in short, that the modernist project of the establishment of human autonomy—in which the human determines her or his own history through the free assumption of an agency that shapes her or his ends—depends, paradoxically, precisely upon passion, upon the acknowledgement that we can be determined *as ourselves* by something—indeed, *only* by something—that is other than ourselves. Or, in short: autonomy is "prevented" by heteronomy. Action is similarly "prevented" by passion.

I am tempting us to move toward the acceptance of a paradoxical relation between elitism and passion in these terms, in which I am arguing that it is passion—passivity—that makes us into exactly the kind of elite required by Stevens as the audience, the possibilities of hearing, the site of receptivity, of and for poetry (and by extension, of all art). Passivity in these terms is consistent both with the establishment of this elite (with all its implications of superiority), and also with the establishment of the human as "humble," as one who "responds" or "receives" (with all the implications of inferiority, and of belatedness). My claim is that it is this paradox that shapes the condition that we call autonomy, or, more important, the possibility of human freedom. Freedom in this sense is not determined by a simple agency or by an existentialist determination of the possibilities of human action (that is to say, it is not characterized by *choice* or by the *acte gratuit*); rather, freedom and autonomy are determined precisely through the fact that we are located always within a preexisting set of human relations, a set that *determines* or even *predetermines* ("pre-vents") our possibilities for becoming human. That is to say, freedom, autonomy, and the very possibility of our becoming human at all are characterized by *passion* and *humility*.

In this, I am effectively advocating that we reconsider the relation between humor in the sense of comedy and laughter and the bodily "humours" as they were conceived in early modern medicine. Poetry, after all, is, among other things, a therapeutic device: like all art, it "attends" us, waits on us. It is like the doctor who is at once our servant and our master, always ahead of us in that she or he knows more about us than we know ourselves, being able to diagnose our condition (and therefore "waiting" for us to catch up, to heal ourselves, to live our lives), yet also always behind us, at our beck and call, attendant on us (needing us to call it forth into being, needing us to call upon it). Yet if poetry is seen as a kind of medicine in this sense, it is reduced to something concerned with mere and basic physical survival, a therapeutic device for keeping the humours—the play of forces that determines our actions and even the very possibility and condition of our acting at all—balanced. In the terms offered recently by Agamben, it is concerned with *zoe*, with "bare life." Yet the terms with which I began, those offered by Stevens, are concerned not with "bare life" but rather with what Agamben calls *bios,* the "way of living." *Zoe* is shared by all animate life; *bios* is something different. We have established that poetry is a means of fashioning a mode of receptivity for the survival not only of humans but also of poetry itself. We need to look more closely now at the *biology* of such passivity or passion.[14]

PASSIONS FOR FAILURE

Passion, we may now say, is a condition of bare life, of living on. Yet this passion cannot be entirely intransitive: we are passionate in relation to something other than the self. For existentialist thought, this becomes the ground for suggesting that the human is human precisely to the extent that she or he "exceeds" herself or himself. That move, especially as it exists in political existentialism, reiterates the ground of a Hegelian aesthetic.

At the start of the *Aesthetics*, Hegel argues that the beauty offered by art is *higher* than that proffered by nature, on the grounds of a certain kind of superfluity or excessiveness. Natural beauty is simply there; but artistic beauty is the product of a spirit, contingent, arbitrary, not necessary:

> The beauty of art is beauty *born of the spirit and born again*, and the higher the spirit and its productions stand above nature and its phenomena, the higher too is the beauty of art above that of nature. Indeed, considered *formally* [i.e., no matter what it says], even a useless notion that enters a man's head is higher than any product of nature, because in such a notion spirituality and freedom are always present. Of course, considered in its *content*, the sun, for example, appears as an absolutely necessary factor [in the universe] while a false notion vanishes as *accidental* and transitory. But, taken by itself, a natural existent like the sun is indifferent, not free and self-conscious in itself.[15]

The important aspect of this is that Hegel here identifies the possibility of aesthetics with the establishment or enactment or realization of a freedom; that freedom is marked precisely by the fact that it is *not necessity*, that it is "in excess" of the way things are given to us. On this basis, a relation can be established between autonomy and aesthetics; the name that we give to that relation has been, traditionally, modernity.

However, I want to argue that this is moving too fast for our present purposes. If we have established that it is a basic, if (self-evidently) *sufficient* condition of human becoming that we live on, then what might we characterize as a further *necessary* condition of that status? The answer is given to us by a kind of tautology: the human is the animal that seeks happiness. Alone among the animals, the human is conditioned by *eudaemonia*. This is totalizing to the extent that it includes its ostensible opposite: if I claim that I want to be unhappy, I am also thereby saying that it will make me happy to be unhappy. That is to say, as soon as we begin to characterize the human beyond the most basic level of *zoe*, into *bios*, it is axiomatic that the *bios* be characterized by eudaemonia.

Teilhard de Chardin wrote about this in his brief essay *Sur le bonheur*, delivered primarily as two lectures in Beijing/Peking in December 1943 (at that time in Japanese—that is, "enemy"—control). He had worked in China, as a palaeontologist concerned with what he called "the phenomenon of man," since the mid-1920s, playing a major part in the discovery of the prehuman (the "becoming-human") fossil dubbed "Peking Man" there in 1929.[16] In his lectures, he starts from the basic presupposition that the human being is marked by this fundamental desire to be happy. What distinguishes the human in this is the fact that as a reflective and a critical being, she or he is not tied to the *immediate* realization of happiness. The capacity for reflection and for criticism leads to the condition in which the human has a perception of the possible and a perception of the future. The consequence of this is that whereas other animals proceed directly toward their happiness, happiness becomes for humans much more problematical, introducing fears and hopes, or obstacles of one kind or another in the pursuit of happiness, the pursuit of the basic characteristic that will make me what I am, a human in the process of being.[17]

In the face of this, Teilhard distinguishes humanity into three types. For each of them, we can see an equivalent in the groups that he would be addressing, in occupied Beijing, at this time; we can also see some possible equivalents in the world of twentieth-century theory and criticism. First, there are *les fatigués,* the exhausted ones; these are pessimists who take the view that it would be better never to have been born. In this category, we might find those made miserable in the war; we might also find thinkers such as Adorno or Cioran (on whom more below) or (but this is much more complicated) Beckett. Second, there are *les bons viveurs;* these, fixated on the intensity of the present moment, are the epicures and hedonists. This group might contain those benefiting commercially from the present Chinese predicament; but it might also include some of those later 1970s anti-psychiatrists who celebrated schizophrenia (Laing, Brown and others), or critics concerned with pleasure (Barthes, say) and thinkers associated with the intensities of desire (Lyotard, Deleuze, the authors of a magic realism). The third group identified by Teilhard he calls *les ardents;* for these, being is inexhaustible, and it is always possible to be more than we are. These are always striving for more and more experience, hungry for life itself and for exceeding themselves. Such a group might include pragmatists such as Teilhard himself, but also those rather neo-Romantic critics who follow the aestheticist line of Hegel: teachers.

For each of these categories, Teilhard identifies a specific characteristic of happiness. For the first, there is the *bonheur de tranquillité,* the happiness of tranquillity; those in this group would advocate a withdrawal into the self, a diminishing of the self in a rather ascetic fashion. The *bons viveurs,* on the other hand, have the *bonheur de plaisir,* and these advocate that we profit from life and savor the moment. Finally, *les ardents* enjoy the *bonheur de croissance* or *bonheur de développement,* the happiness associated with the feeling that we are exceeding our previously greatest capacities, that we are growing and developing more and more, exponentially and indefinitely. For Teilhard, it is this last category who are truly human, for *"l'homme n'est Homme qu'a condition de se cultiver. . . . Etre, c'est d'abord se faire et se trouver."*[18]

These categories are interesting in that, for Teilhard, they are not really equal possibilities. The first two, in fact—bleak pessimism, bland optimism—are not really identified as the condition of being human at all; it is only in the third condition, that of a kind of neo-Romantic self-cultivation, in which the self is always about-to-be, in which it is "living on," or better, characterized by its *survival beyond itself,* that we become truly ourselves, that we become human at last.

Here, then, we are closer to seeing the relation between poetry and survival-as-*bios;* that is to say, we are closer to identifying poetry with the way of living that allows us to exceed our "bare life" or our *zoe.* Yet there remain some questions here. That this is, for Teilhard, a passion, goes without saying; yet his third position exists precisely as a reaction against the predicament in which he and his audience find themselves: at war, in enemy hands, suffering and awaiting deliverance. Thus, we might say, his third condition, the *bonheur de croissance,* with its establishment of the possibility of self-cultivation, of self-development or of *culture* itself, is precisely based upon the preexisting condition of pessimism, of having had to withdraw into the self and find a *bonheur de tranquillité,* that "pre-vents" (comes before, or conditions) that self-cultivation. For Teilhard is lecturing on this precisely because the condition that he advocates is prevented; it is prevented by the feeling that it would have been better never to have been born, the feeling that his audience has regarding the war.

That is to say, the passion for culture here depends precisely upon the passivity that is forced upon the human as a potential victim, as one who faces death. This recalls Pascal, for whom *"tout le malheur des hommes vient d'une seule chose, qui est de ne savoir pas demeurer en repos dans une chambre."*[19] Unhappiness derives from the fact that we have not learnt the spirit of tranquillity. It is this spirit or condition that I am calling here a "critical humility."

It is a humility that comes from the sense of one's own total superfluity, the unnecessity of being, the arbitrariness and absurdity of making a mark, of speaking or expressing when there is nothing to express, and yet the necessity to express it.[20] That is to say, the redundancy here lies in our actually saying anything about a work of art: our task is first and foremost to receive. All agent-oriented criticism is thus, in a particular sense, grounded in a premature utopianism. More fundamentally, it is simply *premature* and, to that extent, *prejudicial*, prejudged—what we used to call "ideological."[21]

Cioran would take a very different view of the condition of becoming human from that advanced by Teilhard. In *The Trouble with Being Born,* Cioran argues that "[u]nmaking, decreating, is the only task man may take upon himself if he aspires, as everything suggests, to distinguish himself from the Creator."[22] For Cioran, that Sartrean existentialist notion that "man is the being whose project is to be God,"[23] is simply wrongheaded; here, he effectively reverses it. It is a consequence of this kind of thinking that *failure* is an absolute necessity: "failure, always *essential,* reveals us to ourselves, permits us to see ourselves as God sees us, whereas success distances us from what is most inward in ourselves and indeed in everything."[24] To Teilhard's demand that we find ourselves, Cioran replies that such a finding is always the discovery of failure, the revelation of failure: the impossibility, as it were, of our ever finding ourselves or ever becoming fully ourselves, fully human. For those of us engaged in the business of aesthetic or cultural criticism, there follows from this logic what could be read as a kind of injunction: "To look *without understanding*—that is paradise. Hell, then, would be the place where we understand, where we understand too much."[25]

Putting this crudely, we might suggest that poetry is not there *for us,* that it is not there to be understood by us, to be centered on us, that we are superfluous to it, unnecessary to its survival. However, we can still—should still—engage with it, be there for it, make ourselves available to it in the sense that we should make ourselves available as a potential audience whose receptivity of it will allow it, and us, to be quickened into being, into our becoming human.[26] The humility that I advocate is simply this first response, the responsiveness that has the quality of firstness about it. It is indebted, obviously, to Beckett. To become human is to fail again, fail better.

BEARING WITNESS

In short, the condition that I advocate here can be called one of "bearing witness." In *Demeure,* Derrida identifies the possibility of witnessing with living on, first in the form of "an essential kind of generality: is the witness not always a survivor?" he asks. His response is interesting for our purposes here:

> This belongs to the structure of testimony. One testifies only when one has lived longer than what has come to pass. One can take examples as tragic or full of pathos as the survivors of the death camps. But what ties testimony to *survivance* remains a universal structure and covers the whole elementary field of experience. The witness is a survivor . . . the one who survives. This surviving speech must be as exemplarily irreplaceable as the instance of the instant from which it speaks, the instant of death as irreplaceable, as "my death," on the subject of which no one other than the dying person can testify. I am the only one who can testify to my death—on the condition that I survive it.[27]

We might think of poetry here as something that can be aligned with "surviving speech," a verbal act that lives on beyond itself, courtesy of a witness, the audience, whose very passivity is the condition that enables it to be quickened into becoming. In short, the humility of the witness, receiving a "surviving speech," is what makes possible the *act* of bearing witness in the first place; it is only through such an act that we can reach the condition of allowing a *survival,* a living on of poetry and of the humanity that receives it.

It has been a kind of commonplace of contemporary theoretical criticism that Derrida long ago dispensed with the notion that there might be an intimacy between the speaking voice and a self that could be somehow located in the speech-act. The subscription to a phonologocentrism was based, it was said, upon a metaphysics of presence that was untenable precisely to the extent that it was metaphysical. Yet it is the case that Derrida himself has remained haunted by this kind of question; in his later work, he relates the questions of "where we speak from" to the absolute liminal point of death.

This takes its most obvious turn when he makes a long-postponed engagement with Blanchot, in *Demeure*. *Demeure* is, in my terms, a "receiving" of *L'instant de ma mort,* a humble passivity before it, an attempt to hear and to bear witness to what it is that "Blanchot" says/writes or makes available in the displaced description and narrative of his own facing of a firing squad, his own "instant/instance of dying." The narrative told by Blanchot is that of a young man who faces death but who gets a reprieve from the execution of that dying, remaining nonetheless haunted forever by the "instant/instance" of "my death." The fundamental question from which Derrida begins to listen is the one that asks how intimate is the relation between Blanchot and this "young man." It is nowhere acknowledged in the text that we have that Blanchot himself is/was the man in the case; Derrida, however, holds also a letter, dated 20 July 1994, from Blanchot, whose words seem clearly to identify Blanchot with the young man in the case. This letter acts as a kind of testimony; the question before us now is whether there is a relation obtaining between testimony, bearing witness— or, as I'll call it here, "confessing"—and passion.

To confess is, in a peculiar sense, to identify oneself firmly with the "I" of one's narrative. "I stole the ribbon" would be, in this case, to forge an identity between the I who speaks the sentence and a person who stole a ribbon at some other place and time. In this case, this composite I is but an effect of the narrative. Thus far, thus commonplace. However, what is of more interest for present purposes is that a confession is an act that demands to be heard, to be *received:* it demands the passivity of a recipient who will remain passive while the confession is being enunciated. Further, its reception must be such that it is accepted, and that it is accepted as truth. This combination, of reception and acceptance, is what we can call a passionate passivity, a passivity that is precisely impassioned in its receptivity. So: "I stole the ribbon" requires an audience that humbly receives that confession, and, in so doing, acknowledges humbly the *absolute singularity* of the I who speaks it. This I can speak only on behalf of itself: if I stole the ribbon, then no one else can have done so. The audience is required to bear witness to the irreplaceable singularity of the speaking I, and, in so doing, acknowledges the I's potentiality for death.

Again, it is Derrida who offers the necessary links here. In *Demeure*, he is at pains to indicate that testimony testifies to an absolute singularity. In testimony, he writes, "you must believe me because I am irreplaceable."[28] This is a clear echo of what he had written some four years previously, when, in *The Gift of Death*, he argues that it is death that marks out such an absolute singularity: "Death is very much that which nobody else can undergo or confront in my place. My irreplaceability is therefore conferred, delivered, "given," one can say, by death. . . . It is from the site of death as the place of my irreplaceability, that is, of my singularity, that I feel called to responsibility. In this sense only a mortal can be responsible."[29] Responsibility here is given by the fact of facing death, even of (in my terms) *receiving* death, as a gift; as in the Cuban missile crisis above. Receptivity faces the death that is there in testimony; as in the case of Stevens's elite.

Passionate speaking allows us to acknowledge that the voice speaks to us; but that it can only do so if it is "responsible," if it is bearing witness and answering; to answer, it must hear what is asked. What is asked, simply, is that the other be heard. Another word describing this situation is "love"; we might here venture a definition of becoming human in these terms given to us by Auden, writing, on "September 1, 1939," of another instant constitutive of the promise of death: "We must love one another or die."

"We must love one another or die." The becoming-human, then, is the loving animal. Teilhard's view of love is useful here to some extent. He considered love to be the "most universal, formidable, and mysterious of cosmic energies," believing that, in a peculiar sense, "love" used humanity to further the end of the Universe's grand evolution toward its (theological) center. It is where he "humanizes" the concept of love, seeing it as something specific to humanity and not just as an abstract play of forces, that he offers us an interesting commentary:

> L'Amour "hominisé" se distinguée de tout autre amour parce que le "spectre" de sa chaude et pénétrante lumière s'est merveilleusement enrichi. Non plus seulement l'attrait unique et périodique, en vue de la fécondité matérielle; mais une possibilité, sans limite et sans repos, de contact par l'esprit plus que par le corps: antennes infiniment nombreuses et subtiles, qui se cherchent parmi les délicates nuances de l'âme; attrait de sensibilization et d'achèvement réciproques, où la préoccupation de sauver l'espèce se fond graduellement dans l'ivresse plus vaste de consommer, à deux, le Monde.[30]

Here, love is concerned with the survival of the species, with living on; but as more than "bare life." Love is that in which we must acknowledge the absolute singularity of the lover and of the loved: in a very specific sense, it is unique on every occasion, nontransferrable, an absolute singularity of an event. The nature of this event is that it transforms passion and passivity (being loved) precisely into action and agency (loving). The lover, as we know from Derrida's work on the politics of friendship, is always "in advance" of the loved:[31] love in this sense is also, like death, a question of responsibility, of the possibility of answering to an occasion, of (in the terms that are germane specifically to this argument) hearing and being a passive/ passionate recipient for poetry. In such passive reception, we can quicken the life of poetry and of the human through the love (the "I like this poem") that is the consequence of a critical humility.

Without this, what is the point of going on?

NOTES

1. Wallace Stevens, *The Necessary Angel* (New York: Vintage, 1965), 29.

2. Ibid., 29–30.

3. I use the word "potential" here in the rather strict sense that it is given in the work of Giorgio Agamben. For a full clarification, see Agamben, *Potentialities,* trans. Daniel Heller-Roazen (Stanford, Calif.: Stanford University Press, 1999), and cf. my "Potential European Democracy," in Brian Dillon, ed., *Agamben*, special issue of *Paragraph* (vol. 25 no. 2; Edinburgh: Edinburgh University Press, July 2002).

4. Kenneth Burke, *Language as Symbolic Action* (Berkeley and Los Angeles: University of California Press, 1966), 20 n. 2.

5. Ludwig Wittgenstein, *Tractatus Logico-Philosophicus,* bilingual ed., trans. C. K. Ogden (Routledge: London, 1992), 184–85: prop. 6.4311.

6. On this apotropaism as a modern phenomenon, see Hans Blumenberg, *The Legitimacy of the Modern Age*, trans. Robert M. Wallace (Cambridge, Mass.: MIT Press, 1983), esp. chap. 2.

7. Thomas Hobbes, *Elements of Law,* published under the title *Human Nature and de Corpore Politico*, ed. J.C.A. Gaskin (Oxford: Oxford University Press, 1994), 43–44.

8. Thomas Hobbes, *Leviathan,* ed. Edwin Curley (Indianapolis: Hackett, 1994), 32.

9. In the work of Kenneth Burke, "motives" play a central operational part. For a useful introduction to this, see Steven Bygrave, *Kenneth Burke: Rhetoric and Ideology* (London: Routledge, 1993).

10. Hobbes, *Leviathan*, 32.

11. For a fuller tracing of the effects of this on European culture, see my *Criticism and Modernity: Aesthetics, Literature and Nations in Europe and Its Academies* (Oxford: Oxford University Press, 1999), esp. chap. 2, "Love as the European Humour."

12. The notion of "prevention" I have in mind here is one to be found in the poetry of George Herbert. Herbert frequently complains that he has been "prevented" from doing as he might by God, in the sense that God has always done it first. He is thus denied authority and autonomy precisely in the very moment when he most fervently tries to assert it; it is this condition of belatedness, in which his entire life is prevented by God's, that Herbert paradoxically finds his subject for poetry. For a fuller explanation, see my *On Modern Authority* (Brighton, Sussex: Harvester-Wheatsheaf, 1987).

13. Jacques Derrida, "Demeure," in *The Instant of my Death*, ed. Maurice Blanchot, and Jacques Derrida, *Demeure*, trans. Elizabeth Rottenberg (Stanford, Calif.: Stanford University Press, 2000), 28.

14. For the distinction between *zoe* and *bios* here outlined, see Giorgio Agamben, *Homo Sacer,* trans. Daniel Heller-Roazen (Stanford, Calif.: Stanford University Press, 1998). Cf. my "Potential European Democracy."

15. G.W.F. Hegel, *Aesthetics,* vol. 1, trans. T. M. Knox (Oxford: Oxford University Press, 1975), 2.

16. On the sinanthrope as "prehominians," see Pierre Teilhard de Chardin, *The Phenomenon of Man,* trans. Bernard Wall (London: Collins/Fontana, 1959), 212–18.

17. Teilhard de Chardin, *Sur le Bonheur / Sur l'Amour* (Paris: Seuil, 1997), 9–10.

18. Ibid., 21.

19. Blaise Pascal, "Pensées," in *Oeuvres complètes* (Paris: Seuil, 1963), 516, liasse VIII, fragment 136 (Lafuma edition: corresponds to fragment 139 in Brunschvicg edition).

20. Here, I am alluding in passing not only to the Pascal fragment from the *Pensées* just cited but also to the preceding fragment (135; 469 in Brunschvicg): "*Je sens que je puis n'avoir point été . . . donc je ne suis pas un être nécessaire,*" but also, more obviously, to Beckett's famous dialogues with Georges Duthuit. Interestingly, Teilhard also has a relevant comment here. Twice in two pages of *The Phenomenon of Man,* discussing the "original forms" in the "birth of thought," he writes: "Man came silently into the world" (pp. 204, 206).

21. On this, see Paul de Man, *The Resistance to Theory* (Manchester: Manchester University Press, 1986), where he puts it thus: "What we call ideology is precisely the confusion of linguistic with natural reality, of reference with phenomenalism" (p. 11). My gloss suggests that ideology is the too-rapid and unreflective—prejudiced—move from reference to phenomenalism in these terms. A fuller exploration of the politics in question here might be found in Norberto Bobbio, *In Praise of Meekness* (Cambridge: Polity, 2000), esp. chap. 1.

22. E. M. Cioran, *The Trouble with Being Born,* trans. Richard Howard (London: Quartet Books, 1993), 6.

23. Jean-Paul Sartre, *Being and Nothingness,* trans. Hazel E. Barnes (London: Routledge, 1969), 566.

24. Cioran, 17.

25. Ibid., 28.

26. It should be noted in passing that the consequence of this kind of humility is very definitely not a self-loathing. As Cioran writes, "He who hates himself is not humble" (p. 26). Such hatred is already a premature agency or action, not passionate enough.

27. Derrida, *Demeure,* 45.

28. Ibid., 33.

29. Jacques Derrida, *The Gift of Death,* trans. David Wills (Chicago: University of Chicago Press, 1995), 41.

30. Teilhard de Chardin, *Sur le Bonheur/Sur l'Amour,* 52–53. ("Truly human love is different from any other type of love because the 'spectre' of its warm and penetrating light has been so beautifully enriched. No longer is there a unique and periodic attraction before achieving material fecundity; but in that reciprocal attraction we find a limitless and restless capacity for contact through the mind rather

than the body: subtle and almost limitless antennae connecting in the midst of the soul's delicate nuances; and the attraction of this reciprocal sensitiveness and achievement, where the concern with rescuing the species gradually loses itself in a greater intoxication, to consume together the World." [Translation by Joëlle Battestini.])

    31. See Jacques Derrida, *Politiques de l'amitié* (Paris: Galilee, 1994), 27–28; and see my commentary on this in my *Criticism and Modernity* (Oxford: Oxford University Press, 1999), 62–67.

Further Reading

Descombes, Vincent. *Modern French Philosophy.* Trans. Lorna Scott-Fox and J. M. Harding. Cambridge: Cambridge University Press, 1980.

Ferry, Luc, and Renaut, Alain, eds. *French Philosphy of the Sixties: An Essay on Antihumanism.* Trans. Mary H. S. Cattani. Amherst: University of Massachusetts Press, 1990.

Finkielkraut, Alain. *In the Name of Humanity: Reflections on the Twentieth Century.* Trans. Judith Friedlander. New York: Columbia University Press, 2000.

Fuss, Diana, ed. *Human, All Too Human.* London: Routledge, 1996.

Gramsci, Antonio. "What Is Man?" In *The Modern Prince and Other Writings.* Trans. Louis Marks. New York: International Publishers, 1957.

Jonas, Hans, "Tool, Image, and Grave: On What Is beyond the Animal in Man." In *Mortality and Morality.* Evanston, Ill.: Northwestern University Press, 1996.

Judt, Tony. *Past Imperfect: French Intellectuals, 1944–1956.* Berkeley and Los Angeles: University of California Press, 1992.

Levinas, Emmanuel, "Humanism and An-archy." In *Collected Philosophical Papers.* Dordrecht: Martinus Nijhoff, 1987.

Lyotard, Jean-François. *The Inhuman: Reflections on Time.* Trans. Geoffrey Bennington and Rachel Bowlby. Cambridge: Polity Press, 1991.

Merquior, J. G. *From Prague to Paris: A Critique of Structuralist and Post-Structuralist Thought.* London: Verso, 1986.

Pearson, Keith Ansell. *Viroid Life: Perspectives on Nietzsche and the Transhuman Condition.* London: Routledge, 1997.

Poster, Mark. *Critical Theory and Poststructuralism: In Search of a Context.* Ithaca, N.Y.: Cornell University Press, 1994.

Sartre, Jean-Paul. *Existentialism and Humanism.* Trans. Philip Mairet. London: Methuen, 1980.

Sheehan, James J., and Morton Sosna, eds. *The Boundaries of Humanity: Humans,*

Animals, Machines. Berkeley and Los Angeles: University of California Press, 1991.

Soper, Kate. *Humanism and Anti-Humanism*. London: Hutchinson, 1986.

Tallis, Raymond. *Enemies of Hope*. London: Macmillan, 1997.

Tester, Keith. *The Inhuman Condition*. London: Routledge, 1995.

Todorov, Tzvetan. *Literature and Its Theorists: A Personal View of Twentieth-Century Criticism*. Ithaca, N.Y.: Cornell University Press, 1987.

———. *Imperfect Garden: The Legacy of Humanism*. Princeton, N.J.: Princeton University Press, 2002.

Wolin, Richard. "Antihumanism in the Discourse of French Postwar Theory." In *Labyrinths: Explorations in the Critical History of Ideas*. Amherst: University of Massachusetts, 1995.

Yarborough, Stephen. *Deliberate Criticism: Toward a Postmodern Humanism*. Athens and London: University of Georgia, 1992.

Selected Bibliography

Adams, Henry. *The Education of Henry Adams: An Autobiography*. Cambridge, Mass.: Riverside Press, 1961.

Adorno, Theodor. *Negative Dialectics*. Trans. E. B. Ashton. London: Routledge and Kegan Paul, 1973.

Adorno, Theodor, and Max Horkheimer. *Dialectic of Enlightenment*. Trans. John Cumming. London: Verso, 1979.

Aristotle. *The Nicomachean Ethics*. Trans. H. Rackham. Cambridge, Mass.: Harvard University Press; and London: William Heinemann, 1934.

———. *De Partibus Animalum*. Trans. D. M. Balme. Oxford: Clarendon Press, 1972.

———. *De Anima*. Trans. Hugh Lawson-Tancred. Harmondsworth: Penguin, 1986.

Barthes, Roland. *Mythologies*. Trans. Annette Lavers. London: Granada, 1973.

Beal, Timothy K. *Religion and Its Monsters*. New York and London: Routledge, 2002.

Beck, Ulrich. *World Risk Society*. Cambridge: Polity Press, 1999.

Beistegui, Miguel de. *Heidegger and the Political: Dystopias*. London: Routledge, 1998.

Berger, Peter L. *Redeeming Laughter: The Comic Dimension of Human Experience*, New York: Walter de Gruyter, 1997.

Bergson, Henri. *Creative Evolution*. Trans. Arthur Mitchell. London: Macmillan, 1911.

———. *Mind-Energy*. Trans. H. Wildon Carr. New York: Henry Holt, 1922.

Bergstrom, Janet, ed. *Endless Night. Cinema and Psychoanalysis: Parallel Histories*. Berkeley, London, and Los Angeles: University of California Press, 1999.

Bhasker, Roy. *The Possibility of Naturalism*. London: Routledge, 1979.

Blackburn, Simon. *Spreading the Word*. Oxford: Clarendon Press, 1984.

Blumenberg, Hans. *Work on Myth*. Trans. Robert M. Wallace. Cambridge, Mass.: MIT Press, 1985.

Brecht, Bertolt. *Poems and Songs from the Plays*. Ed. John Willett. London: Methuen, 1990.

Brentano, Franz. *Psychology from an Empirical Standpoint*. Trans. Antos C. Rancurello, D. B. Terrell, and Linda L. McAlister. London: Routledge and Kegan Paul, 1975.

———. *Sensory and Noetic Consciousness: Psychology from an Empirical Standpoint III*. Trans. Margarete Schättle and Linda L. McAlister. London: Routledge and Kegan Paul, 1981.

Brownlow, F. W. *Shakespeare, Harsnett, and the Devils of Denham*. Newark: University of Delaware Press; London and Toronto: Associated University Presses, 1996.

Buell, Lawrence. *The Environmental Imagination*. Cambridge, Mass.: Harvard University Press, 1995.

Burke, Kenneth, *Language as Symbolic Action*. Berkeley and Los Angeles: University of California Press, 1966.

Callicott, J. Baird, and Fernando J.R. da Rocha (eds.). *Earth Summit Ethics: Toward a Reconstructive Postmodern Philosophy of Environmental Education*. Albany: State University of New York Press, 1996.

Cavell, Stanley. *The Claim of Reason*. Oxford: Oxford University Press, 1979.

Certeau, Michel de. *The Writing of History*. Trans. Tom Conley. New York: Columbia University Press, 1988.

Chappell, T.D.J., ed. *Respecting Nature: Environmental Thinking in the Light of Philosophical Theory*. Edinburgh: University of Edinburgh Press, 1997.

Charles, David, and Kathleen Lennon (eds.). *Reduction, Explanation, and Realism* Oxford: Clarendon Press, 1992.

Chomsky, Noam. *Cartesian Linguistics*. New York: Harper & Row, 1966.

———. *Language and Problems of Knowledge: The Managua Lectures*. Cambridge, Mass.: MIT Press, 1994.

Christie, Ian. *The Last Machine: Early Cinema and the Birth of the Modern World*, London: BFI/BBC, 1985.

Cioran, E. M. *The Trouble with Being Born*. Trans. Richard Howard. London: Quartet, 1993.

Connor, Steven. *Dumbstruck: A Cultural History of Ventriloquism*. Oxford: Oxford University Press, 2000.

Darwin, Charles. *On the Origin of Species*. London and New York: Cambridge University Press, 1975.

Davidson, Donald. *Truth and Interpretation*. New York: Oxford University Press, 1991.

Deleuze, Gilles. *Nietzsche and Philosophy*. Trans. Hugh Tomlinson. London: Athlone Press, 1983.

Derrida, Jacques. *Of Grammatology*. Trans. Gayatri Chakravorty Spivak. Baltimore and London: Johns Hopkins University Press, 1976.

———. "The Ends of Man" *Margins of Philosophy*. Trans. Alan Bass. Chicago: University of Chicago Press, 1982.

———. *Politiques de l'amitié*. Paris: Galilee, 1994.

———. *The Gift of Death*. Trans. David Wills, Chicago: University of Chicago Press, 1995.

———. *Demeure*. Trans. Elizabeth Rottenberg. Stanford, Calif.: Stanford University Press, 2000.

Devitt, Michael. *Realism and Truth*. Princeton, N.J.: Princeton University Press, 1997.

Dewey, John. *The Quest for Certainty: A Study of the Relation of Knowledge and Action*. New York: Putnam, 1960.

——. *Politiques de l'amitié*. Paris: Galilee, 1994.

Docherty, Thomas. *On Modern Authority*. Brighton, Sussex: Harvester-Wheatsheaf, 1987.

——. *Criticism and Modernity: Aesthetics, Literature and Nations in Europe and Its Academies*. Oxford: Oxford University Press, 1999.

Eliot, T. S. *Selected Poems*. London: Faber and Faber, 1954.

Evernden, Neil. *The Social Creation of Nature*. Baltimore: Johns Hopkins University Press, 1992.

Flint, R. W., ed. *Marinetti: Selected Writings*. Trans. R. W. Flint and Arthur Coppotelli. London: Secker and Warburg, 1972.

Foucault, Michel. *The Order of Things*. London: Routledge, 1970.

——. *Power/Knowledge*. Trans. Colin Gordon. Brighton, Sussex: Harvester Press, 1980.

——. *Foucault Live: Interviews 1961–1984*. Trans. Lysa Hochroth and John Johnston, ed. Sylvère Lotringer. New York: Semiotext(e), 1989.

——. *The Foucault Reader*. Trans. Donald F. Bouchard and Sherry Simon, ed. Paul Rabinow. Harmondsworth: Penguin, 1991.

Freud, Sigmund. "General Theory on the Neuroses." In *The Standard Edition of the Complete Psychological Works of Sigmund Freud*. Trans. James Strachey. London: Hogarth Press, 1963, vol. 16 [1916–1917].

Fussell, Paul. *The Great War and Modern Memory*. London: Oxford University Press, 1975.

Gay, Peter. *Weimar Culture: The Outsider as Insider*. Westport, Conn.: Greenwood Press, 1981.

Gellner, Ernest. *Cause and Meaning in the Social Sciences*. London: Routledge and Kegan Paul, 1973.

Geuss, Raymond. *Parrots, Poets, Philosophers and Good Advice*. London: Hearing Eye, 1999.

Godwin, William. *Enquiry Concerning Political Justice and Its Influence on Modern Morals and Happiness*. Harmondsworth: Penguin, 1976.

Goodin, Robert E. *Green Political Theory*. Cambridge: Polity Press, 1992.

Goody, Jack. *The Domestication of the Savage Mind*. Cambridge and New York: Cambridge University Press, 1977.

Gutman, Amy, ed. *Multiculturalism*. Princeton, N.J.: Princeton University Press, 1994.

Hegel, G.W.F. *Aesthetics*. Trans. T. M. Knox. Oxford: Oxford University Press, 1975, vol. 1.

Heidegger, Martin. *Being and Time*. Trans. John Macquarrie and Edward Robinson. Evanston, Ill.: Harper & Row, 1962.

——. *Poetry, Language, Thought*. Trans. Albert Hofstadter. New York: Harper & Row, 1971.

——. *Basic Writings*. Ed. David F. Krell. San Francisco, Calif.: HarperSanFrancisco, 1993.

————. *The Question Concerning Technology and Other Essays*. Trans. William Lovitt. New York: HarperCollins, 1982.

Hobbes, Thomas. *Human Nature and de Corpore Politico*. Ed. J.C.A. Gaskin. Oxford: Oxford University Press, 1994.

————. *Leviathan*. Ed. Edwin Curley. Indianapolis: Hackett, 1994.

Hulme, T. E. *Speculations: Essays on Humanism and the Philosophy of Art*. London: Routledge and Kegan Paul, 1987.

Humphrey, Mathew, ed. *Political Theory and the Environment: A Reassessment*. London: Frank Cass, 2001.

Husserl, Edmund. *Phenomenology and the Crisis of Philosophy*. Trans. Quentin Lauer. New York: Harper, 1965.

Huxley, Aldous. *The Devils of Loudun*. Harmondsworth: Penguin, 1971.

Jacoby, Russell. *The End of Utopia: Politics and Culture in an Age of Apathy*. New York: Basic Books, 1999.

Jay, Gregory S., and David L. Miller (eds.). *After Strange Texts: The Role of Theory in the Study of Literature*. Tuscaloosa: University of Alabama Press, 1985.

Jones, David. *In Parenthesis*. London: Faber and Faber, 1963.

Kahler, Erich. *Man the Measure: A New Approach to History*. Cleveland and New York: Meridian, 1967.

————. *The Inward Turn of Narrative*. Trans. Richard and Clara Winston. Princeton, N.J.: Princeton University Press, 1973.

Kant, Immanuel. *Critique of Pure Reason*. Trans. Paul Guyer and Allen W. Wood. Cambridge and New York: Cambridge University Press, 1998.

Kearney, Richard. *On Stories*. London and New York: Routledge, 2001.

Kerridge, Richard, and Neil Sammells (eds.). *Writing the Environment: Ecocriticism and Literature*. London: Zed Books, 1998.

Khilnani, Sunil. *Arguing Revolution: The Intellectual Left in Postwar France*. New Haven, Conn., and London: Yale University Press, 1993.

Lacan, Jacques. *Ecrits: Selections*. Trans. Alan Sheridan. London: Routledge, 1989.

Lacoue-Labarthe, Philippe. *La Fiction du politique*. Paris: Christian Bourgeois, 1988.

Lawrence, D. H. *Apocalypse*. Harmondsworth: Penguin, 1974.

Levin, Harry. *Refractions: Essays in Comparative Literature*. London, Oxford, and New York: Oxford University Press, 1966.

Levinas, Emmanuel. *The Levinas Reader*. Ed. Seán Hand. Oxford: Basil Blackwell, 1989.

————. *Difficult Freedom*. Baltimore: Johns Hopkins University Press, 1990.

————. *Proper Names*. Trans. Michael B. Smith. London: Athlone Press, 1996.

Locke, John. *Two Treatises of Government*. Ed. Peter Laslett. Cambridge: Cambridge University Press, 1988.

Lyotard, Jean-François. *The Differend: Phrases in Dispute*. Trans. Georges Van Den Abbeele. Manchester: Manchester University Press, 1988.

Mahon, Derek. *Selected Poems*. Harmondsworth: Penguin, 1991.

Man, Paul de. *The Resistance to Theory*. Manchester: Manchester University Press, 1986.

Marcuse, Herbert. *Eros and Civilisation: A Philosophical Inquiry into Freud*. London: Ark, 1987.

Marx, Karl. *Grundrisse: Foundations of the Critique of Political Economy*. Trans. Martin Nicolaus. London: Allen Lane, 1973.

McKibben, Bill. *The End of Nature*. Harmondsworth: Penguin, 1990.

Mead, George Herbert. *Mind, Self, and Society: From the Standpoint of a Social Behaviorist*. Chicago and London: University of Chicago Press, 1962.

Mill, J. S. *Principles of Political Economy*. Oxford: Oxford University Press, 1994.

Miller, James. *The Passion of Michel Foucault*. London: Flamingo, 1994.

Mirandola, Pico della. "Oration on the Dignity of Man." In *On the Dignity of Man: On Being and the One, Heptaplus*. Trans. C. G. Wallace, P.J.W. Miller, and D. Carmichael. Indianapolis: LLA, 1955.

Mohanty, J. N. *Phenomenology: Between Essentialism and Transcendental Philosophy*. Evanston, Ill.: Northwestern University Press, 1997.

Monbiot, George. *No Man's Land: An Investigative Journey through Kenya and Tanzania*. London: Macmillan, 1994.

Mosse, George L. *The Fascist Revolution: Toward a General Theory of Fascism*. New York: Howard Fertig, 1999.

Mulhall, Stephen. *On Film*. London and New York: Routledge, 2002.

Nietzsche, Friedrich. *Beyond Good and Evil*. New York: Random House, 1966.

Nozick, Robert. *Philosophical Explanations*. Oxford: Clarendon Press, 1981.

Papineau, David. *Philosophical Naturalism*. Oxford: Blackwell, 1993.

Pascal, Blaise. "*Oeuvres completes*. Paris: Seuil, 1963.

———. *Pensées*, ed. Philippe Sellier, Paris: Mercure de France, 1976.

Pater, Walter. *Plato and Platonism: A Series of Lectures*. New York: Greenwood Press, 1969.

Petro, Patrice, ed. *Fugitive Images*. Bloomington: Indiana University Press, 1995.

Phillips, Adam. *Houdini's Box: On the Arts of Escape*. London: Faber and Faber, 2001.

Plato. *Republic of Plato*. Trans. Francis Macdonald Cornford. Oxford: Clarendon Press, 1961.

———. *Phaedo*. Trans. David Gallop. Oxford: Clarendon Press, 1975.

———. *The Statesman*. Trans. J. B. Skemp. Indianapolis: Bobbs-Merrill, 1977.

Pound, Ezra. *Selected Poems*. London: Faber and Faber, 1975.

Putnam, Hilary. *Reason, Truth and History*. New York: Cambridge University Press, 1990.

Rajchman, John, and Cornel West, eds. *Post-Analytic Philosophy*. New York: Columbia University Press, 1985.

Ramthum, Herta, ed. *Bertolt Brecht Diaries 1920–1922*. Trans. John Willett. London: Eyre Methuen, 1979.

Reichenbach, Hans. *The Rise of Scientific Philosophy*. Berkeley: University of California Press, 1951.

Rigaut, Jacques. "Un Brillant Sujet." In *Ecrits*. Paris: Gallimard, 1970.

Rockmore, Tom. *Heidegger and French Philosophy: Humanism, Antihumanism and Being*. London: Routledge, 1995.

Rorty, Richard. *Philosophy and the Mirror of Nature*. Princeton, N.J.: Princeton University Press, 1979.

———. *Achieving Our Country*. Cambridge, Mass.: Harvard University Press, 1998.

———. *Philosophy and Social Hope*. Harmondsworth: Penguin, 1999.

Ross, Andrew. *The Chicago Gangster Theory of Life*. London: Verso, 1994.

Sartre, Jean-Paul. *Being and Nothingness: An Essay on Phenomenological Ontology.* Trans. Hazel E. Barnes. London: Routledge, 1969.

———. *Existentialism and Humanism.* Trans. Philip Mairet. London: Methuen, 1980.

Schaff, Adam. *A Philosophy of Man.* New York: Dell, 1963.

Screech, M. A. *Laughter at the Foot of the Cross.* Harmondsworth: Penguin, 1999.

Serres, Michel. *The Natural Contract.* Trans. Elizabeth MacArthur and William Paulson. Ann Arbor: University of Michigan Press, 1995.

———. *Hominescence: Essais.* Paris: Le Pommier, 2001.

Singer, Peter, and Tom Regan, eds. *Animal Rights and Human Obligations.* Englewood Cliffs, N.J.: Prentice-Hall, 1989.

Sokal, Alan, and Jean Bricmont. *Intellectual Impostures.* London: Profile Books, 1998.

Soper, Kate. *On Human Needs: Open and Closed Theories in a Marxist Perspective.* Brighton, Sussex: Harvester Press, 1981.

Sorell, Tom. *Scientism: Philosophy and the Infatuation with Science.* London: Routledge, 1991.

Spurway, Neil, ed. *Humanity, Environment and God.* Oxford: Blackwell, 1993.

Squires, Judith, ed. *Principled Positions.* London: Lawrence and Wishart, 1993.

Stengers, Isabelle. *Power and Invention.* Trans. Paul Bains. Minneapolis and London: University of Minnesota Press, 1997.

Stevens, Wallace. *The Necessary Angel.* New York: Vintage Books, 1965.

Teilhard de Chardin, Pierre. *The Phenomenon of Man.* Trans. Bernard Wall. London: Collins/Fontana, 1959.

Tzara, Tristan. *Seven Dada Manifestoes* and *Lampisteries.* Trans. Barbara Wright. London: John Calder, 1977.

Vogel, Steven. *Against Nature.* Albany, N.Y.: State University of New York Press, 1996.

Weimann, Robert. *Structure and Society in Literary History: Studies in the History and Theory of Historical Criticism.* Charlottesville: University Press of Virginia, 1976.

Williams, Bernard. *Making Sense of Humanity.* Cambridge: Cambridge University Press, 1995.

Wilson, Edmund. *Axel's Castle: A Study in the Imaginative Literature of 1870–1930.* Harmondsworth: Penguin, 1993.

Wittgenstein, Ludwig. *Philosophical Investigations.* Trans. G.E.M. Anscombe. Oxford: Blackwell, 1958.

———. *Culture and Value.* Oxford: Blackwell, 1980.

———. *Tractatus Logico-Philosophicus.* Bilingual ed. Trans. C. K. Ogden. London: Routledge, 1992.

Wolpert, Lewis. *The Unnatural Nature of Science.* London: Faber and Faber, 1993.

Yeats, W. B. *The Poems.* London: Everyman, 1992.

Index

Adams, Henry, 34, 37
Adorno, Theodor, xii, 3, 49, 172
Adorno, Theodor, and Horkheimer,
   Max, 3, 71–5, 79n17, 79n19
Aesop, 46–7
Aesthetics (Hegel), 171
Agamben, Giorgio, 170, 177n3
Alias Grace (Attwood), 108
Alien series, 113–16, 123
Althusser, Louis, 5
Anaxagoras, 43
Animal Farm (Orwell)
anthropocentrism, 20, 21, 68–9
antihumanism, 4–11; theoretical, 7–11
Apocalypse (Lawrence), 34
Apocalypse Now Redux, 113, 117–23
Aristotle, 20, 23, 43, 56, 85, 86, 88, 167
Armstrong, D. M., 87
Arnold, 38
Arnold, Mathew, 32
Ars Magica (Kircher), 99
Auden, W. H., 39, 176
Augustine, 17
Axel's Castle (Wilson), 35

Bachelard, Gaston, 57, 64
Barthes, Roland, 5, 172, 78n9
Bate, Jonathan, 67
Bauhaus, 30, 39
Bauman, Zygmunt, xiii–xiv, 7

Beal, Timothy, 123n3
"The Beast's Confession to the Priest"
   (Swift), 47
Beck, Ulrich, 76, 129
Beckett, Samuel, x, xv, 43, 47, 48, 172,
   174, 178n20
Being and Nothingness (Sartre), 9
Being and Time (Heidegger), 60, 61
Benjamin, Walter, 29, 39
Berger, Peter, 47
Bergson, Henri, xii, 43, 57, 63, 64
Bernhard, Thomas, 30, 50
Bhaskar, Roy, 62
Birth of a Nation, 118
Blanchot, Maurice, 175
Blavatsky, Madame Helena, 36
Blumenberg, Hans, 76
Bobbio, Norberto, 178n21
Bodin, Jean, 103, 131
Brecht, Bertolt, 34, 38, 39
Brentano, Franz, 88–9
Breton, André, 47
Breuer, Josef, 109
Bride of Frankenstein, 116
"Un Brillant Sujet" (Rigaut), 34
Brodkey, Harold, 30
Brunschvicg, Léon, 66n17
Buell, Lawrence, 67
Burke, Kenneth, 167–68
Burns, Robert, 1

Cameron, James, 113, 115
Campbell, Ben, 155
Canguilhem, Georges, 57
Castoriadis, Cornelius, 141
Cavell, Stanley, 116
Certeau, Michel de, 105
Chaucer, Geoffrey, 46
Chekhov, Anton, 38
Chodron, Pema, 124n13
Chomsky, Noam, 18, 23
Christ, Jesus, 43–4, 109, 123
Christie, Ian, 97
Churchland, Paul, 87
Cicero, Marcus Tullius, 17, 45
"Cinema and Psychoanalysis" (Heath), 94
Cioran, E. M., 172–73
Coetzee, J. M., xv
Cohen, David, 133–34
Connor, Steven, xiii, 9
Conrad, Joseph, 2, 117
Constant, Fred, 138, 142
constructivism (nature), 150–51, 159–50
Copernican worldview, 20
Coppola, Francis Ford, 117, 119–20
Crane, Hart, 32, 34
The Crisis of European Sciences and Transcendental Phenomenology (Husserl), 61
Critchley, Simon, xiii, 10
Critique of Dialectical Reason (Sartre), 4
Cube, 6
The Culture of Nature (Alex Wilson), 68

Dada, 37, 50
Dark City, 6
Darwin, Charles, 35, 82
Darwinism, 57
Davidson, Donald, 87
De Anima (Aristotle), 85

Declaration of Egregious Popish Impostures (Harsnett), 104, 105
deep ecology, 67

Delacampagne, Christian, 131
Deleuze, Gilles, 5, 49, 57, 63, 64, 172
Demeure (Derrida), 169, 174–75
Dennett, Daniel, 87
Depraz, Natalie, 63
Derrida, Jacques, 7, 169, 174–76
Descartes—rationalism, 60
Descartes—subjectivity, 21; cogito, 21
Descartes, René, 18, 19, 20, 56, 61, 108; and the cogito, 21; and rationalism, 60; and subjectivity, 21
Dewey, John, 18
Dialectic of Enlightenment (Adorno and Horkheimer), 3, 71, 74, 75
Dilthey, Wilhelm, 59
Discours de la méthode (Descartes), 18
"Do Dogs Laugh?"(Douglas), 44
Docherty, Thomas, xi, 10
Donoghue, Denis, 124n13
Dostoevsky, Fyodor, 2
Douglas, Mary, 44
Doyle, Arthur Conan, 98, 108
Drucker, Peter, 129
Durkheim, Émile, 130

ecocriticism, 67, 70; and myth, 70
Economic and Philosophical Manuscripts of 1844 (Marx), 16
Ecrits (Lacan), 5–6
Ehrenberg, Alain, 134
Elements of Law (Hobbes), 168
Elias, Norbert, 128
Eliot, T. S., 36, 39, 122
"The Ends of Man" (Derrida), 4
Enquiry Concerning Political Justice (Godwin), 1
Erasmus, Desiderius, 17
Eros and Civilisation (Marcuse), 75
Essentialism, 15, 21–4; definition, 23
"Existentialism Is a Humanism" (Sartre), 4
Existentialism, 16, 21, 170 (see also: Humanism, existentialist)
eXistenZ, 6

Fackenheim, Emil J., xiii
The Far Side (Larson), 47

Ferry, Luc and Renaut, Alain, 5
Fichte, Johann, 63
Ficino, Marsilio, 17
Fincher, David, 113
"Flytopia" (Self), 48
Forests (Robert Pogue Harrison), 67
Foucault, Michel, xiv–xv, 3–5
France, Anatole, 127
Fraser, Nancy, 144
Freud, xiv, 8, 9, 40, 93–7, 99, 101, 109, 123n3; and Eros/Thanatos, 73, 78n16; and the Pleasure Principle, 71, 72, 75, 78n16; and the Reality Principle, 71, 72, 75, 78n16; and spiritualism, 97; and the unconscious, 56
Freudianism, 57, 108
Friday the 13th series, 108
Friedman, Jonathan, 144
Frye, Northrop, 30
Fussell, Paul, 31
Futurism, 36–38; Italian, 30; Russian, 30

Galen, 43
Garrard, Greg, 68
Gay, Peter, 39
Gellner, Ernest, 159
Gerontion (Eliot), 36
Giddens, Anthony, 76
The Gift of Death (Derrida), 176
Gillespie, Michael Allan, 129
globalization, xiii–xiv, 128–135 *passim*, 145
Godard, Jean-Luc, 101–2
Godwin, William, 1
Goethe, Johann Wilhelm von, 39
The Golden Bough (Frazer), 120
Goody, Jack, 31
Gorky, Maxim, 97, 100
Goya, Francisco de, 122
Grass, Günter, 30
Great Apes (Self), 47, 48
The Great War and Modern Memory (Fussell), 31
Greenblatt, Stephen, 111n2

Gropius, Walter, 39
Grundrisse (Marx), 79n19
Gulliver's Travels (Swift), 46, 50
Gunning, Tom, 98

Habermas, Jürgen, 130, 141
Hammond, Paul, 100
Hardy, Thomas, 2
Harrison, Robert Pogue, 67
Harsnett, Samuel, 104–10 *passim*
Hazlitt, William, 43
Heart of Darkness (Conrad), 117, 122
Heath, Stephen, 94
Hederman, Mark P., 124n13
Hegel, G.W.F., ix, xii, 35, 63,65n17, 83–88, 170–71, 172; and historicism, 21; and human being, 83–4; and phenomenology, 61
Heidegger, Martin, ix, xii–xiii, 59, 63, 69, 82–6, 167; and antinaturalism, 60–1; and antiscientism, 60; and *Dasein*, 21, 22, 82; and forgetting of Being, 82–3; and human being, 82–3, 84; and National Socialism, 22; and ontic-ontological distinction, 83–4, 85; and the uncanny, 123n3
Heraclitus, 35
Herbert, George, 177n12
Hobbes, Thomas, 168
Hobsbawm, Eric, 131, 133
Høffding, Harald, 17
Hoffmann, E.T.A., 95
Hollington, Michael, 2
The Hollow Men (Eliot), 120, 122
Homer, 71, 78n15, 79n19
Hominescence (Serres), xiii
Horatian satire, 47–9
Houdini, Harry, 98–9
Hugh Selwyn Mauberley (Pound), 34
Hulme, T.E., 2–3
human rights, 1, 139
humanism, 1–11, 15–25, 29–30, 32, 38, 39–40, 127–28; Enlightenment, 19; definition, 7; ethical, 16–17; existentialist, 5; Marxist, 16; philosophical, 16; and philosophy,

humanism (*continued*)
16–17, 19–21; and *paideia*, 17; and
the politics of humanity, 127, 145
humanist tradition, 16, 17, 40
Hume, David, 56
Husserl, Edmund, 23, 59, 89; and anti-
naturalism, 61
Huxley, Aldous, 106–7
Huysmans, Joris Karl, 36, 37

Imagism, 39
Immanuel Kant (Bernhard), 50
In Parenthesis (David Jones), 33
Intellectual Impostures (Sokal and
Bricmont), 63
The Interpretation of Dreams (Freud),
78n16
Interview with the Vampire (Rice), 107
Invasion of the Body Snatchers, 108
"Investigations of a Dog" (Kafka), 47
Irigaray, Luce, 63
Isherwood, Christopher, 39

Jack Maggs (Carey), 108
Jacob, François, 85
Jacoby, Russell, 136
Jaeger, Werner, 22
James, Henry, 34
Jay, Gregory S., and Miller, David L.,
111n2
Jentsch, William, 93–4, 96, 100
Jeunet, Jean-Pierre, 113
Jones, David, 33–5
"Josephine the Singer, or the Mouse-
Folk" (Kafka), 47
Jouve, Pierre Jean, 38
Joyce, James, 30, 38
Jubilate Agno (Smart), 46
Jung, Carl, 31
Juvenalian satire, 47–9

Kafka, Franz, 47, 49
Kahler, Erich, 38
Kant, Immanuel, x, 2, 20–1, 56, 63,
83–6, 88; and ethics, 16; and human
being, 83–4; and the Transcendental
Subject, 84

Kearney, Richard, xiii, 6
Kerridge, Richard, and Sammells, Neil,
67–8
Kircher, Anastasius, 99
Klages, Ludwig, 15
Klossowski, Pierre, 103
Kracauer, Siegfried, 95
Krauss, Rosalind, 97
Kripke, Saul, 23

Lacan, Jacques, 5
Laing, R. D., 172
Larson, Gary, 47
Laruelle, François, 57
Latour, Bruno, 144
Lawrence, D. H., 2, 34, 37
"Legend of the Dead Soldier" (Brecht),
34
Leibniz, Gottfried Wilhelm, 63, 64
Les Six Livres de la Republique (Bodin),
131
Letter on Humanism (Heidegger), 4, 22
Leviathan (Hobbes), 168
Levin, Harry, 30
Levinas, Emmanuel, 1–2, 63
Lévi-Strauss, Claude, 31
Lewis, Wyndham, 2
Life of Brian (Monty Python), 44
"Literature and Science" (Arnold), 32,
33
"Little Shop Girls Go to the Movies"
(Kracauer), 95
Lobkowitz, Nicholas, 143
Locke, John, 151–54
Lorenz, Konrad, 44–5
Lumière brothers (Louis and Auguste),
100–101
Lyotard, Jean-François, 3, 172

Maalouf, Amin, 142
Mahon, Derek, 69
Man and Bird (Derek Mahon), 69
"A Man and His Dog" (Mann), 44
Man Meets Dog (Lorenz), 44
Man, Paul de, 7, 178n21
Mann, Thomas, 30, 38, 39, 40, 44
Marcuse, Herbert, 75–6

Margolis, Joseph, 7
Marinetti, Filippo, 36–7
Marquez, Gabriel Garcia, 30
Marx, Karl, 9, 16, 21, 69–70, 133
Maskelyne, John Neville, 98
Materialism, 56, 58
The Matrix, 6
Maxwell's demon, 108
Mead, George Herbert, 87
Méliès, Georges, 99–101
Merleau-Ponty, Maurice, 57, 63, 64
Metamorphosis (Kafka)
metaphysical realism, 19, 24
Mill, John Stuart, 154, 157, 162n36
M'Naughten rule, 20
"Modern Poetry" (Crane), 32
Mohanty, J. N., 23
Monadology (Leibniz), 64
Monod, Jacques, 85
Montaigne, Michel de, 19, 20
Moore, George, 35
More, Sir Thomas, 17
Mulhall, Stephen, 114
Mullarkey, John, xiii, 7
multiculturalism, 135–42
Mulvey, Laura, xiii, 6
Musil, Robert, 38
Mythologies (Barthes), 78n9

naturalism, 7, 16, 35, 55–64; definitions, 56, 58
La Nature (Merleau-Ponty), 63
Negative Dialectic (Adorno), 3, 5
The Nicomachean Ethics (Aristotle), x
Nietzsche, Friedrich, 2, 9, 37, 64, 108, 123
Nineteen Hundred and Nineteen (Yeats), 34
"The Noble Rider and the Sound of Words" (Stevens), 165
nominalism, 129
Nozick, Robert, 58–9
The Nun's Priest's Tale (Chaucer), 46

Oberstein, Karin Lesnik, 68
The Omen series, 108

On Film (Mulhall), 114
"On the Psychology of the Uncanny" (Jentsch), 93–4, 96, 100
O'Neill, John, 7
The Order of Things (Foucault), xv, 4–5
Orwell, George, 47, 48

Pabst, G. W., 94
Papineau, David, 58, 61, 62
Parallel Lives (Plutarch), 105
Parsons, Talcott, 135
The Parts of Animals (Aristotle), 43, 167
Pascal, Blaise, xii, 173
Pater, Walter, 35
Pearson, Keith Ansell, 63
Peladan, Joseph, 36
Penguins' Island (France), 127
La Pensée Sauvage (Lévi-Strauss), 31
Petrarch, Francesco, 17
Petronius, 47–8
Phaedo (Plato), 85
Phillips, Adam, 98
Philosophical Investigations (Wittgenstein), 87
Philosophical Naturalism (Papineau), 58, 61
"Philosophy as a Rigorous Science" (Husserl), 61
phonologocentrism, 175
physicalism, 56, 61–2
Pi, 6
Pico della Mirandola, Giovanni, 20, 22
Pinker, Steven, 18
Plato and Platonism (Pater), 35
Plato, ix, 17, 22, 23, 35, 56, 84–6, 88; and elenctic (Socratic) dialogues, 81
Platonism, 19
Plessner, Helmuth, 45
Pope, Alexander, 19, 47
Porphyry, 43
The Possibility of Naturalism (Bhaskar), 62
Pound, Ezra, 34, 36, 38, 39

Preface to the Lyrical Ballads
   (Wordsworth), 32, 35, 37
Protagoras, 20
Proust, Marcel, 38
Pythagoras, 43

Quine, W. V., 87

Rabelais, François, 17, 38, 43
Rawls, John, 56
A Rebours (Huysmans), 37
A La Recherche du temps perdu (Proust),
   38
reductionism, 58–9, 62
Reichenbach, Hans, 63
The Republic (Plato), 19, 81
Rice, Anne, 107
Rickert, Corinne Holt, 111n2
Rigaut, Jacques, 34–5
Rilke, Rainer Maria, 69
The Rise of Scientific Philosophy
   (Reichenbach), 63
Robert-Houdin, Jean Eugene, 100
Rockmore, Tom, 4, 61
Rorty, Richard, 134, 145
Rosenberg, Alfred, 15
Ross, Andrew, 70–1
Rousseau, Jean-Jacques, 2

Sachs, Hans, 94
"The Sandman" (Hoffmann), 94
Sartre, Jean-Paul, x, 2, 9, 24, 59, 63,
   167
Satyricon (Petronius), 47
Schelling, Friedrich, 63
Schneider, Monique, 106
Schopenhauer, Arthur, 2, 63, 108
scientism, 62
Scott, Ridley, 113
Screech, M.A., 43
Secrets of a Soul (Pabst), 94
Self, Will, 47, 48
Sellars, Wilfred, 87
"September 1, 1939" (Auden), 176
Serres, Michel, xii, xiii, xv, 108
Smart, Christopher, 46
Sokal, Alan, and Bricmont, Jean, 63

Soper, Kate, xiii, 3
Spencer, Herbert, 34, 63
Spender, Stephen, 39
Spinoza, Baruch, 64
The Statesman (Plato), 81
Statius, Publius Papinius, 51
Stengers, Isabelle, 57, 59
Sterne, Laurence, 38
Stevens, Wallace, 165–67, 169, 170
Sur le bonheur (Teilhard de Chardin),
   171
surrealism, 100
Sutcliffe, Peter, 110
Svevo, Italo, 38
Swift, Jonathan, xv, 46–7, 49, 50
Sylvan, Richard, 150, 156
Symbolism, 30, 35–9
Symons, Arthur, 36

Taylor, Charles, 138–41
Teilhard de Chardin, Pierre, 171–73,
   176
Terence, 107
Tertullian, Christian, 103
The Thirteenth Floor, 6
Thomas, Edward, 69
The Trouble with Being Born (Cioran),
   173
Tzara, Tristan, 34–5, 37–8

Ulysses (Joyce), 38

Varela, Francisco, 63
Varro, Marcus Terentius, 17
Vercors, 127
Vico, Giambattista, 20

Wacquant, Loïc, 145
Wagner, Richard, 118
Walker, D. P., 111n2
Weaver, Sigourney, 114
Weeks, Jeffrey, 142
Weimann, Robert, 30
Weimar Culture (Gay), 39
Weston, William, 104
"What is an author?" (Foucault),
   4–5

Wilde, Oscar, 36
Wildlife Management in the National Parks (Leopold Committee), 153
William of Ockham, 129
Williams, Raymond, 56
Wilson, Alex, 68
Wilson, Edmund, 35
Winckelmann, Johann, 22
Wittgenstein, Ludwig, 21, 49, 87, 167

Wordsworth, William, 32, 37, 38, 40, 69
Work on Myth (Hans Blumenberg), 76
Writing the Environment (Kerridge and Sammells), 67–8

Yeats, W. B., 34–5

Der Zauberberg (Mann), 38
Zoo ou l'assassin philanthrope (Vercors)

About the Editor
and Contributors

Paul Sheehan is a research fellow at Macquarie University, Sydney. He has published in the areas of narrative poetics and the philosophy of literature, including articles on Dickens and Beckett. He is also the author of *Modernism, Narrative and Humanism* (2002).

Zygmunt Bauman is emeritus professor of sociology at the University of Leeds and the University of Warsaw. His most recent publications are *Liquid Love: On the Frailty of Human Bonds* (2003), *Society under Siege* (2002), *The Individualized Society* (2001), and *Liquid Modernity* (2000).

Steven Connor is professor of literary theory at Birkbeck College, University of London. His publications include *The Book of Skin* (Reaktion, 2003), *Dumbstruck: A Cultural History of Ventriloquism* (2000), *Postmodernist Culture* (second edition, 1997), and *The English Novel in History 1950–1995* (1995).

Simon Critchley is professor of philosophy at Essex University. He is the author of *On Humour* (2002) and *Continental Philosophy: A Very Short Introduction* (2001), and the coeditor (with Robert Bernasconi) of *The Cambridge Companion to Emmanuel Levinas* (2001).

Thomas Docherty is professor of English literature at the University of Kent, Canterbury. His most recent publications include *Criticism and Modernity: Aesthetics, Literature, and Nations in Europe and Its Academies* (1999) and *Alterities: Criticism, History, Representation* (1996). He is also the editor of *Postmodernism: A Reader* (1993).

Michael Hollington is professor of English at the University of Toulouse. He is the author of *Dickens' Great Expectations* (1999) and *Katherine Mansfield* (1998), and the editor of *Charles Dickens: Critical Assessments* (four volumes, 1995).

Richard Kearney holds the C. Seelig Chair of Philosophy at Boston College. His most recent publications include *On Stories* and *Strangers, Gods and Monsters: Ideas of Otherness* (both 2002) and *The God Who May Be: The Hermeneutics of Religion* (2001).

Joseph Margolis is Laura H. Carnell Professor of Philosophy at Temple University, Philadelphia. His publications include *Reinventing Pragmatism: American Philosophy at the End of the Twentieth Century* (2002) and *Selves and Other Texts: The Case for Cultural Realism* (2001). He is also the coeditor, with Tom Rockmore, of *The Philosophy of Interpretation* (2000).

John Mullarkey is senior lecturer at the University of Sunderland. His latest book, *Post-Continental Philosophy,* will appear with Continuum Press. He is also the author of *Bergson and Philosophy* (1999) and the editor of *The New Bergson* (1999).

Laura Mulvey is professor of film and media studies at Birkbeck College, University of London. Her recent work includes *Fetishism and Curiosity* (1996), *Citizen Kane* (1992), and a critical commentary for the *Peeping Tom* DVD (1999). She has also codirected six films with Peter Wollen and *Disgraced Monuments* (1994) with Mark Lewis.

John O'Neill is professor of philosophy at Lancaster University. He has published widely on political and environmental philosophy and the philosophy of economics and is the author of *The Market: Ethics, Knowledge, and Politics* (1998). He is also the coauthor (with Ian Bateman and Kerry Turner) of *Environmental Ethics and Philosophy* (2001), and the coeditor (with Tim Hayward) of *Justice, Property and the Environment: Social and Legal Perspectives* (1997).

Tom Rockmore is a professor of philosophy at Duquesne University, Pennsylvania. Among his recent publications are *Marx after Marxism: The Philosophy of Karl Marx* (2002) and *On Heidegger's Nazism and Philosophy* (second edition, 1998). He is also the editor of *New Essays on the Precritical Kant* (2001).

Kate Soper is a professor in the School of Arts and Humanities at the University of North London and has worked as a journalist and translator. She is the coauthor (with Martin Ryle) of *To Relish the Sublime?: Culture and Self-Realisation in Postmodern Times* (2002) and the author of *What is Nature?: Culture, Politics and the Non-Human* (1995) and *Troubled Pleasures: Writings on Politics, Gender and Hedonism* (1990).